TELLING TALES

A Guidebook & DVD

Emily S. Chasse

Neal-Schuman Publishers, Inc.
New York   London

Published by Neal-Schuman Publishers, Inc.
100 William St., Suite 2004
New York, NY 10038

Printed and bound in the United States of America

The paper used in this publication meets the minimum requirements of American National Standard for Information Sciences—Permanence of Paper for Printed Library Materials, ANSI Z39.48-1992.

Library of Congress Cataloging-in-Publication Data

Chasse, Emily S., 1953-
   Telling tales : a guidebook & DVD / Emily S. Chasse.
     p. cm.
   Includes bibliographical references and indexes.
   ISBN 978-1-55570-645-6 (alk. paper)
   1. Storytelling—Study and teaching (Elementary) I. Title.

LB1042.C44 2009
372.67'7—dc22

                                 2009027771

�֍ Table of Contents �֍

❋ Exhibits ❋

Foreword

✳ Bridging Traditional and Technological Communication Networks ✳

The art of communication is at a crossroads in today's environments. One of the roads has a newly structured channel to convey our thoughts, opinions, anecdotes, ideas, information, concerns, and interests. The channel is cyberspace with its array of media in mind-boggling electronic devices to convey messages to unseen recipients. In some situations a meaningful interpersonal relationship between two or more individuals is merely transitory, for the transmitted message lacks *depth* and *substance,* which are vital elements in the art of communication.

It is necessary for the participants to be in each other's presence when they engage in direct communication. It also requires a mastery of effective listening skills by giving careful attention to what is being said. Complementing these skills is the importance of hearing, to extract from the dialog any understanding that may evoke desired responses. Communication also contains nonverbal attributes that are lacking in electronic messaging. Facial expressions may reflect an array of different emotions. In the words of Alexander Smith, eighteenth-century Scottish poet:

> *If we could but read it, every human being carries his life in his face. On our features the fine chisel of thought and emotion are eternally at work.*

Other nonverbal attributes include maintaining proper eye contact, spontaneous gestures with a variety of motions, controlled body language, and a suitable posture.

Storytelling bridges the traditional channels of communication with the technological channels of cyberspace. In its oral traditions

xiii

this art form is as old as the origin of language and predates recorded history. It has overcome challenges of censorship and confronted every new medium of communication from the advent of pictorial images to the most advanced technological wonders. Storytelling possesses irrefutable characteristics that validate its recognition as a vital, living entity in the arts.

Historically rich, storytelling possesses an indestructible appeal as it becomes a connecting link to diverse cultural, ethnic, and religious societies throughout the world. Applying a time-honored practice of the oral tradition, a storyteller communicates, solely, with a self-generated creative artistry and established techniques that contain the same vital elements as delineated in the art of communication.

Practitioners of the art form, storytellers, with their related offerings, are obligated to fulfill its prime prerequisites. Storytelling requires direct, personal contact with responsive listeners. Storytellers are challenged to present selections that contain universal core values of humankind. Listeners must be able to extract from shared listening experiences the ingredients that stimulate desired responses. Regardless of locale or diverse cultures, the lasting appeal of storytelling is its universally accepted purposes.

Storytelling provides entertainment with opportunities to relax in nonstructured environments. It serves as a bridge from the oral renditions to literature with its rich treasury of stories. In its selections it provides concepts that embody ethical and spiritual values without being overly didactic. Storytelling offers vicarious experiences that may satisfy the personal, social, and psychological needs of listeners.

Storytelling has the capacity to stimulate the intellectual and aesthetic spheres of listeners. It perpetuates and keeps alive the heritage and legacies of diverse cultures and religions.

From this conceptual framework of storytelling with artistic and oral renditions, inherent attributes best exemplify the requirements for effective communication. Storytelling requires measurable standards to evaluate its stated purposes. It possesses a stable foundation that has been an enduring presence throughout every historical period of humankind. It offers continuous growth with its limitless appeal to ever-changing environments and cultures.

Recognizing an obligation to continue this artistic legacy, Emily Chasse offers the storytelling resource *Telling Tales: A Guidebook & DVD*. Included in the contents are techniques for a storyteller in story selection, story structure, and performance; specific sources to develop a rich literary background; nonliterary community organizations and media outlets; guidelines for classroom presentations with puppetry plays and tandem storytelling; technological issues; copyright regulations; and suggestions for developing a storytelling course.

Progressing from a storyteller's mastery of techniques related to story characteristics, a need arises to acquire an extensive literary background. Beginning in the home environment are family tales, reminiscences, oral history, and genealogy from which storytellers may use their knowledge of story structure to create personal stories. Beyond this environment are the time-honored gifts from the traditional literary genre. Mythology from Greece and Rome is detailed with its appealing offerings. Epics and legends are interwoven into a tapestry with treasured national and international classics from Babylon, Greece, Finland, England, India, and America.

These offerings are expanded with appealing ballads with their unique classifications, formats, cultural, and historical backgrounds. Completing the traditional classics are the moralistic fables, depicted in the creations of Aesop (Greece), Jean de la Fontaine (France), Ivan Krylov (Russia) and entries from India.

Concluding the text is a proposed syllabus for a storytelling course, as well as informative insights for storytelling in classrooms, the consideration and use of digital storytelling, and the important questions of copyright regulations. Each chapter contains selected stories by the author or designated sources for illustrative purposes. Additional resources include extensive bibliographies and Web sites.

Accompanying *Telling Tales* is a DVD whose contents include an Introduction, Story Selection, Guest Tellers, and Chinese Stories. The tellers reveal distinctively different creative approaches and techniques in relating their stories. Eshu Bumpus shares his original "Storm Story" with a dramatic rendition; duo tellers Ellie Toy and Sharon Lynch retell the delightful tale, "The Tailor," with a tandem presentation; Tom Callinan and Ann Shapiro give a musical interpretation of an originally inspired family ballad; and Emily Chasse retells three Chinese tales, "Why the Sea Is Salty,"" "White Hair Waterfall," and "The Golden Sheng."

Telling Tales: A Guidebook & DVD is a bridge, linking its traditional methods of oral communication to technology with its complex realms of cyberspace.

Spencer G. Shaw, D. Lit.
Professor Emeritus
The Information School
University of Washington

❉ Preface ❉

Storytelling is one of life's most wonderfully enriching experiences; perhaps all the more so because both storyteller and listener benefit from the exchange.

I grew up in a family of storytellers and, from earliest childhood, heard my grandmother's and mother's tales from Europe, as well as stories from my father's side of the family. I learned to tell stories from listening to them. *Telling Tales: A Guidebook & DVD* gives me an opportunity to pass on my enthusiasm to my colleagues today and to future generations.

Much of the material in the pages that follow and on the accompanying DVD, which is included on the back inside cover of this book, is based on the folktelling course I have taught for the past 20 years. I use tales in each of my class sessions because I believe new tellers learn from reading about storytelling as well as *watching* other people and how they tell their tales.

Storytelling—the art of telling tales through words, gestures, sounds, and movement—has been shared throughout all cultures over time. Its popularity has experienced a revival over recent years for a number of reasons. Multiculturalism is served well by the inclusion of stories from various cultural and ethnic groups. Human empathy and our capacity for interpersonal connection are fostered by hearing tales that reflect the human condition. Storytelling in community settings, schools, businesses, religious organizations, and other groups is flourishing among people of all ages. The storytelling community hopes this will continue and that the wonderful tradition of telling tales will grow and thrive.

The Audience

Telling Tales is intended to provide an introduction to the world of telling tales. Librarians, teachers, and others who work with young people will find much useful information here. Because storytelling is not just for young audiences, those who want to share tales with adults will find the content applicable as well.

> The DVD benefits tellers of all experience levels and learning styles, but especially visual learners, because I demonstrate how all these ideas come together in practice.

The book and DVD set is designed for both novices and experienced tellers. Novices will find an explanation of the basics and scripts that will help them get started quickly. More advanced tellers will find useful information, tips, and tales from a wide range of traditions that will help them expand their repertoires.

Organization

This book consists of 13 chapters. The first three chapters provide the fundamentals, including locating and selecting stories and preparing and performing them. Chapters 4 through 8 focus on the major genres of stories that tellers worldwide like to tell and that audiences love to hear. The final five chapters cover a broad range of logistical guidance and advice, ranging from puppetry to copyright considerations. Numerous stories featured throughout the book and on the DVD serve to both illustrate and entertain. At the end of each chapter, there is an annotated list of "Suggested Resources" as well as a "Bibliography."

> The DVD provides a unique opportunity to visualize through video what I have stated in the text of this book and is an integral learning tool.

Following is a thumbnail sketch of each chapter:

> The DVD provides examples of three types of storytelling structure, including telling a number pattern tale with "Jack and the Northwest Wind," telling a chronologic tale with "The Smell of Food and the Jingle of Coins," and telling a combination tale with "Mollie Whuppie."

- Chapter 1, "Background and Basics," welcomes the reader to the world of storytelling. It explains what tales are and where they come from, the benefits of storytelling, and the fundamentals of storytelling structure and technique. This chapter will help a novice teller get started and should be useful to experienced tellers continuing to explore the art of telling tales.

- Chapter 2, "Locating and Selecting Tales," outlines steps for finding and choosing the best tales to tell. It discusses the importance of reading, listening to, and viewing as many tales as possible across the wide range of story types and genres. It describes the need to gain a sense of the story, including its characters, setting, mood, and action. It offers criteria for choosing the right tale and advice on how to prepare a performance for special occasions or before specific audiences.

- Chapter 3, "Preparing and Performing Tales," offers guidelines for organizing the story structure by outlining the tale or by story mapping. It describes ways to enhance a performance by using voice, accents, special clothing, props, and so forth. It also provides advice on practicing before a performance and on how to get the audience involved during the performance.

- Chapter 4, "Storytelling with Classical Mythology," explores the all-important collection of classical myths and the wisdom and creativity they reflect in the tales of the gods and goddesses. While myths have been part of the lore of civilizations worldwide since the beginning of time, *Telling Tales* focuses on the Greeks and the Romans.

- Chapter 5, "Family Tales, Life Experience Tales, Reminiscences, and Oral History," will remind readers of the wonderful tales told to them by their relatives and family friends and of the importance of remembering these stories to pass on to the next generation. It suggests ways to get others to share their tales. The discussion of oral history includes the debate over the pros and cons of oral history, as well as suggestions for preparing for and conducting an oral history interview.

- Chapter 6, "Storytelling with Legends and Epics," describes two genres that almost everyone finds exciting and often inspiring. The discussion of legends focuses on legends about people (including saints, folk heroes and heroines, and Native American legends); those with geographical connections; and finally on tall tales and urban legends. The section on epics provides brief descriptions of well-known epics from around the world.

- Chapter 7, "Ballads," discusses the format of ballads, including meter and rhyme; describes the various types of ballads (nine categories are discussed); and offers a brief overview of

> 💿 The DVD includes a wonderful example of ballad storytelling by Tom Callinan. Performing a ballad that he wrote, Tom Callinan tells a story about his grandmother through song and music.

> 💿 The DVD includes three stories from China that are great examples at showing the intimate connection between China's culture and the integration of those cultural elements into its folktales. The three stories included are "Why the Sea Is Salty," "White-Hair Waterfall," and "The Golden Sheng."

the ballad performing field, with such luminaries as Pete Seeger, Woody Guthrie, Bob Dylan, Joan Baez, and Bill Harley.

- Chapter 8, "Folktale Country Studies," begins with a discussion about folklore, folktales, and fairy tales. It offers ideas for using folklore and folktales as an entertaining way to inform and enlighten audiences about a particular country or culture, emphasizing the importance of making connections between a tale and the geography, history, and social and cultural context of the group or country under study. It closes with sample presentations about China and Poland.

- Chapter 9, "Digital Storytelling," opens the door to the high-tech field of telling tales digitally. It describes exciting options for telling personal tales through the new technologies. It provides an overview of digital storytelling production, including the story itself, the script, the storyboard, recording voice-overs, gathering media resources, and creating the digital story. It ends with a description of how digital storytelling has been used by others.

- Chapter 10, "Other Resources for Locating Tales," describes other sources of story ideas beyond the various genres already discussed. Tales can be spun from news sources, as well as from cultural institutions, traveling exhibits, and displays. The World Wide Web enables you to gather information without even leaving home.

- Chapter 11, "Telling Tales with Young People in the Community and Classroom," describes the wealth of possibilities available to tellers when sharing tales with young people and guiding children and young adults to tell their own tales. The section "Performing Before Children in Schools" suggests ways a teller can work with teachers in a number of areas, including language arts, history, and science. It suggests activities for each discipline. The chapter concludes with sections on children telling tales, helping children with tales, and telling tales to children with special needs.

- Chapter 12, "More Fun! Tandem Telling, Plays, and Puppetry," offers advice on telling tandem tales. It describes how tandem tales can be used in the classroom—and again suggests activities—to enhance young people's language skills, including listening, writing, and speaking, as

> (•) The DVD provides an example of tandem telling, with Ellie Toy and Sharon Lynch telling their version of "The Tailor."

well as social skills and self-esteem. This chapter expands the possible formats available for tellers by including plays and puppetry.
- Chapter 13, "Final Considerations: Storytelling Course, Copyright, Planning Tale Events, Storytelling as a Profession, and a Brief History of Storytelling," explains some areas of storytelling that are important to tellers beginning to perform professionally. It discusses important points of copyright law, planning events, charging fees, giving booktalks, and marketing, and it provides biographical information about several professional tellers. Although the history of storytelling has been woven into the narrative of previous chapters, it is included in this final chapter because I feel that tellers can appreciate the history better when they know how the present fits into the past.

The DVD

The accompanying DVD takes advantage of audiovisual media that allow this guide to go beyond print and readers to hear, watch, and learn from many experienced storytellers. In watching the DVD, readers can learn how gestures, voice modification, and audience participation and enthusiasm all contribute to the good telling of a story. The DVD enables me to instruct and encourage you directly as well as share a wide array of my tales along with more tales told by my friends and colleagues.

The DVD is organized into four different parts: "Introduction," "Story Structure," "Guest Tales," and "Chinese Stories." There is also an option on the DVD to play the stories with or without instruction, so you can play the DVD as an instructional tool or to simply hear the stories right away.

- "Introduction": The introduction provides an overview of the DVD and instruction that make a great storyteller. One of the best ways to become a great storyteller is to see people telling stories because it provides a way to learn how an effective storyteller interacts with the audience and uses different gestures and voice tones. One recommended way to experience storytelling in a setting that provides feedback and constructive criticism is through local community-based storytelling groups.
- "Story Structure": This section of the DVD provides examples of three types of storytelling structure. The first is the chronological story, which is told in a linear sequence from beginning to end. "The Smell of Food and the Jingle of Coins" is an example of a chronological style story. The next story structure is a number pattern style story. The tale of "Jack and the Northwest Wind" is an example of the pattern style tale. The final story structure provided is a combination of the two, called a combination style tale. This is where a chronological story is told within a number pattern story. Another tale, "Mollie Whuppie," demonstrates the combination style story.
- Guest Tales: This section of the DVD is a collection of stories told by some of my colleagues. Eshu Bumpus performing his "Storm Story" is a great example of how gestures, movement, words, and voice modification can be used to tell a wonderful story. Ellie Toy and Sharon Lynch tell their story "The Tailor" in tandem, which is a good way to keep an audience involved and excited. Finally, an example of ballad storytelling is provided by Tom Callinan, "I Never Knew Her Name," the story of his grandmother told through his song.
- "Chinese Stories": This section of the DVD includes three Chinese folktales that show the connections between ancient Chinese culture and cultural elements within Chinese folktales. This way of connecting a country's culture with storytelling occurs in many different countries all over the world.

The three stories that show Chinese culture in storytelling are "Why the Sea Is Salty," "White-Hair Waterfall," and "The Golden Sheng."

I hope you'll find the tips and strategies in this book and their realization on the accompanying DVD to be an effective guide into one of humankind's greatest traditions—one that opens minds, hearts, and imaginations—storytelling.

✳ Acknowledgments ✳

It would be impossible to thank everyone who helped me develop my storytelling skills and love of telling tales. However, I want to mention some of them and those who have helped me during my work in this endeavor and at important times in my storytelling life:

My Neal-Schuman Development Editor, Kathy Blake, who helped me reorganize and highlight my good sections and change and modify the weak sections of my book

My incredible Production Editor, Amy Knauer, who managed to design a wonderful layout and pages with special flair

Charles Harmon and Paul Seeman at Neal-Schuman, who supported and encouraged my book/DVD from the beginning

Elizabeth Lund, my first Neal-Schuman editor

My kind and loving husband, Bill, for his patience, especially when I would claim, "This chapter will only take a few hours to revise . . ."

My wonderful and wise daughter, Sarah Ann, who helped me organize my notes and served as my in-house pre-editor

My grandma, Roxie, and my mother and father for sharing their fun and never-ending supply of tales

My sister, Sally, for her love and support

Central Connecticut State University, for awarding me a sabbatical allowing me to finish rewriting and revising my chapters and DVD

CCSU Burritt Library and all of our wonderful librarians, staff, and students for listening to and about my stories, and always letting me talk about my book, especially Renata Vickrey, for her support and willingness to share her Polish Folktale Project, Theresa Mastrogiovanni, Donna Wallach, Frances Nadeau, and student Dan

Chad Valk, for producing my DVD, and who knew how to film my stories so well and with undying patience, even when I asked, "Please, let me try that tale one more time!"

Matthew Wildman, who introduced me to DVD filmmaking

My storytelling friends, Ellie Toy, Sharon Lynch, Spencer Shaw, Eshu Bumpus, Tom Callinan, and Ann Shapiro

Joseph Bruchac, a kind and thoughtful Native American teller who helped guide me with his wisdom and let me include his story here

The Hartford Friends Meeting for helping and supporting me, my stories, and my book

Christopher McCandless, New England Yearly Meeting of Friends, for help and support

Many, many friends and acquaintances for their ongoing support: Diane and Bill Decker; Evan Greer; Dennis Rouelle; Mike Hammond, lawyer; Albert Marceau; Sylvia; Derek; and Nancy, Hair Company, who always listened as I practiced my tales

Chapter I

✳ Background and Basics ✳

Telling tales can be a tender, fulfilling, and very worthwhile experience for both the teller and the audience. Sharing tales can be thrilling, exciting, and possibly even a little scary. Telling tales can certainly be a way to connect with family, friends, students, and other groups. Lewis Carroll called stories "love gifts." Laura Simms, a storyteller, has said, "A story is not alive unless it is given away" (Livo, 1986: xi).

"Giving away" these "love gifts" can be fun and can make people laugh, cry, smile, or think. Some people are natural tellers, but most need guidance, especially in the beginning. This guidebook will discuss techniques that can be used to select and learn tales to tell; it will explain the structures that many tales follow, and it will outline some of the different types of tales. It will also explain other areas that are important when considering becoming a teller and learning the art of telling tales.

What Is a Tale?

There are many definitions of stories and storytelling, folktales and folktelling. Most types of tales can be either read or told orally. This book will focus on the oral telling of tales. Exhibit 1-1 provides brief definitions of the various types of tales. Some of these story types will be discussed in subsequent chapters.

Where Do Tales Come From?

Storytelling is one of our oldest forms of communication, and most pieces of ancient literature that we still know and read today, such as Homer's *The Iliad* and *The Odyssey,* were originally told orally. Even

1

Exhibit 1-1. What Is a Tale?—Definitions

ballad: A story told in verse.

digital storytelling: Short (2–5 minute) personal narratives combined with digital photos, images, graphics, and music.

epic: A long narrative poem describing the adventures or deeds of a legendary or heroic figure.

fables: Legendary stories in which animals speak and show human qualities and end with a moral.

fairy tales: Stories told by a fairy; narrative of adventures involving fairies, witches, goblins, etc. (A fairy is a mythical being of folklore and romance, usually having human form and possessing magical powers.)

family tale: A story told down through the years among or about family members.

folktales: (a) General term for any of numerous varieties of traditional literature; (b) a characteristically anonymous, timeless, and placeless tale circulated orally among a people ("once upon a time in a land far, far away"); (c) a story from the common folk.

formula tales: Repetitive and predictable tales that repeat a pattern as the narrative unfolds ("BINGO," "There Was an Old Lady Who Swallowed a Fly," etc.).

hero tales: Tall tales of heroes, including Pecos Bill, Annie Christmas, John Henry, Paul Bunyan, etc.

legends: Stories coming down from the past, ones usually thought to be historical though not verifiable.

myths: (a) Stories set in the remote past that deal with the creation of the world, the origin of things, the birth of a culture, a sacred tale; (b) usually a traditional story that serves to unfold part of the worldview of a people or explain a practice, belief, or natural phenomenon; (c) classical myths—The myths dealing with Greek or Roman gods, demigods, and legendary heroes.

nursery rhymes: Rhythmic and musical rhymes for children that often tell stories ("Little Jack Horner," "Humpty Dumpty," "Jack Be Nimble," etc.).

story: An account of incidents or events.

tales: A series of events told or presented; an imaginative narrative of an event.

tall tales: One of the best known types of exaggerated and humorous tales found in America; stories of impossible feats; sometimes told firsthand.

trickster tales: Stories about tricksters full of pranks and mischief.

before these epic poems were written, people in every culture told stories. Telling stories appears to be a cultural universal, common to both primitive and advanced societies.

The Oldest Tale

It is said that the oldest tale, "The Tale of Two Brothers," is of Egyptian origin. It was found written on papyrus in 1185 BC. The original papyrus is now on display at the British Museum in London. (The tale is available online at www.perankhgroup.com/brothers .htm.)

The tale speaks of two eternal issues—first, of jealousy and coveting someone you cannot have; second, of the troubles that arise when a person makes assumptions without knowing the truth. Various versions of this tale have surfaced over the years. The following version is my own:

The Tale of Two Brothers

Once, there were two brothers and they were very close. The older, Anpu, was married and they shared their home with the younger brother, Bata. The brothers worked together in the fields and Bata was a good worker and Anpu appreciated his help. One day, when Anpu was not at home, his wife tried to seduce Bata, and, was rejected. Anpu's wife then accused Bata of having made advances toward her. When Anpu returned home, he heard the story from his wife, grew angry, and wanted to kill his younger brother. Bata heard what Anpu's wife had told Anpu, grew scared and ran away, even though he knew he was innocent. The older brother pursued Bata, and when he found him in the woods, he beat him terribly and left him to die.

Anpu returned home and calmed himself by sitting and drinking a glass of wine. The gods knew the truth of what had happened between the older brother's wife and his brother and they revealed the truth to Anpu.

As Anpu sat the wine turned sour, meaning someone he knew was dying. He realized it must be Bata, who he now knew was innocent of the act of which he accused him, and ran to the woods to try to save his brother before he died. Fortunately he made it in time, saved his brother and returned to their village, telling his wife to leave, because he no longer believed her story.

Source: Adapted by Emily Chasse, who retains the copyright to this version of the story of "The Tale of Two Brothers."

Native American Tales

Native Americans, the indigenous peoples of North America, told tales as a way to teach. Their stories were natural teaching tools. They often talked about the environment and taking care of the land, sky, and water. Some of their stories told of the spirituality of the people and of their culture. Other stories concerned the Native American struggles throughout history.

The tales were originally told in the languages of the tribes, not in English or other languages spoken by the early European-American settlers. Unfortunately, many Native American languages are no longer spoken, and the tales were never translated. That makes it difficult to fully cover the depth and quality of the Native American tales.

There is a Native American tale that comes from the Seneca people. It is called "The Talking Stone," and it shows the importance of storytelling among all people. The tale explains how tales began and why they have been told ever since. The following tale, "The Coming of Legends" is a version of "The Talking Stone." It is by Joseph Bruchac, a Native American storyteller.

The Coming of Legends

Long ago, in the days before people told legends, there was a boy who hunted birds. One day he had been hunting for a very long time and, because it was growing dark, he sought shelter near a great rock. As he sat there, chipping at a piece of flint to make an arrowpoint, he heard a deep voice speak.

"I shall tell a story," the voice said.

The boy was startled and looked all around him, but could find no one. "Who are you?" said the boy.

"I am Hahskwahot," answered the voice. Thus the boy realized that it was the big standing rock which had spoken.

"Then let me hear your story," said the boy.

"First," said the voice of the stone, "you must make me a present of one of the birds you have killed."

"So be it," said the boy, placing a bird on the rock. Then the deep voice told him a story full of wonder, a story of how things were in the former world. When that story was over, the boy went home.

That evening, the boy returned with another bird and, placing it on the rock, sat down to listen.

"Now," said the voice, "I shall tell you a legend. When one is ended, I may tell you another, but if you become sleepy, you must tell me so we can take a rest and you can return the following evening."

Thus it continued. Soon, the boy began to bring people with him and together they listened to the legends told by the standing rock. A great many people now went to the place and listened.

Finally, the voice from the rock spoke to the boy who was no longer a boy but now a man. "You will grow old, but you will have these legends to help you in your old age. Now you have become the carrier of these stories of the former world, and you shall be welcomed and fed wherever you go."

And so it was that legends came into the world.

Source: Bruchac (1985: 12–13). Reprinted with the permission of the author.

Storytelling

The National Storytelling Association defines storytelling "as an art form through which a storyteller projects mental and emotional images to an audience using the spoken word, including sign language and gestures, carefully matching story content with audience needs and environment. The story sources reflect all literature and cultures, fiction and nonfiction, for educational, recreational, historic, folkloric, entertainment and therapeutic uses" (Livo and Rietz, 1987: 7).

Amanda Brotchie (2003), an Australian playwright, writes about elements of stories and storytelling. Brotchie feels traditional storytellers, as well as the storytellers of current film productions, use certain elements in their tales. The elements she lists are frame, characters, plot, structure, and conflict. Her explanation of "the frame" is interesting. She says it is fundamental to any story and refers to the laws that define and govern the universe of the story. Other components work together to provide the drama of the story, but it is the conflict that makes the story most engaging, "as the audience is able to observe a personally confronting or challenging experience—from a safe distance" (p. 99). She says, "The most obvious role of stories is as entertainment: escapism, diversion—a brief holiday from the confines of one's own head" (p. 101).

The Benefits of Storytelling

Because there are numerous benefits to telling tales, it is difficult to list, categorize, or classify them all; also, many of the benefits overlap. Following is a discussion of several important benefits, including cultural, educational, language development, psychological, and spiritual.

Entertainment

In general, telling tales provides entertainment for people, as individuals or as a group. Entertainment is the primary purpose of storytelling, and the audience helps create the story with the teller as it

---

Exhibit 1-2. On a Personal Note: The Shy Child

During a Parent–Teacher Organization (PTO) meeting at my daughter's elementary school, I was invited to share a story with the parents of incoming students about my experience with an initially shy, young girl from the year before. I related a story from the first morning of the little girl's kindergarten class. She had hesitated at the door of the classroom but reluctantly joined the teacher and other children on a braided rug. She was encouraged to join everyone for stories and games throughout the day, and by dismissal time she did not want to leave to return home.

The idea that a timid, shy child had been able to make friends that first day was encouraging to all the parents and eased their fears for their children. All the parents heard that same story together, which made it a starting point for many informal conversations during the meeting that day, as well as assisted in building community within that group. It produced a restful and relaxed tone for the gathering, as stories often do when told well.

---

is being told. Participation in the experience might include subtle eye contact between the teller and audience members, or it might include more vocal interaction or active movement throughout the telling, with jumping, singing, or chanting. Much of this depends on the teller's style; some is determined by the type of audience. The common experience they enjoy together creates a bond that will continue long after the tale has ended.

Helping to Make Sense of the World

Livo (1986: 4) notes, "Story is a universal mirror that shows us the 'truth' about ourselves—who and why we are. When we look into the mirror, we see daily routine and mundane circumstances transformed into something profound . . . 'story' defines humanity." Im, Parlakian, and Osborn (2007: 52), professionals working with children's issues, speak about the power of telling stories: "Through stories, we organize and 'put to voice' our life experiences, and then we pass along our wisdom, history, and culture from one generation to the next." Livo feels stories help us understand the world and make sense of our lives.

Educational Benefits

Children learn many things from hearing stories. The ancient Greeks and Romans, Native Americans, and other ethnic and cultural groups have used stories to teach their children about their customs and traditions and to provide them with other basic information in an effort to pass on their culture. In general, tales demonstrate values and ethical behavior. These aspects of a story are often expressed subtly, but they come through clearly. More overt benefits include sparking the imagination and helping children develop their skills in listening, reading, and writing. It is the beauty of tales to seemingly "teach" without trying.

Two important writers in the field of storytelling and reading speak about the importance of telling tales to children in their development of reading skills. Jeannine Pasini Beekman (2003: 27), recipient of the John Henry Faulk Award for Outstanding Contributions to Storytelling, has found that "Storytelling prepares children for a successful transition to reading by (1) encouraging the art of listening, (2) associating the strange squiggles on the printed page with the words they are hearing, (3) providing opportunities for them to follow events in sequence and predict outcomes, and (4) focusing their attention and giving practice in creative visualization." To the question, "Why read aloud to children?" Jim Trelease (2006: 2), author of *The Read-Aloud Handbook,* responded: "It is the established fact that regular reading aloud strengthens children's reading, writing, and speaking skills—and thus the entire civilizing process."

Teachers/storytellers can open their classes with folk and fairy tales to create a common, positive experience for listeners. Students form mental images of the characters and action. That is the beginning of creative imagination and creative thinking.

If children are given the chance from a very early age to hear tales being told, they are able to practice the art of listening. If children learn this art of listening, it can be transferred to the classroom, where they can apply this skill when they are presented with lessons in the various areas of the curriculum.

Through stories, children enhance their vocabulary, and they also begin to appreciate the beauty of language and to enjoy the rhythm that accompanies the tale. As they hear tales, children learn the meaning of sequencing, the order in which things happen in a story or a piece of music. Children learn the concept of first, second, third, and so forth. They are more able to reconstruct a story or events that happened throughout their day. Therefore, when they speak about ideas or concerns, they can speak more clearly and more expressively about their experiences.

Not only are children's imaginations stimulated when they hear oral storytelling, but they are also more likely to *enjoy* writing to express their ideas. Storytelling can introduce children to patterns of language and extend their vocabulary. It encourages visualization while they listen, as children creatively imagine scenes, action, and characters.

Storytelling has the unique benefit of *not* requiring students to be great readers or writers. Students can become involved in oral history activities, interview subjects, and hear stories from those people. They can strengthen their speaking skills while composing and asking important questions.

Motor Ability and Language Competence

Research indicates a connection between the development of motor ability and language competence. In an article titled "What Infants, Toddlers, and Preschoolers Learn from Play: 12 Ideas," Alice Sterling Honig (2006: 17), a professor of child development, finds that play sharpens cognitive and language skills. She feels that while infants are playing with syllables in their cribs, they are practicing coordination of lips, tongue, palate, and vocal chords. Certainly the way we put words together in stories and tales forms a rhythmic pattern, and it produces a physical response from young children. When a child hears nursery rhymes or folktales with repetitive lines like "I'll huff and puff, and BLOW your house down" or "Jack Be Nimble, Jack Be Quick," you can observe their bodies moving with the rhythm.

Lynne (E.F.) McKechnie, an associate professor who teaches children's literature and provides library services for children, observed a story hour for infants and very young children to see how very young children responded. As she watched a librarian read a story and show a large illustration of a lion paired with another picture showing the lion making its characteristic roar, she observed: "Louise (8 months) is smiling in anticipation of the page turning." When the librarian turned the page, she and all the mothers in the room pretended to roar like lions:

> Louise excitedly waved her arms up and down while smiling broadly. While Louise could not yet talk, or even roar like the adults in the room, her smiles and body movements speak clearly to her engagement with this shared story. Anticipation, an important emergent literacy skill, was evident in Louise's smile. While she was not yet able to speak, Louise "roared" in her own way through her energetic arm waving. In a similar fashion, two other young children, Mark and David, danced their way through a story. (McKechnie, 2006: 193)

Cultural Benefits

Telling tales of various groups helps keep alive and furthers understanding of the cultural heritage of a people. Children learn to accept and respect the traditions and customs of the people of other countries and ethnic groups.

One teacher, Betsy Santino, used folktales to help her third and fourth grade students experience other cultures. Students discussed similarities and differences in versions of "Cinderella" from several different countries. They heard, read, and compared the "Cinderella" stories and used a chart to fill in the comparisons. A Venn diagram allowed her students to compare variations simultaneously. Santino (1991: 70) felt that the students benefited by developing multicultural awareness and that the tales helped "demonstrate that people from different cultures share a need for love, hope, and security."

Psychological/Therapeutic Benefits

In *The Uses of Enchantment: The Meaning and Importance of Fairy Tales,* Bruno Bettelheim describes how hearing folktales aids chil-

---

Exhibit 1-3. On a Personal Note: Respect for Other Cultures

Children and adults enjoy hearing stories, especially when the stories relate to their country/ethnic group of origin. I visited a fifth grade classroom when they were studying Japan and told a Japanese tale, "Peach Boy." When I finished, a small child of Japanese descent spoke up: "Oh, my grandma tells me that story all the time! It's one of my favorites." It felt like the other children were looking at him with admiration, but the child looked embarrassed and got very quiet. I told him how pleased I was to hear what he had said and was glad to hear that his grandma told him Japanese tales. I asked if there were others and he said, "Yes. She tells a lot of stories." Before I left, I suggested to the classroom teacher that she should find out if the grandmother would be willing to come to the class and share other stories with the children. The child's grandmother was pleased to come to the classroom and share stories with the children. It served to further heighten that boy's place in the classroom.

A week later, the classroom teacher told me that she had often had to stop other children from picking on that child because he is small and usually very quiet. But, since I had told the tale in her class and the boy had responded, she thought most of the other children were now treating him differently and with respect.

---

dren in their maturation. Bettelheim (1977: 278) discusses "the struggle for maturity" and notes that "difficult developments must be undergone, hardships suffered, dangers met, victories won. Only in this way can one become master of one's kingdom."

Spiritual/Religious Benefits

A religious or spiritual gathering of any kind can benefit from a storyteller of religious or spiritual tales. Some stories are spiritual in a broad sense, with no specific religious affiliation.

In 1885, Leo Tolstoy (1998) wrote a tale, "The Questions," which felt very spiritual to me. I revised it to make it my own story and told it at the 2007 Connecticut Storytelling Festival in New London in April of that year. It was met with approval, and several in attendance spoke of their reactions. Jon J. Muth (2002) wrote and illustrated a wonderful picture book version of "The Three Questions," published by Scholastic Press. In my version, "Neely's Three Questions," some events differ from those in Tolstoy's tale, but the base and impact of the story have remained the same.

Neely's Three Questions

Feeling overwhelmed with all she thought she needed to do, Neely thought, "If I only had the answers to three important questions, I would always know the right things to do." The three questions Neely wanted to have answers for were:

When is the best time to do things?

Who is the most important one?

What is the right thing to do?

Neely decided to ask her friends and she started by asking her good friend Jacob the first question.

"Jacob, how do I know the right time to do things?" "Neely, I'm surprised at you! You just have to keep a calendar so you know the exact right time to do something. Don't you have a calendar that tells you?" "Hm-m-m," she thought. She had a calendar and it was always OVER-FILLED with things to do. No, that might be okay for Jacob but it wasn't her answer. "Thank you, Jacob," she said, "but I'm still looking for what is right for me."

She went to her friend Joni's house. "Joni, how do I know who is the most important? So I know who to do things for?" "Neely, I'm surprised at you. You choose to do things for the person that can do something good back for YOU . . . so, each of you gets something good."

"Thanks, Joni. But, I don't think that is right for me. I'm going to keep looking."

She went to David's house to ask him the third question, how she would know the right thing to do. David said, "Well, Neely, it's too hard to decide for yourself. I think it takes a committee to decide what needs to be done, what is the RIGHT thing to do." Once again, Neely didn't think that was the answer for her.

So, she went home and that night, with all her thoughts about the three questions and with a storm raging outside,

Neely had a very hard time sleeping. But, in the morning, she knew her next step. "I need to ask someone very wise. My friend Eve is the oldest and wisest person I know. She has had a very hard life but she still has an incredibly positive attitude. She is always smiling and she gives great advice." Neely walked up the hill toward Eve's small house with branches and twigs and a couple of trees in her path. It had been a horrible storm, but now it was sunny and people were outside clearing their yards.

As she approached Eve's house Neely saw Eve out collecting branches and twigs. "Eve, are you okay? I'm glad to see no trees went down on your house. But, stop, sit down, and let me pick up the branches." "Oh, Neely, yes, I'm fine. Would you get some of the little twigs, too? They help make such a great fire. But, come talk with me." Neely laughed and said, "Eve, you always look at the bright side of things. We've just had a major storm and you see it as a great way to get material to start fires in your fireplace this winter." But, she started picking up twigs and branches and telling Eve about her wish to find the answers to her three questions:

> When is the best time to do things?
> Who is the most important one?
> What is the right thing to do?

Neely explained that her friends had given her suggestions but that they didn't feel right for her.

Eve sat down on a rock and started to think about those questions. Neely was stacking the twigs and branches in piles next to one of the trees.

Suddenly Neely saw a boy of about 12 running in front of the house holding his hand, which looked like it was bleeding. She recognized him as a child from Eve's neighborhood and she ran out calling to him. The boy stopped and Neely quickly took off her jacket and held it against the cut on his palm to stop the bleeding. "How did this happen? I recognize you but I don't know your name."

He said, "I'm Johann and my mother and I meet at home every afternoon when I get out of school and she comes home from work. I saw there were dishes in the sink and I wanted to surprise her by washing them and having them stacked clean when she got home. But, I stuck my hand in the soapy water in the sink and my hand got immediately cut on something. I wanted to catch her as she came home down this street." He and Neely started walking back to his home so he could show her the dishes in the sink. Neely reached carefully into the sink and pulled out two pieces of a broken glass jar.

She also took some soap and cleaned Johann's cut just as his mother came in. She saw the blood on the floor and Neely cleaning Johann's hand. "Thanks for taking care of Johann's hand, but what happened?" Johan explained and they put a Band-Aid on his hand. His mother thanked Neely for helping Johann.

Neely said good-bye and started walking back to Eve's house. When she saw Eve, she explained what had happened and asked if she'd had any ideas for Neely's questions.

"You answered them yourself, Neely! Don't you see?" Neely looked confused, so Eve explained.

"You saw a chance to help me and THAT WAS THE RIGHT TIME. You came here and you helped the person you were with (ME) and that was THE RIGHT PERSON, and you helped me, which was THE RIGHT THING TO DO!!!

Then you saw a child was hurt and went to help him— RIGHT TIME (right then), RIGHT PERSON (the one you're with), and RIGHT THING TO DO (help him).

So, you've answered all three questions twice today!" Neely realized what Eve was saying, smiled, and thanked her.

Source: Adapted by Emily Chasse, who retains the copyright to this version of the story of "Neely's Three Questions."

Telling stories to a group gathered for a time of worship or spiritual sharing can offer a useful message to those gathered. It can also contribute to group cohesiveness. Often, a strong story can provide a wonderful opening for a meeting or session. It can focus on any theme(s) the event might have.

Story resources for religious or spiritual groups are numerous. The Bible, Koran, or other religious texts can be used to learn certain stories. Discussions can be curriculum based, or they can focus loosely around a topic. A religious leader may include stories in his or her sermon or talk, or the stories may be included as part of a Sunday school lesson or a religious education lesson plan.

Story Structure

All tales have structure. Learning to identify the type of framework is one of the most critical steps when learning a story. Knowing the structure provides the teller with a clear memory device. The more a tale conforms to a structure, the easier it is to learn. This helps the teller prevent memory "blanking." Blanking occurs when a teller forgets a character, an item, or the next section of the story and cannot continue. Tellers need to feel confident that they can tell the story.

Tellers can keep index cards of the story, notes about the story, or a simple outline of the story in their pocket or nearby if they want. However, most tellers would rather not depend on them. Consulting these "cue" cards may help the teller remember the needed words, but it can ruin the flow of the tale. When tellers are able to remember the story, they can work with the characters and their actions and the tale comes to life. New tellers might be tempted to memorize a tale, but memorization can produce a stilted and stiff story.

In the past, stories tended to be repetitive, most likely so they could be more easily remembered. Before written language and the invention of the printing press, information was remembered in various ways. People might have stored items in their memory as a list or collected them as groups. For example:

Things to do:

1. Meals—Pick some lettuce and a few potatoes; fill a pitcher with water from the stream, ask a neighbor for a couple of carrots.
2. Children—Get the boys up to plow; ask Sarah to help with breakfast. Tommy needs a new pair of boots.
3. House—Chop wood for the fire.

In the past, people often told stories to their children or to each other. Parents or siblings would delight children or adults with fairy tales, scary stories, legends, and other types of tales told orally. Most children grew up knowing how to tell a tale because they had heard many tales told. When learning to tell tales, it is helpful to watch how other people tell. Watching people perform tales and hearing or reading information about storytelling can help children and adults learn to tell stories.

The structure or pattern of a tale serves as the base that the tellers can use to develop the tale for themselves. Their final version should keep the base or the basic storyline, but within that structure they can expand and modify the tale. The teller can change minor elements such as names and/or places. This technique can be very useful when telling to a child or group of children.

In the past, numerous authors have written about and described story structure. Most notably, Vladimir Propp (1968), Claude Levi-Strauss (1963), Alan Dundes (1978), and Norma Livo (1986) are credited with exploring the structures of myths and tales. Claude Levi-Strauss explores myths and observes that they contain a series of events that are combined to form a pattern that tells a story. Vladimir Propp, of Russia (1895–1970), analyzed many of his country's folktales, or *szazka,* and identified common themes within them. Allen Dundes (1964: 110) looks at North American Indian folktales and notes that "American Indian folktales are structured and should no longer be considered as haphazard and random conglomerates of free-floating motifs." In his book, *Essays in Folkloristics,* the chapter "The Number Three in American Culture," Dundes (1978: 130) states, "Of course, American Indians are not particularly bothered by what appears to us as an exaggerated use of four or five repetitions, just as we are not irritated by our own equally persistent use of threefold repetitions."

Norma Livo's (1986) description of structures is extremely complete and thorough. She describes her ideas about story structure in *Storytelling: Process and Practice*. This resource is currently out of print, but many libraries have copies for circulation.

Other story structure discussions are available. Lois Stern (2001) covers story structure in literature for children in *Literature and the Young Child, Part One: Ages 3–5. Overview/Developing Sense of Phonics and Story Structure*. She focuses on books but covers many picture books that are based on folk and fairy tales, especially in the first two sections of the document. She explains how children learn about story structure and recognize that tales have a beginning, middle, and end.

Story Structure Types

This section covers the three main story structures with additional structure information. It also discusses various ways the structures can be presented.

> The accompanying DVD includes examples of these story structures: number patterns, chronological, and pattern-type combination.

Type One: Number Patterns

Tales are often set to patterns of numbers. Many ethnic, cultural, and religious groups have tales that reflect "sacred" numbers. For instance, many European tales use the number pattern three. Native American tales often use the number patterns of four, five, and seven, and Asian cultures tend to use the number pattern of seven. Number pattern tales offer events that are repeated over and over in the story. Examples of "number pattern of three" tales include the following:

1. "Goldilocks and the Three Bears": Goldilocks breaks into the three bears' house while they are away on a walk. She tries their
   porridge (too hot, too cold, just right!),

chairs (too hard, too soft, just right!), and
beds (too hard, too soft, just right!).
The ending comes when the bears return and are not too
happy to find Goldilocks asleep in Wee Bear's bed!

2. "The Three Little Pigs": The wolf tries to destroy the three
pigs' houses so he can eat them but:
He blows down the straw house, but they run to the
wood house.
He knocks down the wood house, but they run to the
brick house.
He huffs and puffs, but he can't blow the brick house
down.
So, in the end, he gives up!

3. "The Three Billy Goats Gruff": Separately, the three Billy
Goats try to cross the troll's bridge, but the troll threatens
each of them. Each Billy Goat convinces the troll that the
next Billy Goat will be bigger and tastier, and the troll allows the first two to cross the bridge. However, when the
third Billy Goat wants to cross, he doesn't let the ugly troll
get in his way and does away with the troll for good.

The number pattern of five tales includes "The Brementown
Musicians" (German). The number pattern of seven is found in "The
Fisherman and His Wife" (German), and the number pattern of nine
is found in "The Fat Cat," a Danish tale.

The number pattern story structure unfolds by repeating the
events over and over a certain number of times. The story moves forward, but a section of the story is repeated the required number of
times. For example, in the story of the three bears, Goldilocks tastes
each bowl of porridge, then sits in each chair, and then tries sleeping in each of their beds before she finally falls asleep in one bed,
and, when discovered by the bears, she leaps out the window and
runs away, never to be seen again (Langley, 1993).

"The Fisherman and His Wife" also follows a number pattern,
but it includes more elements. "The Fisherman and His Wife"
follows the number pattern of seven. The "fish prince" granted the
fisherman's wife's wishes for bigger and bigger houses with added
benefits (servants, furniture, kitchen pots and pans, etc.), but

it ends when she asks to rule the world. When the fisherman returns home, he finds his wife sitting in front of their original hut (Grimm, 1993). The patterns in both "Goldilocks and the Three Bears" and "The Fisherman and His Wife" stories move *forward,* and then, at some point, after the number elements have been told, they end.

Some stories, after the number elements have been told, repeat the elements in the *reverse* direction. The following folktale, "The Fat Cat," moves forward and then reverses and unfolds backward.

The Fat Cat

Forward: Once upon a time there was an old woman and she lived with her Cat in a small hut. The old woman loved making soups. One day she starts a pot of soup but realizes she needs one more ingredient. She asks the Cat to watch the pot of soup while she goes to the village for the needed ingredient. "I'd be glad to!" replied the Cat.

But, as soon as the woman was gone, the Cat eats the soup and the pot, too. He is feeling rather full, so he goes for a walk. He meets up with Skohottintot and Skohottintot says, "My, what have you been eating, my little cat? You are SO FAT!" The Cat immediately eats Skohottintot!

The Cat continues walking and each time he meets someone, each remarks on his weight with the same line, "My, what having you been eating, my little cat? You are SO FAT!" Immediately, the Cat eats them and continues walking. After Skohottintot, he eats Skolinkenlot, a flock of five birds, seven dancing girls, a parson with a crooked staff, and the lady with the pink parasol. But, when he meets a woodcutter with his ax, the woodcutter says the Fat Cat will not eat him and, in fact, he slices open the Cat's belly. Then [**reversing** the story], out comes the woman with the pink parasol, the parson and staff, the seven dancing girls, the flock of five birds, Skolinkenlot, Skohottintot, the pot and the soup.

Source: Adapted by Emily Chasse. "The Fat Cat" is a traditional Danish folktale. Both Margaret Read MacDonald (2001) and Jack Kent (1971) have published picture book versions of the tale.

> The accompanying DVD presents "Jack and the Northwest Wind," which uses a three-part number pattern structure.

"The Fat Cat" has a number pattern of nine, and, after the teller has told about all the elements, the elements are told in **reverse.** Note the difference. In "Goldilocks and the Three Bears" and "The Fisherman and His Wife," the story doesn't reverse. It ends and Goldilocks leaves, or it returns to the beginning and the Fisherman returns to find his wife in front of their original house, the shed. That is the end. None of the elements are told in reverse.

Type Two: Chronological

The simple chronological structure type contains a series of events arranged in the order of their occurrence. In this type of story, there is no number pattern. The following tale is an example of a simple chronological structure type.

Ruined Man's Wealth Restored through a Dream

Once upon a time there was a wealthy man from Baghdad who lost all of his money. He became quite destitute and dejected. But one night he dreamed a voice told him to go to Cairo where he would find his fortune. While he was sleeping during his first night in Cairo, he was attacked by a band of robbers. He screamed, alerting the neighbors, who called the Chief of Police. The poor man was put in jail, and the town official asked who he was and why he was in Cairo.

> The poor man explained about his dream, but the town official just laughed and said it had been a bad idea to try to find his fortune in Cairo. In fact, he himself had had such a dream, but he hadn't been foolish enough to follow that dream. The official's dream had counseled him to dig under a courtyard fountain in Baghdad and he would find a large amount of coins.
>
> The poor man returned to Baghdad and dug under the fountain in the middle of the village square. He located a packet containing hundreds of gold coins, enough wealth to provide for the poor man and his family for the rest of their lives.
>
> *Source:* Adapted by Emily Chasse from Burton (1885: 289–290).

Other chronological tales include the following:

- "How the Sea Became Salty," from *Chinese Folk Tales,* by Louise and Yuan-Hsi Kuo (1976)
- "Gohei Saves His Village," from *Fun and Festival from Japan,* by Alice Gwinn (1966)

> 💿 The accompanying DVD presents "The Smell of Food and the Jingle of Coins," which uses a chronological story structure.

Type Three: Pattern-Type Combinations

Some tales combine structures. These might include stories with a number pattern for the main story joined with a chronological story within the story. "Mollie Whuppie" is a pattern-type combination tale. The story uses a "number pattern" of three, with a short chronological tale during the third section.

Knowing a story's structure helps a teller learn a story and remember it. Whether the story is a number pattern story, a number pattern story with reversal, a chronological story type, or a pattern-type combination tale, knowing the structure can help the

> 💿 The accompanying DVD presents "Mollie Whuppie," which uses a combination story structure.

teller remember the story, even when it is a long and complicated tale. When tellers feel confident that they understand the idea of story structure and recognize many of the general ones described here, they can begin to look further at the way a story unfolds and how it affects the way a story is told.

Summary

The telling of tales has been a worldwide phenomenon since the beginning of time, and storytellers have presented stories to people of all ages. Many benefits are derived from storytelling. These include providing entertainment; helping us make sense of the world; allowing people to share customs, traditions, and moral codes; promoting and furthering understanding of the cultural heritage of a people; promoting children's development of reading, writing, language, and motor skills; serving psychological and therapeutic needs; and fulfilling spiritual and religious needs.

All stories have some type of structure, and it is important that tellers understand structures and recognize their importance when learning and organizing the tales they will tell. The three main types described in this chapter were (1) number pattern, (2) chronological, and (3) pattern-type combinations. Chapters 2 and 3 outline steps for novice tellers to follow when finding stories, learning them, and performing them well.

Suggested Resources

Print Resources

Cassell, Justine. 2007. "Virtual Peers for Literacy Learning." *Educational Technology* 47, no. 1 (Jan/Feb): 39–43.
Cassell feels the ability to read and write is incredibly important to academic success. She describes an approach to teaching literacy that involves natural storytelling by children.

Compton, Karen. 1991. "Folklore in the *ESL* Classroom." *Southern Folklore* 48, no. 1: 57–67.
English as a Second Language (ESL) students have strong interest in discussing their memories involving folklore and folktales. Compton

found that discussing games, legends, jokes, and other memories of folklore from their childhoods was extremely beneficial to the ESL students in achieving their behavioral goals in communication.

Curenton, Stephanie M. 2006. "Oral Storytelling: A Cultural Art That Promotes School Readiness." *Young Children* 61, no. 5 (September): 78–89.
There are many positive aspects of storytelling in developing school readiness. Curenton feels childhood educators can use storytelling as an age-appropriate and culturally sensitive tool to promote transition to school.

Dixon, Roger and Odette N. Gould. 1998. "Younger and Older Adults Collaborating on Retelling Everyday Stories." *Applied Developmental Science* 2, no. 3: 160–171.
Dixon and Gould studied the collaboration and retelling of everyday stories between younger and older adults. This type of storytelling led to greater understanding and acceptance between the groups.

Eastman, Mary Huse, ed. 1870–1963. *Index to Fairy Tales, Myths & Legends.* Boston: Boston Book.
Indexes to tales can help a teller locate certain stories or find tales on particular subjects. [No ISBN]

Grimm, Jacob. 1993. *Grimm's Complete Fairy Tales.* New York: Barnes & Noble.
This edition of Grimm Brothers' stories includes 200 of their well-known tales. ISBNs: 0880295198; 9780880295192

Grugeon, Elizabeth and Paul Gardner. 2000. *The Art of Storytelling for Teachers and Pupils: Using Stories to Develop Literacy in Primary Classrooms.* London: David Fulton.
In this practical handbook, the authors encourage teachers to incorporate storytelling in their classrooms and across the curriculum; to help children develop their own storytelling abilities; and to discover how telling stories can improve literacy. ISBNs: 1853466174; 9781853466175

Haven, Kendall. 2000. *Super Simple Storytelling: A Can-Do Guide for Every Classroom, Every Day.* Englewood, CO: Teacher Ideas Press.
Many basic storytelling exercises can be used to encourage storytelling in the classroom. Haven lists some and gives a step-by-step introduction to learning how to tell tales. ISBNs: 1563086816; 9781563086816

Honig, Alice Sterling. 2006. "What Infants, Toddlers, and Preschoolers Learn from Play: 12 Ideas." *Montessori Life* 18, no. 1: 16–21.

Honig believes the way we put words together in stories and tales forms a rhythmic pattern, which produces a physical response in young children. When a child hears nursery rhymes or folktales with repetitive lines like, "I'll huff and puff, and BLOW your house down" or "Jack Be Nimble, Jack Be Quick," you can observe their bodies moving with the rhythm.

Im, Janice, Rebecca Parlakian, and Carol Osborn. 2007. "Rocking and Rolling: Supporting Infants, Toddlers, and Their Families. Stories— Their Powerful Role in Early Language and Literacy." *Young Children* 62, no. 1: 52–53.

"Through stories, we organize and 'put to voice' our life experiences, and then we pass along our wisdom, history, and culture from one generation to the next" (p. 52). Im feels stories help us understand the world and make sense of our lives.

Ireland, Norma Olin. 1973. *Index to Fairy Tales, 1949–1972: Including Folklore, Legends & Myths, in Collections.* Metuchen, NJ: Scarecrow Press.
ISBNs: 0873051017; 9780873051019

———. 1985. *Index to Fairy Tales, 1973–1977: Including Folklore, Legends & Myths, in Collections.* Metuchen, NJ: Scarecrow Press.
Indexes to tales can help a teller locate certain stories or find tales on particular subjects. ISBNs: 0810818558; 9780810818552

Ireland, Norma Olin and Joseph Sprug. 1989. *Index to Fairy Tales, 1978–1986: Including Folklore, Legends, & Myths, in Collections: Fifth Supplement.* Metuchen, NJ: Scarecrow Press.
ISBNs: 081082194X; 9780810821941

Lehrman, Betty. 2005. *Telling Stories to Children: A National Storytelling Guide.* **Jonesborough, TN: National Storytelling Network.**
Lehrman gives basic information on finding tales and learning to tell them. She looks at the different types of tales and the various techniques for telling, including adding movement and sound. She describes the elements of planning successful storytelling programs, as well as many additional elements of storytelling fun. It is a small but compact volume of information available from the National Storytelling Network for a very reasonable price. ISBNs: 1879991349; 9781879991347

MacDonald, Margaret Read. 2005. *Twenty Tellable Tales: Audience Participation Folktales for the Beginning Storyteller.* **Chicago: American Library Association.**
A list of storytelling books wouldn't be complete without this resource by Master Storyteller Margaret Read MacDonald. In this book,

she shares 20 tales from all over the world that are easy for beginners to learn. She also includes advice on learning, rehearsing, and presenting the tales as each teller builds a collection of his or her own stories. ISBNs: 0838908934; 9780838908938

Maguire, Jack. 1998. *The Power of Personal Storytelling: Spinning Tales to Connect with Others.* New York: J.P. Tarcher/Putnam.
Maguire explains the importance of tales in overcoming "feelings of isolation, emptiness, and frustration" and inviting participation in human society and sharing the wonders of being human. He offers ideas for sharing stories with various community groups. He also describes finding or starting up a community storytelling group, and he outlines important points (e.g., timing, location, content of meetings) and simple rules to help the storytelling group meetings run smoothly. ISBNs: 0874779308; 9780874779301

Rockwell, Anne F. 1975. *The Three Bears & 15 Other Stories.* New York: Crowell.
Many of the stories referred to in this chapter can be found in Rockwell's book of stories. ISBNs: 0690005970; 9780690005974

Sprug, Joseph W. and Norma Olin Ireland. 1994. *Index to Fairy Tales, 1987–1992: Including 310 Collections of Fairy Tales, Folktales, Myths, and Legends: With Significant Pre-1987 Titles Not Previously Indexed.* Metuchen, NJ: Scarecrow Press.
Indexes to tales can help a teller locate certain stories or find tales on particular subjects. ISBNs: 0810827506; 9780810827509

Online Resources

Connecticut Storytelling Center homepage.
www.connstorycenter.org (accessed April 22, 2009).
The Connecticut Storytelling Center (CSC) was founded in 1984 and is based at Connecticut College in New London, Connecticut. CSC's mission is to promote the art of storytelling in all its forms and to serve storytellers and story listeners throughout the state of Connecticut.

National Storytelling Network: The World Enriched Through Storytelling.
www.storynet.org (accessed April 22, 2009).
The National Storytelling Network (NSN) serves individuals and organizations that use storytelling in health and healing, business, law, education, religion, and environmental issues. NSN also publishes a magazine and a directory of storytellers, and it sponsors a national conference.

"The Tale of Two Brothers."
www.perankhgroup.com/brothers.htm (accessed April 22, 2009).
  This site includes the oldest tale, "The Tale of Two Brothers," which is
of Egyptian origin. It was found written on papyrus in 1185 BC.

Storyfest: The Arts of Myth and Ritual in Sacred Story and Pilgrimage Travel.
www.storyfest.com (accessed April 22, 2009).
  Storytelling Travel Adventures to Mythic Sites & Legendary Destinations offers a chance to participate in virtual journeys to mythological places or register for a Master Class in Sacred Storytelling. The tours include personal guides and mentors for the journey.

Bibliography

Beekman, Jeannine Pasini. 2003 "Telling and Crafting Stories for Young Listeners." *Storytelling Magazine* 15, no. 3: 29–31.
Bettelheim, Bruno. 1977. *The Uses of Enchantment: The Meaning and Importance of Fairy Tales*. New York: Vintage Books.
Brotchie, Amanda. 2003. "Story and Storytelling." *Australian Screen Education* 31 (Winter): 98.
Bruchac, Joseph. 1985. *Iroquois Stories: Heroes and Heroines, Monsters and Magic*. Trumansburg, NY: Crossing Press.
Burton, Richard F. 1885. *The Book of the Thousand Nights and One Night: A Plain and Literal Translation of the Arabian Nights Entertainments*, vol. 4. [S.l.]. Printed for the Burton Ethnological Society for members only.
Caduto, Michael J. and Joseph Bruchac. 1988. *Keepers of the Earth: Native American Stories and Environmental Activities for Children*. Golden, CO: Fulcrum.
Cassell, Justine. 2007. "Virtual Peers for Literacy Learning." *Educational Technology* 47, no. 1 (Jan/Feb): 39–43.
Compton, Karen. 1991. "Folklore in the *ESL* Classroom." *Southern Folklore* 48, no. 1: 57–67.
Cunningham, Caroline. 1939. *The Talking Stone, Being Early American Stories Told before the White Man's Day on This Continent by the Indians and Eskimos*. New York: Knopf.
Curenton, Stephanie M. 2006. "Oral Storytelling: A Cultural Art That Promotes School Readiness." *Young Children* 61, no. 5: 78–89.
De Wit, Dorothy, ed. 1979. *The Talking Stone: An Anthology of Native American Tales and Legends*. New York: Greenwillow.
Dundes, Alan. 1964. *The Morphology of North American Indian Folktales*. Helsinki, Finland: Suomalainen Tiedeakatemia, Academia Scientiarum Fennica.
———. 1978. *Essays in Folkloristics*. Meerut, India: Folklore Institute.

———. 1980. *Interpreting Folklore.* Bloomington: Indiana University Press.

Grimm, Jacob. 1993. *Grimm's Complete Fairy Tales.* New York: Barnes & Noble.

Gwinn, Alice E. 1966. *Fun and Festival from Japan.* New York: Friendship Press.

Honig, Alice Sterling. 2006. "What Infants, Toddlers, and Preschoolers Learn from Play: 12 Ideas." *Montessori Life* 18, no. 1: 16–21.

Im, Janice, Rebecca Parlakian, and Carol Osborn. 2007. "Rocking and Rolling: Supporting Infants, Toddlers, and Their Families. Stories— Their Powerful Role in Early Language and Literacy." *Young Children* 62, no. 1: 52–53.

Isbell, Rebecca, Joseph Sobol, Liane Lindauer, and April Lowrance. 2004. "The Effects of Storytelling and Story Reading on the Oral Language Complexity and Story Comprehension of Young Children." *Early Childhood Education Journal* 32, no. 3 (December): 157–163.

Kent, Jack. 1971. *The Fat Cat.* New York: Scholastic Book Services.

Kuo, Louise and Yuan-Hsi Kuo. 1976. *Chinese Folk Tales.* Millbrae, CA: Celestial Arts.

Langley, Jonathan. 1993. *Goldilocks and the Three Bears.* New York: HarperCollins.

Levi-Strauss, Claude. 1963. *Structural Anthropology.* Translated from the French by Claire Jacobsen. New York: Basic Books.

Livo, Norma. 1986. *Storytelling: Process and Practice.* Littleton, CO: Libraries Unlimited.

Livo, Norma J. and Sandra Rietz. 1987. *Storytelling Activities.* Littleton, CO: Libraries Unlimited.

MacDonald, Margaret Read. 2001. *Fat Cat: A Danish Folktale.* Little Rock, AR: August House.

Maguire, Jack. 1985. *Creative Storytelling: Choosing, Inventing, and Sharing Tales for Children.* Cambridge, MA: Yellow Moon Press.

McKechnie, Lynne E. 2006. "Observations of Babies and Toddlers in Library Settings." *Library Trends* 55, no. 1: 190–201.

Muth, Jon J. 2002. *The Three Questions.* New York: Scholastic Press.

Propp, Vladimir. 1968. *Morphology of the Folktale.* Austin: University of Texas.

Santino, Betsy H. 1991. "Improving Multicultural Awareness and Story Comprehension with Folktales." *Reading Teacher* 45 (September): 77–79.

Stern, Lois. 2001. *Literature and the Young Child, Part One: Ages 3–5. Overview/Developing a Sense of Phonics and Story Structure.* Opinion paper. EBSCO ERIC ED 450420.

"Tale of Two Brothers." Available: www.perankhgroup.com/brothers .htm (accessed February 7, 2009).

Tenggren, Gustaf. 2003. *Tenggren's Golden Tales from the Arabian Nights.* New York: Golden Books.

Tolstoy, Leo. 1998. *Walk in the Light & Twenty-three Tales.* Farmington, PA: The Plough. Available: www.katinkahesselink.net/other/tolstoy-3-questions.html (accessed February 7, 2009).

Trelease, Jim. 2006. *The Read-Aloud Handbook.* New York: Penguin Group.

Chapter 2

❊ Locating and Selecting Tales ❊

Most tellers find certain types of tales or structures that they especially like to tell and that they feel comfortable performing. This chapter helps novice tellers begin to find the best tales for them. It will expand upon the following five steps, which are useful to novices who are beginning their storytelling journey:

1. Read and listen to a wide variety of tales.
2. Find a tale you really love and that feels like it is one you could learn and would like to tell to others.
3. Read the story for sheer pleasure and re-read it until you feel like you have a sense of the story, characters, setting, mood, and action. You will also gain a sense of how you will tell it using different voices, actions, and gestures.
4. Look for similar structures used within different tales. It is an important aspect for learning tales.
5. Select the right story for you, as you consider your audience, the event, and other significant aspects of the occasion.

Read and Listen to a Variety of Tales

Storytellers need to know many stories in various types and formats. The more stories tellers hear or read, the better able they will be to select their own tales for retelling. The various types of tales include fables, fairy tales, folktales, classical myths, legends, realistic adventures, family tales, and formula tales. Exhibit 1-1 in Chapter 1 provides definitions of different story types.

Tales of all sorts are available in different formats, including print, microfilm, DVDs, videotapes, audiocassettes, and computer files. Tales are used for fun, entertainment, and educational purposes, as well as to celebrate holidays and other special occasions.

They can be found at such places as public libraries, school and college libraries, historical centers, Native American centers, and storytelling centers, as well as on the Internet and from special library collections. Materials will include folktale collections, books on legends, mythology anthologies, and books that include and discuss folktales from various countries. There are also numerous reference books on storytelling.

It can be helpful to locate a book about an individual tale, but sometimes collections of tales from a particular author or from a specific country or books that include stories from a particular group of people are good places to start. You can find some suggestions at the end of this chapter.

Folktales and Fairy Tales

New tellers may want to start reading or hearing tales of the folktale variety. Augusta Baker and Ellin Greene (1987) recommend this in their book *Storytelling: Art & Technique.* They note: "These stories come from the folk—workers, peasants, and just plain people. They are as old as the human race. Though they were told primarily to amuse, they also contain the key to the ideas, customs, and beliefs of earlier peoples, for life was told in tale, not explained in a philosophy. Thus the folktale is enhanced by simplicity and directness— and this is the way it should be" (Baker and Greene, 1987: 33).

Fairy tales are similar to folktales but use more magical events, places, and characters. "Cinderella" has a fairy godmother who works magic; "Jack and the Beanstalk" includes magic objects, such as the tablecloth (food), the chicken (golden eggs), and the play-away club (hammer anything that needs to be pounded); and "Baba Yaga" has a magic hut that walks on chicken legs.

Collections

Many people in North America are familiar with the folk and fairy tales from England's Joseph Jacobs and Andrew Lang, France's Charles Perrault, Germany's Brothers Grimm, Denmark's Hans Christian Andersen, and Norway's Peter Christen Asbjørnsen. Although these tales were not written by these authors, the authors gathered the tales and placed them in collections. We do not know for certain where most tales originated, but we are fortunate to have this rich legacy of tales that were preserved by the collectors in these five countries. There are collections from other countries, but these five are notable and recognizable by many children and adults in the United States.

Norwegians Peter Christen Asbjørnsen, a trained zoologist, and Jorgen Moe were both tutors and began collecting stories in the 1800s. They are best known for their tales "East of the Sun and West of the Moon" and "The Three Billy Goats Gruff."

Charles Perrault is known for his Mother Goose nursery rhymes and has given us the polished and lively tales of "Cinderella," "Sleeping Beauty," and "Little Red Riding Hood." Some of Perrault's French stories were retold as tales in the Brothers Grimm collection.

Joseph Jacobs and Andrew Lang intended their tales for the enjoyment of children. The stories tended to be cheerful and fun and include "Goldilocks and the Three Bears," "Henny Penny," and "Three Little Pigs."

Jacob and Wilhelm Grimm were both accomplished scholars in Germany. Wilhelm was an artist and gifted storyteller, whereas Jacob, a university professor, was dedicated to his studies. Their stories were enthusiastically read and shared. They collected their tales from many people, including friends and relatives. Among their tales are "Rapunzel," "Cinderella," and "Little Red Riding Hood."

Some tellers and adults fear the Grimm tales are harsh and, at times, too brutal for children. Many other people feel children understand "real" versus "imaginary" and believe the stories are fine to tell. "Psychoanalysts also hold that 'the child through the comparison between the fantastic and the real, gradually learns to test reality. When the child realizes that the fairy tale is fictitious, he learns to enjoy it as fiction' (Barchilon and Petit 1960, 26)" (Arbuthnot and Sutherland, 1972: 141).

Find a Tale You Love

After reading, hearing, and watching many tales, as a novice teller, you will begin to realize that you are drawn to certain types of tales, story structures, or other criteria and that you are developing preferences for certain types of stories and/or story structures. You will begin to recognize tales that are right for you and to select some favorites. These stories will feel comfortable, and you will want to share them with others. This process entails developing self-knowledge.

Some tellers develop certain *habits* of story choice—for example, leaning toward three-part or five-part tales; tales involving animals, as in Brer Rabbit or other stories with animal characters; stories about strong female characters, and so forth. These habits are fine, especially with beginning tellers. They help provide a level of comfort for a new teller.

Tellers may also develop preferences for stories that allow certain types of paralinguistic effects, such as jumping movements, fast action, loud voices, singing, dancing, or low-key movements. Tellers may develop reputations for their styles of telling, and a listener may remark, "Oh, that is the teller who practically dances her way through her story!"

Tellers should choose stories that reflect their values and beliefs and avoid those that don't. For example, some tellers never tell stories they feel are sexist or that cast females in a bad role. They have the right to choose their stories and would probably not enjoy telling those stories or be able to tell them in an entertaining way.

The idea of who *you* are and what types of stories *you* like to tell are the most important considerations. The story will have only as much meaning as you give it. So, begin by finding a tale that you love and want to share. Later you can expand your repertoire and add different types of tales and/or story structures.

Exhibit 2-1. On a Personal Note: Story Preferences

When I first started telling tales to children, I found that I preferred stories with the number pattern of three. Number pattern of three stories is common among European folk and fairy tales, such as "Goldilocks and the Three Bears," "The Three Billy Goats Gruff," and "The Three Little Pigs." This was the pattern structure in most of the stories I had been told as a child, and I was comfortable with it. When I started telling more stories, I expanded my ability to tell tales of many different types and story structures.

Gain a Sense of Story, Characters, Setting, Mood, and Action

Tellers should read the story for sheer pleasure and re-read it until they feel they have a sense of the story, characters, setting, mood, and action. Novice tellers should try reading a tale or listening to a recording of a tale at different times and in different locations. This can assist novice tellers as they imagine the story in their minds and they choose to portray the character and setting in various ways.

Storytellers will choose the way they want to portray the various elements. Do they want the main character to be funny, light, and happy? Will they describe the setting as colorful or dark? Should the character move quickly with many small, flighty movements or slowly with deliberate actions? Their choices help set the tone of the tale.

Many tellers find it helpful to practice telling the tale to themselves while they are, say, driving, swimming, or walking. It is a fun way to practice while you are doing other things you like to do.

The story will be revealed through your words, expressions, and movements. So, let yourself enjoy the story and think about how you might use different voice levels and volumes for emphasis. You can start to plan your gestures and actions and consider how you will introduce the setting, mood, and characters.

Be Aware of Story Structures

Novice tellers will notice similar structures in the tales they read. Make a mental note of which structure a tale follows based on the discussion about story structures in Chapter 1. This will help you select a story you would like to learn. For example, you might select a number pattern story structure, which you would tell one episode at a time. If it is simply a chronological story, you would just need to remember how the story progresses, and, with practice, you would present it in that order. A pattern-type combination combines the two structure types, so it would require remembering both the number pattern and the chronological order of events. It may sound difficult at first, but tellers get used to learning the stories they want to tell. It takes a lot of practice, but it gets easier the more stories you learn.

Criteria: Selecting the Right Tale

Apart from being a tale that you love, that holds a special meaning to you, and that you want to share with others, there are some other, more objective, criteria to consider when selecting a tale to tell.

Objective Criteria

The tale should have a single, clear theme that is well-defined. It can have subthemes, but it must have one theme that is central to the story.

"The Black Geese of Baba Yaga" tells a story with a theme of keeping a promise. It tells of a young girl who promises her mother she will watch her little brother while the mother is running an errand in the village. The girl's mother has warned her that the black geese of Baba Yaga have been seen flying overhead, so the girl needs to watch her little brother very carefully. If the black geese see her little brother playing by himself, they may carry him off to Baba Yaga for her dinner.

Elena sees her friends playing nearby and goes off to join with them, intending to watch her little brother from afar. However, Elena goes with her friends to a new location and forgets to watch her little brother. When she returns home, she finds him missing and assumes the black geese of Baba Yaga saw him playing by himself and carried him off to Baba Yaga for her dinner.

The theme of this story involves promises and how Elena can live up to the promise she made to her mother. The tale is wild and fun and involves Elena's attempt to find and bring her little brother home before Baba Yaga eats him for her dinner. On her journey to rescue her brother, she generously stops three times to help out when needed. Her generosity can be seen as a subtheme, and the results help her in her quest. Alison Lurie (1980) provides us with this fun and exciting tale in *Clever Gretchen and Other Forgotten Folktales*.

The tale should have a simple, but well-developed plot.

To have a well-developed plot, a story should include the following:

- A brief opening that introduces time, setting, characters, and an element that arouses anticipation (e.g., "Once upon a time in a land far, far away, there was a . . .)
- Actions that tell the story through word pictures and build quickly to the climax
- An ending that resolves the conflict, releases the tension, and leaves everyone feeling satisfied. Examples of good endings occur in "Old One Eye," from *Grandfather Tales*: "Well, that one-eyed rogue jumped out of the chimney corner and run for his life, and him and his two buddies left that country in a hurry" (Chase, 1948: 207); and "And the rich old lady she cut her off a piece of that fish and eat it, and went on to bed and slept sound" (Chase, 1948: 207)

The tale should include a small number of characters who are believable or, in the case of many traditional folktales, represent stereotypical qualities such as good, evil, beauty, not-so-bright, greed, etc.

Examples include the following:

"Clever Elsie" and "Jack and the Beanstalk" (good but not-so-bright)
"Wicked John and the Devil" (mean)
The stepmothers in "Cinderella" and "Snow White and the Seven Dwarfs" (evil)

The style is in the telling, and each teller should develop his or her own style.

Styles may include humor, surprise, added rhythmic sounds, flowing or staccato movements, repetitious phrases, outrageous facial display, or a soft and warm expression.

The rendition must be faithful to the source material.

Minor elements (a character's name, setting, description of a character, etc.) can be changed, but the story base must remain the same.

The story must have dramatic appeal that is characteristic of a drama, with vivid gestures, voices, and motions, causing trepidation, anticipation, and much excitement.

The conflicts and emotions involved in the tale are what make a good story, and people enjoy the drama and flair that is part of a good story told well. "The Black Geese of Baba Yaga" is slightly scary and a great story for young people above the age of five.

> ☉ Another good example is Eshu Bumpus's story "The Storm," which is included on the accompanying DVD. This original tale is exciting and very scary and involves an escape from a huge gorilla. It is a perfect example of dramatic appeal, and Bumpus plays it to the hilt.

Another example of a tale with a dramatic storyline is "Simon's Splendid Pocket Watch." Adults and adolescents appreciate the dramatic moments when the narrator meets the family of Simon, the soldier he shot while serving in the Civil War. The narrator is returning Simon's pocket watch to the family, as Simon had requested before he died.

Finding the Best Tale for a Specific Person or Group

Certain characteristics of individuals or groups must be considered and should guide tellers in their choice of tales. Characteristics include the following.

Special Situations

The Ages or Sophistication Levels of Children or Adults in the Group

Most stories do not discriminate by age, but some hold greater appeal and are more appropriate for certain ages and levels of sophistication. See later for more on ages.

Special Events

Special events often offer opportunities to tell related stories. A celebration of a new bridge, park, or library would be a perfect time to locate a story that would fit the specific event. The same is true for holidays, such as Christmas, Passover, or Presidents' Day.

Themes

Various school classes, groups, clubs, or agencies might choose to select a theme for a celebration. A teller would need to discover as much as possible about the group and the theme when selecting a story.

An example of using a special theme is an afternoon program of winter stories for elementary school children that could be combined with outdoor activities (e.g., sledding, skating, making snowmen), indoor crafts (e.g., painting, drawing, working with clay), and snacks. The tales could be interspersed with the activities and snacks. This program could be offered at a school or library and might include some of the following tales:

"Jack and the Northwest Wind"
"Why the Bear Is Stumpy Tailed"
"Snow White and the Seven Dwarfs"

Type of Group

Groups may be school classes, Sunday school groups, town meetings, parent–teacher organizations, clubs, and so forth. The groups could be gathered for specific programs, such as for library story-hours and senior center entertainment.

Location

The type of physical space and the actual location are extemely important when preparing for a storytelling performance. A teller may be appearing in a classroom, church, library, home, senior center, institution, or outdoors in a park, schoolyard, campground, or around campfire.

Sometimes a teller has to plan tales for a group or event he or she knows little about. It can be one of the skills a teller develops over time. A teller can also attempt to learn general stories that can be told to almost any group, age, or event.

Exhibit 2-2. On a Personal Note: Challenging Locations

Telling tales outdoors can present one of the most challenging situations. Outdoor noises can be very distracting to you as the teller and to your audience and their ability to concentrate on your stories. I've had positive experiences telling legends to a town festival celebrating the town's history. The organizers of the event gave me a special outdoor location with clearly marked boundaries so no one would walk through the area talking or causing my listeners to be distracted by their movements. That was a very positive experience, and I was asked back for several years until the festival changed and stories no longer fit with the purpose.

However, I also have had situations where the venue wasn't conducive to storytelling. One festival where I was invited for several years to perform tales for young children was especially problematic. It didn't have a specific area for me to perform in, and the children always had other activities available. I felt that I was competing with "bubble-blowing," finger painting, face-painting, singers, and more. It was a wonderful festival, but it wasn't a good space for storytelling, until we found a separate place for it.

Age Levels

Even though stories don't, in essence, discriminate by age, certain stories are more appropriate for specific age levels.

Birth to 2 Years

Interesting sound patterns and nursery rhymes are fun at this age. Rhythm and rhyme are the most important elements. Young children like simple nursery rhymes, and they can be bounced on a lap or can clap with the rhyme. Nursery rhymes often tell a simple story. Examples include "Jack and Jill," "Little Jack Horner," "Eensy, Weensy Spider," and "Patty-Cake."

3 to 5 Years

It is fun to use very simple stories in which children can participate. A lot of rhythm and repetition are appropriate and enjoyable to children of this age. Examples include "Bear Hunt," "The Gingerbread Man," and "There Was an Old Lady Who Swallowed a Fly."

The rhythm comes from the repetition of words and phrases in a set pattern. "Little pig, little pig, let me come in. Not by the hair on my chinny, chin, chin." Or "Run, run, run, as fast as you can. . . . Can't catch me, I'm the Gingerbread Man!"

Young listeners still want interesting sound patterns. Their stories can include simple traditional stories with direct plots. Examples include "Goldilocks and the Three Bears," "Stone Soup," and "The Three Little Pigs." The bears are silly and do funny things like sit in chairs and sleep in beds! They also say funny lines like the wolf's "I'll huff and I'll puff and I'll blow your house down" or "Who's been sleeping in my bed?"

6 to 9 Years

Stories can be a little more complicated for this group, and the following would be appropriate: "One-Eye, Two-Eyes, Three-Eyes," "Jack and the Northwest Wind," and "The Fisherman and His Wife." Tall tales such as those about America's own Paul Bunyan or Pecos Bill are enjoyed by children in this age group. The exaggerated humor is appreciated, but younger children may have a hard time accepting the outrageousness.

10 to 14 Years

Preteens and teenagers want stories that are even more complex and elaborate. "Mollie Whuppie," "The Smell of Food and the Jingle of Coins," and "Wicked John and the Devil" are good choices. It would also be a good time to start legends and classical mythology. Children at this age are developing a sense of reason and judgment, and they find legends, epics, and hero tales fun and interesting.

Augusta Baker and Ellin Greene say that a retelling of *The Odyssey,* as well as tales of Robin Hood and King Arthur, would be appreciated by children in this age group. Some might feel that these stories aren't really folktales, because we know the authors and therefore they cannot be considered anonymous. However, they are considered literary tales. They are legendary stories, and tellers can choose the best way to tell them (Baker and Greene, 1987: 32).

For children 10 to 14 years old, school systems often cover wide geographic areas, and including a local or state legend would make an excellent choice. Most states have their own collections of folktales and legends. Children and young adults have often heard these legends from family members and like to retell them to their peers and teachers.

Adolescents like the idea that they have connections to other people and places. Many legends and folktales have similar stories that merge from different locations. Local legends that show up in different locations are especially appealing to young people. Ghost stories and humorous tales are also appealing with this age group.

15 to 18 Years

Stories for this age group can be longer and more sophisticated than those shared with younger children. Young people of these ages would enjoy "The Golden Sheng," from *Chinese Folk Tales* by Louise and Yuan-Hsi Kuo (1976), and "The White-Hair Waterfall," from *The Magic Boat and Other Chinese Stories* by M.A. Jagendorf and Virginia Weng (1980).

Adults

Adult listeners enjoy tales that are even longer and more complex. Stories that involve personal interpretations, such as many of the Greek myths, or tales from ancient China or Japan are welcomed by young or older adults.

Storytellers have found it rewarding to share tales with adults about people who have faced challenges immigrating to this country. Peter Coan (1997) includes interviews with people about their experiences coming to America.

Summary

Novice tellers should read and listen to a wide variety of tales. They will find ones they love and that they would like to share with others. All tellers develop preferences for certain types of stories and select ones that will allow them to use gestures, movements, and other effects to tell the story well. They should choose tales that reflect their values and beliefs, as these are the ones they will tell with joy and enthusiasm.

Having an awareness of story structure enables a teller to select tales that offer a sense of drama, told through the story's characters, setting, mood, and action. After considering certain criteria involving the plot, theme, characters, and style, tellers will present tales in their own manner, always keeping to the original base of the story. The intended audience and the event's location and theme will help tellers in selecting their stories.

Suggested Resources

Coan, Peter M. 1997. *Ellis Island Interviews: In Their Own Words.* New York: Facts on File. ISBNs: 0816034141 (hardcover); 9780816034147 (hardcover); 0816035482 (softcover); 9780816035489 (softcover)
Coan lets readers share the experiences of immigrants to America.

Schimmel, Nancy. 1992. *Just Enough to Make a Story: A Sourcebook for Storytelling.* Berkeley, CA: Sisters' Choice Books and Recordings. ISBNs: 093216403X; 9780932164032
Schimmel, a professional storyteller, offers wonderful advice to teachers, librarians, community leaders, and anyone else who wants to tell stories to children or adults. She covers choosing, learning, and telling stories, as well as choosing the appropriate medium when telling tales.

Young, Terrell A. 2004. *Happily Ever After: Sharing Folk Literature with Elementary and Middle School Students.* Newark, DE: International Reading Association. ISBNs: 0872075109; 9780872075108
The oral tradition of storytelling is important in early and middle levels of education. This guide provides an overview, explores the use of storytelling in the classroom, and looks at traditional literature across cultures.

Bibliography

Anderson, H.C. 1986. *Anderson's Fairy Tales.* New York: Grosset and Dunlap.
Arbuthnot, May Hill and Zena Sutherland. 1972. *Children and Books.* Oakland, NJ: Scott Foresman.

Asbjørnsen, Peter Christen. 1969. *East of the Sun and West of the Moon; Twenty-one Norwegian Folk Tales.* New York: Viking Press.

Baker, Augusta and Ellin Greene. 1987. *Storytelling: Art & Technique.* New Providence, NJ: R.R. Bowker.

Barchilon, Jacques and Henry Petit. 1960. *The Authentic Mother Goose Fairy Tales and Nursery Rhymes.* Denver: A. Swallow.

Bauer, Caroline Feller. 1977. *Handbook for Storytellers.* Chicago: American Library Association.

Chase, Richard. *Grandfather Tales.* 1948. Boston: Houghton Mifflin.

Coan, Peter M. 1997. *Ellis Island Interviews: In Their Own Words.* New York: Facts on File.

Grimm, Jacob. 1993. *Grimm's Complete Fairy Tales.* New York: Barnes & Noble.

Jacobs, Joseph. 2002. *English Fairy Tales; and, More English Fairy Tales.* Santa Barbara: ABC-CLIO.

Jagendorf, M.A., and Virginia Weng. 1980. *The Magic Boat and Other Chinese Folk Stories.* New York: Vanguard Press.

Kent, Jack. 1971. *The Fat Cat.* New York: Scholastic Book Services.

Kuo, Louise, and Yuan-Hsi Kuo. 1976. *Chinese Folk Tales.* Millbrae, CA: Celestial Arts.

Lang, Andrew. 1994. *A World of Fairy Tales.* New York: Dial Books.

Livo, Norma. 1986. *Storytelling: Process and Practice.* Littleton, CO: Libraries Unlimited.

———. 1987. *Storytelling Activities.* Littleton, CO: Libraries Unlimited.

Lurie, Alison. 1980. *Clever Gretchen and Other Forgotten Folktales.* New York: Crowell.

Maguire, Jack. 1987. *Creative Story: Choosing, Inventing, and Sharing Tales for Children.* Cambridge, MA: Yellow Moon Press.

Perrault, Charles. 1993. *The Complete Fairy Tales of Charles Perrault.* New York: Clarion Books.

Chapter 3

❋ Preparing and Performing Tales ❋

Learning to tell tales is a fun and entertaining process, but novice tellers should consider some guidelines as they prepare performances with stories that both meet their own personal needs and are appropriate for individual audiences and types of events. This chapter discusses some of the important points to consider.

Preparation is paramount. To perform stories in front of an audience with confidence, a teller must be ready. The audience will be better able to share the teller's excitement and delight with the tales if the teller displays a sense of control and composure. This doesn't mean that a teller will never make a mistake or forget a line; it does mean that he or she can fix a mistake or compensate for a forgotten line and remain in control of the story.

After a teller feels comfortable with the steps outlined in Chapter 2, there is a second set of steps to learn for preparing for the actual performance:

1. Organize the story by writing down the key points or making an outline on small index cards that can be reviewed before the performance. Alternatively, you can prepare a story map. You should not try to memorize the story.
2. Choose a friend or family member to be the audience for your first performance. Tell them to make comments and suggestions on the presentation, and then use their ideas as you continue to work on the story.
3. Consult with other tellers and storytelling groups to learn about how they prepare their tales and hone their presentation skills.
4. Once you are comfortable telling a few tales, perform with storytelling groups and, possibly, schedule folktale performances with local libraries or schools.

Preparing the Story to Tell

When you have selected a story and feel comfortable with the way you plan to tell it, you should organize the story. Having the organization in mind is a good way to learn and remember it. Two common organizational techniques are (1) writing the key points down or making an outline on index cards and (2) mapping the story.

Some tellers simply make photocopies of the stories they have learned so they have a collection of the printed tales. Whatever technique you use, it's best to have something written down that you can re-read before a performance.

It can be a comfort to know you have the stories in your pocket or hidden elsewhere while you are telling them. It is also useful to maintain a collection of these story cards (or notes saved in another form) or maps so you can refer to them when asked to perform tales in the future. Hopefully, you won't need them, but, just in case. . . .

Organizing the Story Structure

Story cards and story mapping are useful techniques for tellers in planning and organizing the telling of a tale. Both techniques help them "see" the organization or structure of a tale. The techniques can also be used to help a child see the organization when he or she is introduced to a story. Adults could show the child an outline, such as the following example for "Goldilocks and the Three Bears," or they could fill out a mapping form with the child.

Outlining the Tale: "Goldilocks and the Three Bears"

Following is an example of a simple outline of the story of "Goldilocks and the Three Bears":

A.   Once upon a time in a land far, far away, there lived three bears in a neat, cozy cottage in a forest.
     1. Big—Papa Bear
     2. Medium—Mama Bear
     3. Little—Baby Bear

B. One morning they woke up and were hungry. They made porridge (a lot like oatmeal) and poured it into three bowls.
    1. Big bowl for Papa Bear
    2. Medium bowl for Mama Bear
    3. Small bowl for Baby Bear
C. They each tasted their porridge but declared it too hot to eat! So, they went for a walk in the woods while it cooled. While they were gone, a little girl with golden curls walked by their cottage and smelled the delicious porridge. "Mm-m-m," said Goldilocks. She looked in the window and did not see anyone, so she walked to the front door and went inside without even knocking! The bears were very trusting and never locked their doors. Goldilocks saw the three bowls of porridge and decided to take a taste of each of them.
    1. Papa Bear's bowl was "TOO HOT!!!"
    2. Mama Bear's bowl was "TOO COOL!!!"
    3. Baby Bear's bowl was "JUST RIGHT," and she ate it all up!
D. Goldilocks needed a rest, so she walked into the living room and saw three chairs.
    1. Papa Bear's big chair was "TOO HARD!!!"
    2. Mama Bear's chair was "TOO SOFT!!!"
    3. Baby Bear's chair was "JUST RIGHT," and she rocked and rocked and rocked and broke it all to pieces!
E. Goldilocks needed to take a nap, so she walked to the bedroom.
    1. Papa Bear's bed was "TOO HIGH!!!"
    2. Mama Bear's bed was "TOO LOW!!!"
    3. Baby Bear's bed was "JUST RIGHT," and she crawled in and pulled the covers over her head and fell asleep!
F. While Goldilocks slept, the bears came home and noticed that someone had been in their house.
    1. Papa Bear said, "Someone's been eating my porridge!"
    2. Mama Bear said, "Someone's been eating my porridge!"
    3. Baby Bear said, "Somebody's been eating my porridge and ate it all up!"
G. They went to the living room.
    1. Papa Bear said, "Somebody's been sitting in my chair!"
    2. Mama Bear said, "Somebody's been sitting in my chair!"

    3. Baby Bear said, "Somebody's been sitting in my chair and broke it all to pieces!"
H. They walked into the bedroom.
    1. Papa Bear said, "Somebody's been sleeping in my bed!"
    2. Mama Bear said, "Somebody's been sleeping in my bed!"
    3. Baby Bear said, "Somebody's been sleeping in my bed and she's still here!"
I. Goldilocks heard the bears and sat up and saw them. She then hopped out of bed, ran to the window, leaped out, and ran off . . . never to be seen again! And, that's the story of "Goldilocks and the Three Bears."

Story Mapping

Story mapping involves arranging the parts of the story in a manner that helps the teller remember them. The map is a graphic representation of the tale that allows the teller to visualize the organization. It can take the form of a box (as shown in Exhibits 3-1 and 3-2) or a web.

    Examples of story mapping can be found in books about storytelling—for example, Flack (1997), Hoke (1999), Livo (1986), and Livo and Rietz (1987)—or on the Internet.

Exhibit 3-1. Story Map

BEGINNING	_____	_____
Introduce anonymous time	Introduce anonymous place	Introduce characters and state the conflict
MIDDLE	_____	_____
1st episode	2nd episode	3rd episode
END	_____	_____
1st resolution	2nd resolution	3rd resolution
CONCLUSION	_____	_____

Exhibit 3-2. Story Map of "Goldilocks and the Three Bears"

INTRODUCTION

Once upon a time, in a land far, far away, there were three bears. The bears woke up one morning, were hungry, and fixed porridge. The porridge was too hot, so they went out for a walk in the woods. While they were out, a young girl with golden curls walked by their cottage and smelled the porridge. Without even knocking, she opened the front door and went into the kitchen.

BEGINNING

Goldilocks was hungry so she started tasting the bears' porridge.

Goldilocks tasted Papa Bear's bowl. TOO HOT!	Goldilocks tasted Mama Bear's bowl. TOO COLD!	Goldilocks tasted Baby Bear's bowl. It was just right and SHE ATE IT ALL UP!

MIDDLE

Goldilocks wanted to sit down so she went to the living room and tried the bears' chairs.

Goldilocks sat in Papa Bear's chair. TOO HARD!	Goldilocks sat in Mama Bear's chair. TOO SOFT!	Goldilocks sat in Baby Bear's chair. It was just right and she rocked and BROKE IT ALL TO PIECES!!!

END

Goldilocks was tired, went to the bears' bedrooms, and tried the bears' beds.

Goldilocks tried Papa Bear's bed. TOO HIGH!	Goldilocks tried Mama Bear's bed. TOO LOW!	Goldilocks tried Baby Bear's bed. And FELL FAST ASLEEP!

CONCLUSION

The bears come home and see what has happened.

Papa Bear, "Someone has been eating my porridge!"	Mama Bear, "Someone has been eating my porridge!"	Baby Bear, "Someone has been eating my porridge and THEY ATE IT ALL UP!"
Papa Bear, "Someone has been sitting in my chair!"	Mama Bear, "Someone has been sitting in my chair!"	Baby Bear, "Someone has been sitting in my chair and THEY BROKE IT ALL TO PIECES!"
Papa Bear, "Someone has been sleeping in my bed!"	Mama Bear, "Someone has been sleeping in my bed!"	Baby Bear, "Someone has been sleeping in my bed and SHE IS STILL HERE!!!"

Goldilocks wakes up, realizes what has happened, jumps out of the bed, leaps out the window, and runs away, never to be seen again!

Do Not Try to Memorize the Story

It is important to stress from the beginning that you should *learn* the story and not try to memorize it. Memorizing it makes it hard to tell without sounding stilted, stiff, and unnatural. Learning the story usually involves reading it many times, hearing it, and practicing telling it.

The only stories that need to be memorized are *literary* stories that were originally written and not told orally. Those stories were never part of the oral tradition, and their authors are known. For those stories, because the words don't change, a teller needs to commit the story to memory. That type of telling is not covered in this book, although the memorization of epics is mentioned in Chapter 6.

One exception to this rule pertains to tales of the *oral* tradition. If a chant or a poem or some other very small amount of special wording plays an integral part in the story, those words should be memorized. For example, in "The Golden Sheng," a Chinese tale mentioned in Exhibit 8-2, two lines need to be memorized. Mulberry Boy, one of the main characters, hears the dragon calling to

> "The Golden Sheng" is performed on the accompanying DVD.

his sister, Little Red Maiden, with the lines, "Waa-waa, foolish maiden. To marry me you say 'Nay.' Well, drill, drill, drill away, you will drill the rock every day and, if you do not drill through the mountain, your life I will not spare."

Mulberry Boy answers with the line, "Evil dragon, evil dragon, torturing my sister. . . . Day after day, I will play on my golden sheng, never will I stop, and your life I will not spare!" (Kuo and Kuo, 1976: 20). These lines are very important to the action in the story and need to be memorized and told, as part of the story, exactly as you heard the tale or saw it written in a book.

Although stories were originally told orally, many have since been written down, and certain words and phrases have been retained. These words and phrases need to be included with the exact words when the story is retold.

Planning the Storytelling Performance

Other important elements need consideration when planning a storytelling performance. These include how you will use voice, gestures, paralinguistic effects, kinesthetics, and props and how you can increase opportunities for the audience to participate. You should choose how much action, sounds, voices, narration, singing, chanting, or jumping to use. It is important to balance these effects with the actual story. Too much action without enough of a story isn't useful or fun. Not all stories need special effects, but there may be times when effects are an enhancement. The same is true for singing or chanting. Finding the right balance takes time and experience. You need to be flexible, because the balance may change, depending on the group or the size of the group.

Paralinguistic Effects

The *Oxford English Dictionary* (2009) defines paralanguage as "the non-phonemic but vocal component of speech, such as tone of voice, tempo of speech, and sighing, by which communication is assisted. [and] Sometimes also taken to include non-vocal factors such as gesture and facial expression." When tellers call out the sound the wind is making, they are using paralinguistic effects. Tellers can choose to incorporate motions and gestures, enhancing the paralingistic effects they are using in the story.

Appearance and Clothing

A storyteller's appearance is extremely important for performances. Tellers want their audiences to be drawn to them, and one way to accomplish this is by wearing bright, exciting clothing and styles. Colorful beads, belts, scarves, and so forth are fun and useful, too.

Voice

A teller's voice can reflect the strong and scary growling of the troll in "The Three Billy Goats Gruff" (Galdone, 2006); the kind, sweet, caring voice of Joshua's mother in "Joshua and the Genie"; or the wise and funny sound of Pandora in Barbara McBride-Smith's new version of the Greek tale by that name.

Joshua and the Genie

Joshua was a good boy. He had a lot of friends, was very bright, liked to read, was good at sports, enjoyed singing and music, and more. But he wanted to have something very special about him. His friend Anna could tell stories so well, and when she started telling stories, everyone wanted to hear them. Joshua wished he could tell stories like Anna. It really made Anna special.

And his friend Richard could stick out his arm and "Whoosh" catch a fly or "Whoosh, whoosh," more than one fly. Joshua wished he could catch flies like Richard. It really made Richard special.

His mother noticed Joshua moping around one day, thinking about having something special about him. "Joshua, what's wrong? You look sad."

"I wish I had something special about me. Anna is special because she can tell stories, and Richard is really special because he can catch flies with one hand! I don't have anything special about me."

"Oh, Joshua, I'm sorry you're feeling that way, but I don't think it's true and I think you're very special. You're funny and bright and you are a great reader. It's a beautiful day, so why don't you walk down to the pond, skip a few stones, and stop worrying about it?"

So Joshua walked around the pond and started skipping stones. Suddenly he saw a bottle sticking out of the sand. He pulled it out of the sand, brushed the side, and pulled out the cork. POOF! Out popped a genie.

"Your wish is my command."

"Who are you?"

"You released me from the bottle when you pulled out the cork. Now, you can have any three wishes."

"WOW!" Joshua was so excited. A genie and three wishes! He thought about it and very quickly said, "I want to be able to tell stories like Anna . . . no, I want to tell them BETTER than Anna."

"Your wish is granted."

The next day, everyone wanted to hear Joshua's stories. They were really good . . . moving, funny, and sometimes, even a little scary. Even the principal pulled up a chair and enjoyed the tales. But after a while, Joshua got tired of telling stories. He'd been doing a lot of reading about genies and had found out that genies were good and helpful when someone had wishes left to use, but as soon as the wishes had all been granted genies could turn on a person. They would become mean and nasty. Joshua thought that was pretty scary so he didn't want to use his last wish until he really needed it.

One day as he walked home from school, he saw his dog on the front porch and his dog saw him and got really excited. He bounded down the stairs and ran across the street. Just then Joshua saw a car squealing around the corner heading straight for his dog. It looked like the car was going to hit his dog. He ran to his house, up the stairs to his bedroom, and pulled the cork out of the bottle.

"Your wish is my command."

"Please don't let my dog die. Please don't let him die."

Just then, Joshua's mother called up the stairs, "Joshua, your dog is okay. That car just nicked him a little, but he's fine."

Joshua breathed a sigh of relief but then he noticed the genie. He was getting bigger and bigger, uglier and uglier, and his teeth were getting longer and longer. He started growling at Joshua.

Joshua thought fast. "Oh, yeah. It's easy for you to get bigger and look meaner. That's not hard for you."

"You're right and I will!" said the genie. The genie grew larger and larger and his teeth got longer and sharper.

Joshua said, "But it would be impossible for you to get smaller. I bet you can't do that."

"I can do anything I want!" And the genie started to get smaller.

"Oh, yeah, a little bit smaller is nothing. But to get really small, like a mouse . . . or a fly. You can't do that."

The genie looked at Joshua defiantly and started shrinking . . . smaller and smaller and smaller until he was the size of a fly. Joshua reached out his hand and "Whoosh" caught the genie fly!

Then Joshua went to the shelf, pulled out the cork, and stuffed the genie into the bottle. Next, he walked down to the pond and buried the bottle in the sand. And who knows? Maybe, you'll be the one to find it there, brush off the sand, pull out the cork, and . . .

Source: Written by Emily S. Chasse.

Repetition

There are opportunities to include repetitious language in a story as a technique to get children to participate. After you say the words as part of the story, you can signal the audience to join in the next time those words are used. "Little Pig, Little Pig, let me come in!" and "Not by the hair on my chinny, chin, chin" are two examples from "The Three Little Pigs." Because this occurs three times in the story, children laugh louder each time it is called out.

Language: Accents and Dialects

When a story comes from a certain country or region or from a specific ethnic group, the words or sounds a teller uses can reflect that dialect. Accents enhance a story when they are performed *skillfully*—for example, a good southern accent when telling "Wicked John and the Devil" (Chase, 1948: 29), or a good British accent when telling "The History of Tom Thumb" (Crossley-Holland, 1987: 155).

In Irish tales such as "Finn MacCoul and His Fearless Wife" (Byrd, 1999), "Tim O'Toole and the Wee Folk" (McDermott, 1990), or "Fiona's Luck" (Bateman, 2007), the teller should use a credible Irish brogue.

However, a poor accent can ruin a story. Norma Livo (1986: 115) notes that it is hard to copy dialect from words written on a page. In cases where stories need to be told in the dialect of a particular ethnic group, people from that ethnic group could be offended by a person outside the group attempting to copy their dialect. Many storytellers suggest that tellers listen—either in person or on a tape—to someone who speaks the dialect and then practice it until they have perfected a natural accent. Tapes are available in some college and university libraries, and a local theatre group might have recordings that you could borrow.

If you have any doubt about your ability to perform the tale comfortably and convincingly with an accent, don't attempt it. Tellers should present the tale in the way they feel most comfortable. As Livo (1986: 97) has noted: "A character's language done in the teller's own dialect is more believable than a poorly rendered accent."

Stage Dressing, Props, Furniture, and Lighting

Preparing the stage for a teller's performance can be simple or more complex. Some tellers prefer to perform without anything extra on the stage or in the performance space. Others like to use curtains, chairs, stools, pillows, kitchen pots and pans, or other objects.

A storyteller from Hartford, Connecticut, uses a small folding stepladder in her stories in a variety of ways, leading to laughter from her audience. This technique is very individual and another teller might not be able to "pull it off" in the same manner.

A teller should appear in sufficient light, but the light should not shine directly in the teller's face. If performing outdoors, the teller should make certain that the sun doesn't shine in his or her face or on the faces of audience members.

Practice Performances

When you are finally ready to try an actual performance, select a few family members or friends to watch you tell your tale. The first time, it would help to ask for them for positive comments only. The next time, allow them to make mild criticisms and suggestions and use their comments to make any revisions, and then practice it with those changes. It can be hard, at first, to work with critical—even if valid—comments, but it is the best way to refine your storytelling performance.

Seek out storytelling groups in your local area and watch them tell their tales, and then join them in informal storytelling performances. You will gain a great amount of wisdom and helpful suggestions from other storytellers. It is a wonderful way to work on your presentation skills.

Public Performances

When you feel ready to share a few tales publicly, continue working with your storytelling group and consider scheduling small performances with local libraries or schools. Your storytelling group can guide you in further paid performances. See Chapter 13 for information on the storytelling profession.

Audience Participation

The amount and type of audience participation depends on the teller; the age, and the sophistication of their audience; and the teller's comfort level with ad-libbing or improvising. The Danish tale "The Fat Cat" tells of a woman making porridge and of her need for her cat to help care for the pot of porridge while she runs an errand to obtain more of a certain herb or spice for the mixture. After she leaves, the cat eats the entire pot of porridge and the pot! The teller can wear a large sheet around his or her neck and body and store all the characters the cat encounters and eats while he goes out for a stroll because he is feeling so full. While on his walk, he keeps eating each person, animal, and object that he meets after they comment on his huge size. The audience members participate by assuming the roles of the people, animals, or objects, and are swept under the sheet each time the cat eats one of them. The cat grows even fatter, and audience members find it hysterical; the children under the sheet laugh and laugh until the cat meets a woodsman who puts an end to the consumption by slicing the cat's belly with his ax, and releasing all the children (characters) from under the sheet.

The returning woman fixes the resulting cut with a Band-Aid, gives the cat a swat on the rear end, and returns to her kitchen to start another pot of porridge. This is an old Danish tale, which is recounted in the picture book *The Fat Cat* (Kent, 1971).

If the teller is female, she should wear long pants or a long skirt, and she can add a large sheet when the cat starts eating the people, animals, and objects. The teller may be more comfortable if he or she asks a teacher or another adult to monitor the activity under the sheet. The resulting story can show participatory storytelling at its best.

Another possible format could involve a large poster of the cat with a large hole cut out for the cat's mouth. Children could help by "feeding" pictures of the animals, people, and objects into the cat's mouth.

Participation such as this can be a lot of fun for both the teller and the audience, but it doesn't always need to be this active or rambunctious! Sometimes it can be as subtle as eye contact between teller and audience members; soft audience chanting and small movements (e.g., as part of the story of "The Gunniwulf" [told in Chapter 12]); or chants during the telling a nursery rhyme such as "The Gingerbread Man" (Baumgartner, 1998).

Props

The use of props is also very individualistic. The tale of "Jack and the Northwest Wind," which is provided later in this chapter, can be told without props, or the teller can wear a hat and take it off and brandish it, as appropriate. Or, if they wish, they can use a tablecloth, a stuffed chicken, and a small wooden club.

To use props effectively, you need to keep the following key points in mind:

1. Remember that the story is the most important component of the performance.
2. Don't use props that are so large and unwieldy that they are hard to control.
3. Don't use props that attract too much attention.
4. Make sure that the props are well integrated with the story.
5. Props shouldn't be a crutch. You should know the story well enough to be able to tell it without props. They should be an added treat, something special for that tale.
6. Use props with only a few stories, or perhaps use them only with certain audiences.

A teller might want to have certain objects available each time a storytelling session is scheduled. Blankets, rugs, shawls, or quilts are soft ways of marking the beginning of a session. Aprons, bags, key rings, knapsacks, eyeglasses (real or pretend), are also prop-like objects to signal that it's time for storytelling. Any type of clothing—including hats, shirts, necklaces, beads, carved, painted sticks—can serve the same purpose. Or, a storyteller may invite audience members to join the teller on the quilt. It is another form of ritual, and it can be a comfort for you and your audience to understand that it holds a special meaning and that the telling will now begin!

Designing and Redesigning Tales

As tellers begin to feel comfortable with stories, they might want to create their own tales for themselves or for someone else to tell. They can choose to design or create a new tale based on one of the

---

Exhibit 3-3. On a Personal Note: Stones

In several tales I tell, stones play an important role. They may be an important part of the story or I may just keep a few of them in a leather bag and ask a child from the audience to select one so I know which story to tell next. This can serve a couple purposes. As I tell my stories, I might see one child who I think needs an extra boost. Or, it might be a special treat for a child who has been especially attentive. Being selected to choose the stone that signifies the next story is often seen as an honor and is sought after by the children.

story structures from Chapter 1 that they know and like to tell. Or, they can redesign a tale based on a traditional tale they already know and like.

Tellers can use a story structure they already know. It could follow a number pattern, chronologic, or pattern-type combination. Tellers can fill in the story, following the criteria described in Chapter 2. Basically, it would include a theme, plot, opening, actions, characters, and setting, and it should have dramatic appeal and a satisfying resolution. Remember, after a short opening, keep descriptions of setting and characters simple. Have it build quickly to a climax. Maguire's (1985) *Creative Storytelling: Choosing, Inventing, and Sharing Tales for Children* is a very useful and fun guide that can help you create and compose tales from old, new, and original stories.

You can also redesign a new version of a tale based on a traditional tale. You would change the story but retain its base, thus creating a new version of an old tale. My version of "Jack and the

> (◉) "I present my version of "Jack and the Northwest Wind" on the DVD that accompanies this guidebook.

Northwest Wind," provided below, might have reflected my concern for my own young child when I composed it in early 2001. I revised it while keeping the base of the story but changed some simple items and focused on the mother's concern for her son's safety.

The "Jack Tales" is a series of stories about a boy who is well-meaning but not very bright. He tries to do the right thing and always attempts to help his mother and his family. His attempts do not always work out the way he expects. The tales are often fun and exciting, and they end with a good conclusion.

Jack and the Northwest Wind

Jack was a good boy and always tried to help out his mama and family whenever he could. His daddy was gone a workin' and Jack, his mama, and his brothers slept in a small room with as many blankets as they could find. But on nights when that Northwest Wind blew in the cracks and crevices of the walls, they were SO COLD.

Jack decides to go in search of the hole where the Northwest Wind comes from and plans to plug it up with his hat so it could no longer blow through the cracks and crevices of their house. His mama and brothers laugh and tell Jack he is wrong and there isn't any such hole where the Northwest Wind comes from. But Jack takes off one day with his hat and walks and walks, looking for that hole where the Northwest Wind comes from.

In mid-afternoon Jack meets a man who asks, "Who are you and where are you going?" Jack tells him and the man explains that there is no such hole and urges Jack to join him for lunch and take a present from the man back to his mama. Jack says his mama loves presents and he and the man share lunch. Afterward the man shows Jack a gift of a tablecloth for his mama. Jack says, "Wonderful! My mama will love a new tablecloth." "Jack, it's not just ANY tablecloth; it's a MAGIC tablecloth. . . . Watch!" The man throws it into the air, saying "Spread, tablecloth, spread" and the tablecloth comes down covered with food. Jack is delighted and says how much his mama will like it.

The man warns Jack that there are boys at the bottom of the hill who will want to talk but they are nothing but trouble, so he should walk on by. But when Jack gets to the bottom of the hill, the boys run out, asking who he is and what he has tucked under his arm. He tells them who he is and pretends it is just an old tablecloth, but the boys question him again and he can't keep a secret and tells them about the magic tablecloth. He demonstrates the "Spread, tablecloth, spread" command and the boys get so excited they beg Jack to stay and let them show their father when he gets home. Jack says he needs to start for home but says he'll wait a few moments. Unfortunately, while he is waiting, he falls asleep and it gives the boys the time to switch Jack's tablecloth for an old one of their own. When Jack wakes up the next morning he doesn't notice the tablecloth isn't his own, says goodbye, and walks home. Of course, when Jack shows what he thinks is the magic tablecloth to his mother, it doesn't work. His mother is not surprised and says, "Jack, there is NO MAGIC."

A few days later Jack decides to try to find the Northwest Wind again and he sets off to find it. In mid-afternoon he meets the same man again and he convinces Jack again to share lunch with him. They have a nice meal and the man says he has another present for Jack's mama. He shows Jack a chicken and Jack says his mama would love to have a new chicken, but the man tells Jack it is not JUST a chicken, but a magic chicken. He demonstrates the command, "Lay, chicken, lay" and the chicken lays a golden egg. As Jack heads home, the man warns him again not to wait when the boys at the bottom of the hill stop him to talk. But when Jack reaches the bottom of the hill, the boys run out, ask how he is doing, and what he has under his arm. Jack tries to hurry on and not stop to talk but he can't help himself. He tells the boys he has a magic chicken and demonstrates the "Lay, chicken, lay" command. After the chicken lays a golden egg, the boys convince Jack to wait for their daddy so he can see the magic chicken. Even though Jack knows he should go straight home, he waits, and falls asleep while the boys replace his magic chicken with one of their own that is not magic.

When Jack heads home the next day he doesn't realize it isn't his magic chicken. His mama is glad to see him safely at home but when he tries to demonstrate the magic chicken, it doesn't work. "Jack," his mama says, "There is NO MAGIC." He is disappointed but it isn't long before he decides to try again to find the hole where the Northwest Wind comes from and plug it up with his hat.

As he is traveling and looking, he comes across the same man who has stopped him before. He offers Jack a meal and a present for his mother again. After their meal the man shows him a small club of wood and says it is magic. It looks like a very small baseball bat and can chop wood, knock apart wood for kindling, or pound nails into a piece of wood. He just has to say the magic words "Play-a-Way, Play-a-Way, Play-a-Way, Club," and it does whatever it is asked to do. Jack realizes it could help his mama and family so he thanks the man, takes the club, and heads for home. The man warns him again not to stop at the bottom of the hill and talk to the boys, but of course he stops, and Jack has to show off his play-a-way club. The boys convince him to wait for their daddy and he does, but he falls asleep and doesn't see them replace his play-a-way club with a piece of wood of their own. However, when the boys' father gets home, he hears them demonstrating how the play-a-way club can knock wood into kindling. Jack realizes what is happening and decides the boys must have also taken his magic tablecloth and chicken. He calls out "Play-a-Way, Play-a-Way, Play-a-Way Club, knock down this house if they don't give me back my tablecloth and chicken right now."

The boys know Jack saw what was going on and realize he has figured everything out. Jack grabs his play-a-way club and the boys give him back his tablecloth and chicken. Jack runs all the way home with his treasures to show his mama.

His mama says, "Jack, I'm so glad you are home and safe!" But Jack says, "Mama, wait until you see what I have!" He shows her the magic tablecloth with "Spread, tablecloth, spread!" and the chicken, saying, "Lay, chicken, lay," and the Play-a-Way Club knocking wood boards to cover the holes in the walls of the house. His mama starts to say, "There is NO MAGIC" when she sees the tablecloth and the golden egg, and the Play-a-Way Club. "Well, Jack, I guess there is MAGIC!" And that's the story of Jack and the Northwest Wind.

Source: Adapted by Emily Chasse, who retains the copyright to this version of the story of "Jack and the Northwest Wind."

There are many versions of "Jack and the Northwest Wind," and it is considered to be in the public domain. The general rules for copyright can be found at www.librarycopyright.net, and they should be closely considered when planning commercial storytelling performances. Copyright is also covered in Chapter 13.

Summary

The teller and the audience will enjoy the storytelling experience when the teller has organized, prepared, and practiced sufficiently. The teller's language, voices, gestures, accents, and actions need to be well planned so the performance can progress smoothly.

Opportunities for audience participation can add to the event and may be subtle—with soft chants—or more overt—with loud voices or singing and shouting. Added effects of props or rituals can enhance the storytelling experience. Overall, when the teller has planned ahead and feels confident with the tale, the experience should prove successful.

The next chapter explores the challenges and rewards of storytelling with classical mythology.

Suggested Resources

Flack, Jerry. 1997. *From the Land of Enchantment*. Englewood Cliffs, CO: Teacher Ideas Press. ISBNs: 1563085402; 9781563085406

There are many ways to use folk and fairy tales when teaching children, and Flack outlines creative ideas involving stories for the classroom. He also includes a section on story mapping.

Hoke, Judy. 1999. "The Realm of Fairy Tales: An Original WebQuest for Grades 4–5." www-ma.beth.k12.pa.us/jhoke/jhwebquest/storymap.htm (accessed February 7, 2009).

An outline of a story map helps children organize the story elements of their tale. Hoke includes the characters, setting, problem, major events, and the solution that results in the outcome of the tale.

Lipman, Doug. "eTips from the Storytelling Coach." www.storydynamics .com/Home/etips1.html (accessed April 24, 2009).

Lipman, a storyteller, musician, and teacher, coaches other storytellers using principles modeled by his father and some of his most helpful teachers as well as his own experiences. He writes an e-mail newsletter, which he offers for free.

Sierra, Judy. 1996. *The Storytellers' Research Guide.* Eugene, OR: Folkprint. ISBNs: 0963608940; 9780963608949

Sierra provides extremely useful advice for beginning or advanced tellers. She includes research basics, gives ideas on ways to select stories, and clearly explains copyright issues.

Bibliography

Bateman, Teresa. 2007. *Fiona's Luck.* Watertown, MA: Charlesbridge.

Baumgartner, Barbara. 1998. *The Gingerbread Man.* New York: DK Ink.

Byrd, Robert. 1999. *Finn MacCoul and His Fearless Wife: A Giant of a Tale from Ireland.* New York: Dutton Children's Books.

Chase, Richard. 1948. *Grandfather Tales: American-English Folk Tales.* Boston: Houghton Mifflin.

Crossley-Holland, Kevin. 1987. *British Folk Tales: New Versions.* New York: Orchard Books.

Flack, Jerry. 1997. *From the Land of Enchantment.* Englewood Cliffs, CO: Teacher Ideas Press.

Galdone, Paul. 2006. *The Three Billy Goats Gruff.* New York: Clarion Books.

Hoke, Judy. 1999. The Realm of Fairy Tales: An Original WebQuest for Grades 4–5. Available: www-ma.beth.k12.pa.us/jhoke/jhwebquest/storymap.htm (accessed February 7, 2009).

Kent, Jack. 1971. *Fat Cat: A Danish Folktale.* New York: Scholastic Book Services.

Kuo, Louise and Yuan-Hsi Kuo. 1976. *Chinese Folk Tales.* Millbrae, CA: Celestial Arts.

Livo, Norma. 1986. *Storytelling: Process and Practice.* Littleton, CO: Libraries Unlimited.

Livo, Norma and Sandra Rietz. 1987. *Storytelling Activities.* Littleton, CO: Libraries Unlimited.

Maguire, Jack. 1985. *Creative Storytelling: Choosing, Inventing, and Sharing Tales for Children.* Cambridge, MA: Yellow Moon Press.

McBride-Smith, Barbara. 2005. *It's Not Easy Being a Goddess: A Yellow Rose of Texas Tells the Greek Myths in Her Native Tongue.* Little Rock, AR: August House Publishers.

McDermott, Gerald. 1990. *Tim O'Toole and the Wee Folk: An Irish Tale.* New York: Viking.

Oxford English Dictionary. Available: http://dictionary.oed.com (accessed February 7, 2009).

Chapter 4

✳ Storytelling with Classical Mythology ✳

Myths, in general, originated among groups of people from various civilizations and locations. People from Africa; Egypt; North, Central, and South America; Asia; Europe; the Middle East; and Oceania have their own myths, and many of those myths mix and overlap. Discussion of mythology in this chapter is limited to the field of classical mythology. Classical mythology covers the myths dealing with Greek or Roman gods, goddesses, demigods, and demigoddesses, and with the mortals with whom they were said to have interacted. Classical mythology is of utmost importance to the world of storytelling, as these myths provide the basis for most tales, legends, and stories told worldwide.

The Ancient peoples told stories as they sought answers to life's vital questions, including their role in the world and how they should behave. Long before Christ (fourteenth century BC), the ancient Greeks sought explanations for natural wonders and answers to mysterious questions. The Greeks were very creative, and when they looked up at the stars, they saw visions of animals, insects, and objects, imagined where these figures had come from and why they had appeared, and they formed tales about those figures they saw in the sky.

Myths are rooted in human behavior, even when such behavior is exhibited by gods and goddesses who are, of course, not human. Myths can be used—as they were among the ancient Greeks and Romans—to educate and enlighten. They are especially meaningful to children and young people. While children as young as elementary school ages might find stories about gods and goddesses appealing, it is often middle school and high school students who are most attracted to the fantastic characters and creatures of classical myths. Although some enterprising teachers present stories and information on classical mythology to younger children, most schools offer formal instruction during the middle school years. Myths offer creative ways to teach different aspects of social studies, language arts, mathematics, and a multitude of other areas. Chapter 11 includes activities dealing with classical mythology that can be used in the classroom.

Classical myths promote an understanding of ethics and morals, and of the motivations behind the characters' actions, providing insights into people's behavior. By listening to and reading such ancient tales, children vicariously experience challenging situations; they learn how to deal with hard times and face defeat, and how to gain knowledge from all of it. Young people can watch love bloom or falter; they can see pride, jealousy, curiosity, and envy; and they can see the outcomes and consequences of actions stemming from those emotions. Some of the gods and goddesses reflecting emotions include Eros, the God of Love; Gelos, the God of Laughter; Lyssa, the Goddess of Rage; and Philotes, the Goddess of Friendship. Other Greek and Roman gods can be found, with descriptions, at Greek and Roman Mythology, http://ancienthistory.about.com/library/bl/bl_myth_table_romangods.htm.

The story of Narcissus is an excellent example of a myth that demonstrates some of the benefits of good morals. Narcissus was very handsome, but also very vain. He rejected those who admired and cared about him. One day, he saw his refection in a pool of water and fell in love with himself. He kept gazing at his image and lost all interest in food and drink until he finally wasted away to nothing and died.

Librarians, teachers at all levels, social workers, psychologists, community workers, child and young adult caregivers, and others should thus share classical myths with young people. It is preferable to tell the myths orally without a book, but they can be read aloud if the adult doesn't feel equipped to tell the myths without a print source.

Before proceeding any further, we should start with some basic terms and definitions, which can be found in Exhibit 4-1.

Exhibit 4-1. Terms and Definitions
classical mythology: The myths dealing with Greek or Roman gods and god-desses, demi-gods, and demi-goddesses.
demi-god: Those male characters with one parent a god and one a mortal. A mythological being thought to possess less power than a god but approaching that status.
demi-goddess: A female demi-god.
gods: Beings with more than human attributes and incredible powers. Beings be-lieved to control a certain aspect of the world (Poseidon, Ruler of the Sea; Zeus, Ruler of the Sky; Hades, Ruler of the Underworld, etc.).
goddesses: Female gods, holding supreme powers (Venus, Goddess of Beauty; Athena, Goddess of Wisdom; Aphrodite, Goddess of Love, etc.).
myth: A story that is not true but not completely false. "Plato refers to 'muthos' to denote something not wholly lacking truth but for the most past fictitious" (Cuddon, 1998: 525). "Plato recognized the power that resides in myth, and warned his followers to beware of its seductive charm" (Cotterell, 2005: 10).
mythology: The definition of the word *mythology* is very broad. *American Heritage College Dictionary* (2002: 921) definitions include the following: a body of myths associated with an individual, event, or institution; a body or collection of myths belonging to a people and addressing their history, deities, ancestors, and heroes.

Greek Mythology

The Greeks were wonderful tellers of myths. They were curious about why things happened, and they told stories to try to explain actions, events and phenomena that occurred in their natural world that seemed strange or unusual. The Greeks were creative. Looking at the stars and the constellations, they saw pictures and told stories about them. So many questions led to many stories.

There are stories associated with many individual constellations. A few of the most well-known stories are covered here.

It is said that Zeus, King of the Gods, fell in love with Callistro, a beautiful young woman who was a hunter. When Zeus's wife, Hera, found out, she was furious and changed Callistro into a bear. Zeus heard what Hera had done, and to protect Callistro from further abuse, he sent her into outer space as Ursa Major, the Great Bear. Ursa Major contains seven bright stars that make up the Big

Dipper, which has the distinct shape of a ladle. Zeus turned Callistro's son, Arcas, into a little bear and sent him to join his mother as Ursa Minor, the Little Bear. Ursa Minor has a ladle shape as well, and is known as the Little Dipper.

Orion, the great hunter, was said to be the tallest and most handsome of men. A distinctive line of three stars forms his belt. There are many stories about Orion but, in one, Orion fell in love with Artemis, the Greek Goddess of Hunting. Artemis's brother, Apollo, didn't think much of Orion, so he tried to change things. He dared Artemis to prove what a great hunter she was by shooting at a figure a long way away from them. She shot her arrow well and killed the figure, who turned out to be Orion. Artemis was terribly sad when she found out and sent Orion into the sky so everyone would see and remember him.

Greek myths tend to fall into two categories: *creation* myths and *explanatory* myths. Creation myths try to explain how the world began and how man and woman were created, as well as explain the existence of gods and goddesses. The Greek story of Creation is told later in this chapter.

Explanatory myths try to interpret natural events and strange phenomena of nature, such as the following:

- Why did the sun appear in the morning, move across the sky, and fall away over the edge of the world at night?
- Where do the colors come from as the sun disappears?
- How were beautiful lakes formed that look like they could only be made by a giant foot stomping down on the earth? and Where was that giant?
- Why does the sky make such noise sometimes when it rains?

One myth about nature concerns the discovery of fire. Prometheus, the son of one of the Titan gods, was told by Zeus to create man from earth and water. Prometheus finished that task, grew close to man, and wanted to help man out however he could. But Zeus wanted to keep man from gaining power, especially in terms of fire. Prometheus, who didn't always agree with Zeus, decided to give man the secret of fire and stole it from Mount Olympus, giving it to the mortal men on Earth.

There are no exact, agreed-upon dates for the beginning or end of the ancient Greek civilization, but it developed and expanded beginning in approximately 3000 BC. Their power had waned by 145 BC, when their power fell to the Roman Empire. The Greeks had felt the Roman presence for more than a century.

Roman Mythology

Roman civilization emerged in the fifth century BC and continued to the fourth century AD. When Rome took control of Greece, the Romans accepted the Greek gods and goddesses and the accompanying mythology. But, they gave the gods and goddesses new names and added a few new myths of their own. For example, the name of the Greek god Zeus—Lord of the Sky, Gods, and Thunder—became the Roman god Jupiter. Exhibit 4-2 provides the names of a few of the many other gods and goddesses with both Greek and Roman names.

More changes of the gods' and goddesses' names can be found at the Greek and Roman Mythological Gods Web site at http://ancient history.about.com/library/bl/bl_myth_table_romangods.htm.

Many of the Roman myths focus on the founding of Rome by Romulus and Remus, and other tales about Rome. They include the

Exhibit 4-2. Examples of Gods and Goddesses with Greek and Roman Names

Greek	Roman	Domain
Aphrodite	Venus	Goddess of Love and Beauty
Athena	Minerva	Goddess of Education, Science, and War
Demeter	Ceres	Goddess of the Corn, Earth, Harvest
Eros	Cupid	God of Love
Nike	Victoria	Goddess of Victory
Pan	Faunus	God of Flocks
Poseidon	Neptune	Ruler of the Sea
Zeus	Jupiter	Ruler of the Sky

story of Cloelia, a Roman girl who was held hostage by the Etruscans but escaped and swam across the river Tiber and led other Roman girls to safety. Romulus and Remus, a myth dating from 400 BC or so, was the tale of twin sons born to a Latin princess and Mars, the Roman God of War who is also associated with agriculture and fertility. The twins' uncle tried to drown them, but they were saved by a she-wolf and a woodpecker. The twins were able to overthrow their uncle, and they decided to found a new city on the spot where they had been rescued, but they fought bitterly over what to name it. Each stood on a hill, and a flock of birds flying over Romulus signalled that the gods felt the new city should be named after him. In *Roman Myths,* Michael Grant (1984: 107) cites a common tale about Remus: "Remus, by way of jeering at his brother, jumped over the half-built walls of the new settlement, whereupon Romulus killed him in a fit of rage, adding the threat, 'So, perish whoever else shall overleap my battlements!'" Once Romulus had killed Remus, he became king. As Rome's leader, he was able to add large sections of land and many people to his domain, and after his death, the Romans worshipped him as the deity Quirinus.

The Western Roman Empire began its decline in the fifth century AD, and the Eastern Roman Empire joined it when Constantinople fell in 1453. The Greek civilization influenced the modern world in the arts, science and medicine, and philosophy. The world continued to gain from the Romans in terms of libraries, museums, architecture, language, technology, and the legal profession.

Telling Tales of Classical Myths

Learning to tell Greek and Roman myths may seem overwhelming at first to tellers who may have focused primarily on folk and fairy tales. Many myths are lengthy and more complicated than other stories, and thus they take longer to learn, plan, and prepare for performances. However, if storytellers start with some shorter classical myths, they can enjoy telling them and add other, more complex myths later. It helps to have a background in classical mythology when venturing into this area. If tellers want to obtain a basic understanding, they can choose from a great selection of standard works in this area, some of which are included in the Suggested Resources at the end of this chapter.

A short classical myth that would be good to begin with is the story of Pan. Pan is the God of Flocks and Shepherds (Bulfinch, 2003: 9) and "woods and fields" (Bulfinch, 2003: 166), and he is said to have goat's feet and to protect pastures and shepherds (Bell, 1982: 321). When Pan was born, he was so pathetically ugly that his mother took one look at him and ran away, screaming. She had suffered a "panic" attack. The program could continue with a brief description of Pan and his powers.

Another classical character, Pandora, makes a great tale, and after reading several versions of Pandora, tellers could compose their own personal account of the story. Pandora, the first woman, was given gifts by all the gods, including Zeus, the supreme deity in Greek mythology. Zeus gave her a box, but told her she was not to open it. She was so curious that she finally opened it, releasing all the ills of the world: poverty, shame, sickness, and so forth. But, deep down inside the hateful box was the only thing that has helped sustain humanity in hard times—hope and peace, the latter of which is symbolized today as a dove. In her book *Mythology,* Edith Hamilton (1969: 88) says that for Pandora, "the source of all misfortune was not her wicked nature but her curiosity."

Classical myths have been well integrated into American pop culture. Mythological figures and classical names appear in the news, on television, in movies and films, in books and magazines, on the Internet and the World Wide Web, and in comics. They are also used as brand names for commercial products, in advertisments, in logos, and more. In the *Dictionary of Trade Name Origins,* Adrian Room speaks about the importance of words in trade names— for example, "a number of names from mythological sources, such as Ambrosia, Apollinaris (via a place name), Cerebos, Dyane, Flora, Hermesetas, Milo, Pan, and Zephyr" (Room, 1982: 13). Other brand names include Ajax cleanser, Milky Way candy bars, and Nike athletic sportswear and equipment.

The Greeks had many wonderful myths, beginning with their story of creation. Many versions of this Greek myth are available in print, on the Web, and in other media formats from various sources. The following is my own adaptation:

The Greek Story of Creation

In the beginning there was nothing—no earth, no water, no sky, no sun, moon, or stars . . . only space. The Greeks called this "CHAOS." To them this meant a void, a "yawn."

From chaos came a force—nature. Nature saw possibilities and appealed to a powerful god to help. He agreed to help and separated the sea from the land and the heavens from both. This caused a deafening clap of thunder as he spoke the word. Flames leapt high in the air and formed the skies. Beneath them the earth sank to the bottom. The seas boiled, swarmed, and rolled around.

She (nature) appealed to a lesser god to help tame them all. They took water from the seas and made peaceful rivers. They raised the earth in places, making hills and mountains. Lakes and valleys were formed. The god smoothed some of the earth for fields, made stony plains for sheep, and scattered seeds so forests would grow to shelter the animals.

As earth and heavens met there sprang Uranus and Gaea and they had many children. Their firstborn were the twelve giant TITANS, also known as the elder gods. The Titans, six boys and six girls, Cronus, Rhea, Iapetus, Oceanus, Hyperion, Themis, Thea, Mnemosyne, Phoebe, Coeus, Tethys, Crius. Later, a thirteenth Titan was added, Dione.

The Titans Cronus and Rhea are the parents of Zeus and the other Olympian gods and goddesses. Later other children were born—the Cyclops, and more. Uranus hated them and threw them into Tartarus—the deepest pit in the Underworld.

Gaea was furious and urged the Titans to overthrow their father, but only the youngest, Chronus, was brave enough. He attacked Uranus with a sickle and banished him from earth. Chronus (Saturn) replaced his father as Lord of the Universe. Chronus married his sister Rhea and they had many children (Olympians), but Chronus was afraid his children might try to overthrow him as he had done to his father, so he ate them all.

Rhea was furious and had hidden the youngest one, named Zeus. Everyone protected Zeus and he married Metis. Rather than do away with Chronus, Metis mixed a potion and gave it to him, telling him it would make him undefeatable. Instead it made him throw up all his unharmed children: Hestia, Demeter, Hera, Hades, and Poseidon, etc. They were reunited and joined their brother Zeus.

That was JUST THE BEGINNING!!!

Source: Adapted by Emily Chasse from the following sources: Josepha Sherman (2003: 34–36); *Encyclopedia Mythica* gives a similar version, which can be found on the Internet at www.pantheon.org/areas/mythology/europe/greek/greek_creation_myths.html. YouTube also carries many versions of the Greek story of creation.

If we had lived in the eighth or ninth centuries BC, we might have heard Homer or another traveling bard reciting poetry—for example, *The Iliad* or *The Odyssey. The Iliad* tells the story of the war between the Trojans and the Greeks, ostensibly fought to retrieve Helen (the wife of Menelaus) from Paris, a son of the king of Troy who had stolen her from Menelaus, the king of Sparta. Certainly it was not that simple, but it makes a good story.

Locating Performers

The Greek and Roman myths are special fields in storytelling and require the skills of a gifted storyteller. It is pleasing to hear directly from one of those tellers and some of them are available. Storytellers of this type are located throughout the United States and tell Greek and Roman myths to young people and adults. They may not be easy to locate individually, but a storytelling group or center would be able to suggest the names of some performers to contact. Among the storytellers who tell tales of classical mythology are Odds Bodkin and Barbara McBride-Smith.

Odds Bodkin, who is also a musician, offers workshops and programs involving the telling of a wonderful collection of folk and fairy tales, legends, epics, and myths from all over the world. He performs the *The Odyssey* and *The Rage of Hercules,* among other works. His performance of *The Iliad: Book 1* has been successfully performed at colleges and universities. Bodkins uses his voice and musical instruments (12-string guitars, Celtic harp, grand piano, and other instruments) to convey his tales, and he has won many awards for his work throughout the country. Contact information for Bodkins can be found at the end of the chapter.

Barbara McBride-Smith, a teacher, school librarian, theological seminary instructor, traveling storyteller, and writer, has crafted many wonderful stories, including some of the Greek myths. She tells the story of Pandora and other Greek myths in a funny, irreverent way. Her versions of Greek myths can be found in her book, *Greek Myths, Western Style: Toga Tales with an Attitude* (1998), and on her recordings, *It's Not Easy Being a Goddess* (2005), *The Button Box* (2005), and *Good Old Boys and the Women Who Love Them* (2005), which are available from August House and other commercial vendors. Her book of myths was chosen by the American Library Association as a "Top Ten Title" for adult new readers.

Summary

Classical mythology is of tremendous importance to the world of storytelling. Telling Greek and Roman myths can be rewarding for a storyteller, and they should be included in a teller's repertoire of tales. These tales of gods and goddesses reflect very human behavior, and they are enjoyed by children and adults of all ages. There is an art to telling classical myths, and it is best to begin with shorter myths and add more lengthy and more complicated ones later on.

Chapter 5 discusses the important areas of telling tales in the family, tales from a person's life experiences and reminiscences, and storytelling as a way to record oral history.

Suggested Resources

Cruikshank, Wendy. 2001. "Fabulous Fun with the Greek Myths." *Instructor* 110, no. 5 (Jan/Feb): 58–61.

Lessons that combine language and culture while learning about Greek myths are fun and helpful to use with elementary-aged children. The ideas offered here involve reading, language arts, acting, speaking, and creative arts.

Greek Mythology for Students. Ten-volume set (videos or DVDs) for grades 4–8, 23 min, with Teacher's Guides, available from the Library Video Company. www.libraryvideo.com/sm/greekmyth.asp.

The ancient Greeks told a wealth of compelling stories that attempted to explain the mysteries of the world around them. These myths have been retold over and over and embellished by storytellers, capturing the drama of the heroes, monsters, and gods that are still recognized in the world today! *Greek Mythology for Students* is an animated video series that captures the drama of the Greek myths. A host introduces each story and highlights its connection to the world of today.

McBride-Smith, Barbara. 1998. *Greek Myths: Toga Tales with an Attitude.* Little Rock, AR: August House. ISBNs: 0874835240; 9780874835243

McBride-Smith tells Greek myths irreverently and with a lot of wisdom and humor. Young people and adults appreciate her style and the way she brings the Greek myths into the twentieth century.

———. 2005. *The Button Box: Stories about Mama.* Little Rock, AR: August House Audio. Compact Disc. 48 min, 20 sec. ISBNs: 0874837626; 9780874837629

———. 2005. *Good Old Boys and the Women Who Love Them.* Little Rock, AR: August House Audio. Compact Disc. 51 min, 21 sec. ISBNs: 0874837634; 9780874837636

Ross, Cynthia. 1993. *A Literature Unit for D'Aulaire's Book of Greek Myths.* Huntington Beach, CA: Teacher Created Materials. ISBNs: 155734423X; 9781557344236

Ross expands the Greek myths outlined by the authors Ingri and Edgar D'Aulaire into vocabulary, literature, science, and art activities for young people. Creating a volcano, paper weaving in the style of Athena, making astronomy notebooks, and acting out Greek plays are some of the exciting adventures Ross offers to teachers for classroom use.

Rzeszotarski, Jodi. 2007. "Literature/Research: Greek Mythology Who's Who." *School Libraries Media Monthly* 24, no. 2 (October): 13–16.

The library media specialist or teacher introduces the study unit and the students are assigned a god or goddess to research. The students identify, select, and evaluate print and World Wide Web resources that can be used when investigating classical mythology and use those sources to prepare projects that are assigned by their classroom instructors.

Shearman, Josepha. 2003. *Mythology for Storytellers: Themes and Tales from around the World.* Armonk, NY: M.E. Sharpe. ISBNs: 0765680564; 9780765680563

Mythology is very important to storytellers, and Shearman discusses what and why tellers need to know about myths and information about their retelling. He includes over one hundred important myths.

Summers, Cynthia Soslan. 2000. "The Boy Who Fell from the Sky." *Literary Cavalcade* 53, no. 5 (October): T2.

The story of Icarus, his father, Daedalus, and their attempt to escape from the island of Crete is described. Daedalus, an inventor, had made wings for his son out of wax and warned Icarus not to fly too close to the sun. Icarus ignored his father's warning, his wings melted, and he was plunged into the sea. Works by painter Michael Ayrton about this myth are displayed on the WWW, and an accompanying activity involving art, reading, and vocabulary is described.

Web Resources

Classical Myth.
http://web.uvic.ca/grs/bowman/myth (accessed May 1, 2009).

This site draws together the ancient texts and images available on the Web concerning the major figures of Greek and Roman mythology.

Mythweb.
www.mythweb.com (accessed May 1, 2009).

This site is devoted to the heroes, gods, and monsters of Greek mythology.

"Some Basic Facts about the Classical Constellations."
http://cosmopolis.com/star-myths (accessed May 1, 2009).

Star myths of the Greek and Romans are described and illustrated, with facts about the classical constellations and information on exploring constellation charts. The site also includes links to other astronomy-related sites.

Minneapolis Institute of Art. "World Myths & Legends in Art."
www.artsmia.org/world-myths (accessed May 2, 2009).

Artwork has been inspired by myths and legends. This interactive site allows exploration of this art by themes and cultures.

Perseus Digital Library.
www.perseus/tufts.edu/hopper (accessed May 1, 2009).

Founded in 1987, the Perseus Digital Library is designed to bring a wide collection of materials to regions throughout the world. It contains information on Greek and Latin classics, art and architecture, archeology, Egypt, literature (including Shakespeare and Marlow), and the Edwin C. Bolles Collection (a Digital Archive on the History and Topography of London, and Greek and Roman history).

Bibliography

American Heritage College Dictionary. 2002. Boston: Houghton Mifflin.

Bell, Robert E. 1982. *Dictionary of Classical Mythology Symbols, Attributes, and Associations.* Santa Barbara: ABC-Clio.

Bulfinch, Thomas. 2003. *Mythology.* New York: Gramercy Books.

Cotterell, Arthur. 2005. *The Encyclopedia of Mythology: Classical, Celtic, Norse.* London: Hermes House.

Cuddon, J.A. 1998. *A Dictionary of Literary Terms.* Oxford, UK: Blackwell.

Encyclopedia of Myths: Roman Mythology. Available: www.mythencyclo pedia.com/Pr-Sa/Roman-Mythology.html (accessed April 24, 2009).

Grant, Michael. 1984. *Roman Myths.* New York: Dorcet Press.

Greek and Roman Mythology. Available: http://ancienthistory.about .com/library/bl/bl_myth_table_romangods.htm

Hamilton, Edith. 1969. *Mythology.* New York: New American Library.

McBride-Smith, Barbara. 1989. *Greek or Whut? Myths—Down Home and Irreverant—For Adults and Teens.* Little Rock, AR: August House. Cassette tape.

_____ 1998. *Greek Myths, Western Style: Toga Tales with an Attitude.* Little Rock, AR: August House.

———. 2005. *The Button Box: Stories about Mama.* Little Rock, AR: August House Audio. Compact Disc. 48 min, 20 sec.

———. 2005. *Good Old Boys and the Women Who Love Them.* Little Rock, AR: August House Audio. Compact Disc. 51 min, 21 sec.

———. 2005. *It's Not Easy Being a Goddess: A Yellow Rose of Texas Tells the Greek Myths in Her Native Tongue.* Little Rock, AR: August House Publishers. Compact Disc.

"Romulus and Remus." 2008. *Encyclopædia Britannica.* Encyclopædia Britannica Online. Available: http://0-search.eb.com.csulib .ctstateu.edu/eb/article-9083869 (accessed October 27, 2008).

Room, Adrian. 1982. *Dictionary of Trade Name Origins.* Boston: Routledge & Kegan Paul.

Sherman, Josepha. 2003. *Mythology for Storytellers: Themes and Tales from around the World.* Armonk, NY: Sharpe Reference.

Contact Information

Odds Bodkin:
Phone: 603-938-5120 or 800-554-1333
Fax: 603-938-5616
e-mail: mil@oddsbodkin.com
Web site: www.oddsbodkin.com

Barbara McBride-Smith:
www.territorytellers.org/Profiles/BarbaraMcBride-Smith

Chapter 5

⁂ Family Tales, Life Experience Tales, Reminiscences, and Oral History ⁂

Family tales, life experience tales, and reminiscences involve personal stories told for the benefit of friends and family members. Oral histories also concern stories remembered from a personal perspective, and they are generally recorded for their historical value.

Family tales are stories about people, places, or events that have happened to family members or are connected to someone in a family. These stories are told informally to others, usually when the family is gathered together and is sharing memories.

Life experience tales are personal stories about memorable things that have happened to a person. They can be shared with anyone individually or in a group.

Reminiscences are stories remembered, recalled, or recollected and are often attributed to older people. Typically, they might be thought of as tales about "the way things were" or "the way it used to be." In the online *Resource Handbook for Lay Ministries,* Elisabeth Lopukhin (1991: n.p.) states that "towards the end of life, reminiscing becomes essential for a healthy old age. Everyone needs to feel that an impact had been made, to leave something of one's self behind."

Personal tales can be especially compelling, and many personal tales are waiting to be told. These may be family stories, firsthand accounts of historical events, or tales of meaningful experiences from people's lives. Family tales can concern individual family members or family events and traditions; they can be modern or based on events that occurred long ago. Oral history and recorded historical accounts from personal knowledge may shed new light on historical events. Written life experience tales or reminiscences hold additional value, as these story forms are often entertaining, moving, thoughtful, or sad.

Family Tales

Family tales allow wonderful memories to be shared with family members across generations. Adults and children alike enjoy hearing tales about relatives they never knew but wish they had, and they are glad that they are at least able to hear their stories. Possibly there were crazy great-grandmothers, wild grandfathers, jolly aunts and uncles, or cousins who sounded like a lot of fun.

Sharing family tales can be a fun and enlightening activity for children, parents, aunts, uncles, cousins, and grandparents. It often involves the same stories being told again and again and again. These stories, usually informally or casually told, can create irreplaceable and lasting bonds among family members. Often spontaneous and unplanned, these tales may include family history and information that is new to some family members. These stories may be told while huddled around an old box of withered and crumbling photos, an old and forgotten photo album, an old box of miscellaneous photos, or an extensive collection of digital photos. These tales expand family members' knowledge of events that have affected the family and often reflect the family's traditions, value system, or an individual or family's moral code. A family that chooses to pick, prepare, process, and can fruits or vegetables would want to pass that information on to the younger generation, who can continue the family tradition when the older generation can no longer perform those tasks. Such knowledge and skills can be passed on through sharing the canning experience with multiple generations. The shared experience would often also include hearing the stories from past years. Lessons on the canning of strawberry jam would include stories of past years, such as the number of berries picked, the family members involved, the recipes used, and the temperature in the strawberry fields and the hot kitchen.

Whenever or however they are told, these types of tales encourage communication among family members. When people took part in activities in which they produced handicrafts or cooked or baked, more stories were told. Activities of baking pies and cooking huge Sunday dinners, sewing quilts for new babies or newlyweds, or canning produce involved telling stories while completing those tasks.

Whereas traditional folk and fairy tales usually use simple, brief openings, such as "Once upon a time in a land far, far away," family stories should include more specific time frames (e.g., "Your grandma was 16 in 1929 when she started working for the shoe factory and she . . . "), and they should be specific in terms of places (e.g., "The railroad ran from Mason City to Des Moines, in central Iowa, when your grandpa had a run-in with a hobo . . .").

Telling Family Tales

In his book *Telling Your Own Stories,* Donald Davis (1993) encourages family members to make careful use of their descriptive skills. He points out that we can create scenes, events, and people by "making use of descriptive smells, sounds, tastes, and tactile sensations" (p. 25).

Davis guides the reader through the important steps of telling family tales. Central to the plot will be some sort of crisis. It does not need to be a life-and-death matter, but it must be a significant happening in the course of an individual's life. A crisis may involve a new job and the things that inevitably occur simultaneously as a family searches for a new home and place to live, discovers the challenges of a new community, or experiences the stress of the actual move with children, pets, and possessions.

Davis encourages a teller to be specific about times and places, so the listener can visualize the setting and follow along with story and characters. It is important to set the scene with a full description of the kind of place and people in a story before anything takes place in the plot. Captivated listeners will pay attention, allowing you to focus on the telling of your story.

Davis includes wonderful prompts in his book that will get you and your relatives started telling about events in their lives. Davis outlines a useful section he calls "A Story-Form Format." His format includes the main character, a possible problem, the crisis, insight gained, and affirmation of the result. Davis's format would be a good place for a novice teller of family tales to start, although not all family tales will fit the same format.

Tellers can gather stories from family members at any time. To get a relative talking, it's best to ask questions that elicit specific information, such as the following:

- "Tell me about your favorite teacher."
- "Describe any pets you had when you were young."
- "Did you ever get into trouble at school?"

Once a person starts speaking, other family members will be apt to add more information. Take unobtrusive notes and ask permission to record their stories.

Types of Family Tales

Everyone in the family can tell tales, which can be of any type and told at any time. Family members may share personal tales of immediate family members or relatives' experiences relating to schools, holiday celebrations, pets, games played, family vacations, or other memories.

Examples might include stories of tough teachers who required much work and research. A person selecting a teacher requiring less work may later regret making that choice. Long-distance vacations involving car trips with many children, pets, fatigue, and/or fun will stir memories. Memories of summer evenings playing games of hide-and-seek as the sun went down will evoke similar stories. It seems that most people can remember when they found out the truth about Santa Claus, where they were when they heard the news of President Kennedy being shot, or what they were doing when they heard about the terrorist attacks on September 11, 2001.

Often, when people are asked if their family members told stories, they will laugh and say, "Oh, yeah . . . but, not your typical three bears story!" That probably means their family didn't tell traditional folk and fairy tales but that they did pass on various types of family tales. Because the younger generation will be the family storytellers someday, they should try to remember the stories told to them by their parents and grandparents in order to continue the family tales tradition (Davis, 1993: 6).

My grandmother loved to tell tales about her life to any family member who wanted to listen. They were very entertaining, and I have always loved hearing different parts of her story. Following is her story.

My Grandma, Roxie

My Grandma Roxie . . . what a woman! No, they didn't use that word in the same way we do, now . . . what a lady! . . . better . . . But let me tell you about my Grandma Roxie and maybe we can come up with the best word to describe her.

Roxie would laugh about times she got in trouble as a child. "Boy, I really got it that time!" I assumed that meant a spanking but she never really said what it meant. The story I remember from her early childhood days took place when she was four or five years old. She and her family lived at the edge of a small town in Kentucky and one day she was thinking about a pair of shoes she'd seen downtown. Her momma and daddy were out in the back weeding the garden and she decided to walk downtown and get those shoes. Actually she called them black patent leather slippers but when I asked what she meant she said they were wonderful black patent leather shoes. She took off without telling her parents and ran down to the shoe store. Her daddy was the sheriff and everybody knew Sheriff Huff. She strolled into the shoe store and pointed to the shoes in the window. "I want those black patent leather slippers and my daddy said to put them on our bill." The owner of the store knew her daddy and he pulled the pair from the window for Roxie. He started to try them on her but Roxie took them from him and said that was "Okay. I know they fit." She quickly put them on and started to walk home. She knew before she had gone far that she had made a big mistake. They were not the right size and her feet were killing her!

She had to go home and tell her parents what she had done. She really got it that time!

When she was a little bit older, there was a Sunday when her momma and daddy were going to church and were planning on bringing the new preacher man and his wife home for lunch. Her momma asked her and her little sister, Myra Lou, to watch the pot roast and make sure it didn't burn. They went to church and before long Roxie and Myra Lou were having a great time but never checked the pot roast . . . until they smelled it burning! Then they checked and it was black. Myra Lou said, "Roxie, what are we going to do? Momma will be so mad!" Roxie thought about it and said, "I've heard that we can sprinkle pepper on the burned part, no one will be able to tell that it is burned." So, Roxie and Myra Lou poured pepper on the pot roast. But, when their momma opened the front door, she knew immediately what had happened. "Roxie!" She really got it that time!

The next time she "really got it" she was 16 years old. Her momma and daddy were worried about Roxie because they didn't like her boyfriend, Jesse. Roxie's father took her aside one day and told her they would like her to stop seeing Jesse. "But, Daddy . . . we're in love!" Her father told her that he knew she thought she loved Jesse but he knew some things about Jesse and didn't want her to see him anymore. Also, did she know her momma's sow had just had piglets? "Yes," Roxie said she knew and "Weren't they cute?" Her daddy told her that her momma and he had de-cided that if Roxie stopped seeing Jesse, they would give her one of the piglets. In fact, she could pick out the one she wanted. Roxie was delighted . . . at first. Piglets are livestock and owning livestock was wonderful, but then she thought about giving up Jesse. "I don't know, Daddy. I love Jesse." Then he told her she didn't really have a choice. She had to stop seeing Jesse. Roxie said she would and then said she wanted to pick out her own piglet. She and her daddy went to the barnyard and she picked out a cute piglet.

That night, as she was falling asleep, she heard a soft knocking at her window. "Knock, knock."

"Who's there?" she called quietly.

"It's me, Jesse. Come out and talk to me."

"I can't. I told my daddy I would stop seeing you."

"Roxie, come to the window." She climbed out of bed, walked to the window, and she and Jesse started talking and finally he convinced her to climb out of the window.

"Roxie, we're in love! We can't stop seeing each other."

"But Jesse, they gave me a piglet."

"Really? That's good! But Roxie, let's run away and get married. We can bring the piglet with us!"

"But Jesse, who would marry us? Everybody knows my daddy and they would guess we were running away."

"We can run to the river and swim across it to Tennessee. No one would know us or your daddy there."

"Okay, Jesse. But that's a long way to the river."

"We can steal . . . borrow your momma's horse."

"No, Jesse."

"Sh-sh-sh. We'll return it later."

Roxie wasn't so sure at first; but then she thought about her love for Jesse and they really wanted to get married. They were in love, so, she told Jesse "Yes," got dressed, and quietly got her momma's horse out of the barn. Then she and Jesse rode to the river with the piglet under her arm. They swam the river but Roxie lost one of the buttons on her skirt and had to hold it together with her left hand while she raised her right to get married at the Justice of the Peace when the sun came up.

When it was all over and word got back to her momma and daddy, they disowned Roxie and she couldn't go back home. It was sad, but she and Jesse started a life together and had their first child. That changed everything and the word came that they were welcome back at home. Years went by and everyone saw that Sheriff Huff had probably been right. Roxie might have been better off if she hadn't married Jesse because he had a drinking problem and was an alcoholic. Life was hard for both Roxie and Jesse but they had four children, and although their lives were hard, the children had a pretty good life and felt loved by both parents. Eventually Roxie divorced Jesse when the youngest was in high school and she moved to Fort Wayne, Indiana, with the children.

When my sister, brothers, and I were children, neither one of my parents ever spoke ill of my Grandpa Jesse. We went to see each of them every summer. Roxie was a waitress in Fort Wayne and Jesse had a small place in the country in southern Indiana. We loved to visit each of them and they gave us children wonderful times when we were with them. Grandpa Jesse knew every wildflower and small animal and bug on his property and he told us about them when we visited. He would take us to the small pond and show us the little fish and insects there.

When Roxie got older, my parents helped her buy a small cottage on a lake outside Fort Wayne and she loved it. She had a pontoon boat and could go out fishing whenever she wanted. As a college student in Ohio, I would often drive across the border to visit her in her little cottage on the lake outside Fort Wayne. One time I brought my boyfriend, John, to visit with me. At one point, we were helping get lunch ready and Mac Davis came on the radio singing his song, "Stop and Smell the Roses." Roxie started singing with him and I said, "Roxie, you really like Mac Davis, don't you?" "Honey, I wouldn't kick his shoes out from under my bed." "Grandma!" I said, embarrassed in front of my boyfriend. But, she just laughed and helped us fix lunch.

She never gave up her independence and it caused her trouble sometimes. One winter day she noticed a small leak in the cottage ceiling and decided to fix it. She put up the ladder and climbed up on the roof to fix the leak, which she did. When she went to climb back down, she saw the ladder had fallen over. She hadn't heard it because the snow was so soft. The lake residents lived there primarily in the summer but not that many spent the winter on the lake. Her closest neighbors were Mr. Huston and his wife but she could see they had gone in town to run errands. They were the only neighbors near enough to call to and they were gone. Roxie had to sit on top of her roof the entire afternoon in the frigid weather until the Hustons pulled in and Mr. Huston saw the ladder was down. He ran over calling to Roxie, "Are you up there, Roxie? Are you okay?" Roxie called down that she was fine but freezing and Mr. Huston climbed up to help her down.

"Roxie. Don't you EVER climb up there by yourself without calling me to help."

Roxie promised, but who knows?

She was independent, a fighter, a rebel, and always wonderful . . . my Grandma Roxie.

Source: Emily Chasse, who retains the copyright to this story of "My Grandma, Roxie."

Discussions of family tales and family history can branch off into the area of genealogy. While genealogy allows technical research into the lineage of a family and may help clarify family tales, it doesn't involve actual storytelling or the tales themselves, so this guidebook will not cover genealogy. However, family members should be aware of resources such as the *Family Genealogy and History Internet Education Directory,* which is available at www.academic-genealogy.com. This Web site gives information and relevant links about family history records, genealogy and family history, and related areas.

Katherine Allen (1987) devised a special program for encouraging awareness of a family's history using an intergenerational exchange of information about the family members' life experiences, values, and the patterns that make up their heritage. The program is an inexpensive and positive approach to exploring family processes and history. Her method is appropriate for people in a variety of situations, including senior citizens, church groups, community groups, and people of all ages.

Older and younger members reveal insightful and meaningful information, resulting in the discovery of facts and fictions about their families of origin. Allen includes two exercises to assist practitioners and families interested in exploring this type of oral history and lists discussion questions and suggestions to stimulate further work with other oral traditions. She also finds that stereotypes held by younger family members about older members tend to diminish as they get to know them and hear their stories.

Life Experience Stories and Reminiscences

Life experience stories and reminiscences differ from oral history stories, because their focus is on personal tales that aren't especially historically significant. They are stories about the lives of people living in the present—although they may tell of events that occurred in the person's past. Often these narratives are stories about significant experiences in a person's life.

It might seem that a life experience tale would be easy to present to others, but, in fact, it takes time to organize those memories. Connie Regan-Blake, a gifted storyteller from North Carolina, "encourges people to be aware of their surroundings when they're looking at memories, not only the images but the smell and touch and sound of things. All those things help bring back memories" (Mooney and Holt, 1996: 36). The person telling the story needs to choose the important story elements from memory. The key elements to include in life experience stories are the following:

- It should include the other people who are involved, the time period, and the setting.
- It should have a beginning, a middle, and an end (like all good stories).
- Something of significance should happen.

The following story relates an important experience from my time in high school.

A Girl's High School Equal Rights Experience

In 1970, before TITLE IX was passed (in 1972), my high school offered sports clubs for girls (synchronized swimming, for example), but not competitive team sports for girls. When I heard the boys were able to practice running on the indoor school track at lunchtime, I wanted the same opportunity.

Assuming there would not be an issue with my decision, I started putting on my shorts and T-shirt and running on the track after lunch. It wasn't long before I was called into the principal's office.

I thought I had a good case and wasn't especially worried about presenting it to the principal, but just being in the principal's office could always cause some anxiety. His office always had the scent of disinfectant, and I sat there quietly while hearing the large institutional wall clock tick off the minutes.

He finally entered, sat at his desk, and informed me that the option to run at lunchtime was only offered to the boys' track team. I protested, saying my grades were good and I didn't need the extra time for homework, I liked running, thought it would be good for my health, and felt girls should be able to have the same options as the boys. I was the only girl I knew who wanted to run at lunch anyway, as far as I knew.

The principal said he still didn't like the idea, but that he would think about it. The next day, when I opened my locker, there was a fresh, new team sweat suit folded neatly in the bottom. I'm not certain if it was put there by the principal or the track coach, but they both gave me broad smiles that day so I knew things were OK. I enjoyed running at lunch the rest of that spring.

Source: Emily Chasse, who retains the copyright to this story of "A Girl's High School Equal Rights Experience."

Another area of life experience stories involves reminiscences. To reminisce is to recall events for your own enjoyment or to tell of those past experiences to other people. Reminiscence can mistakenly be attributed exclusively to older adults, whereas in fact people of any age can reminisce.

Librarians, teachers, and others serving as storytellers want to offer storytelling to individuals and groups of all ages, including elderly adults, and these tellers also may want to listen to stories from audience members. Older adults might bring memories from their childhoods or from their life experiences. Some of the older people may need special help dealing with difficult personal memories, and other professionals should be called on to provide that help when needed.

There are many ways to enjoy family tales and memories of life experiences with children and adults. It is clear that these stories need to be passed to members of the next generation and should be recorded in print, or in electronic format, whenever possible.

Oral History

Other tales of historic value include oral history. The *Oxford English Dictionary* (1989: 885) defines oral history as "[the collection or study of] tape-recorded historical information concerning matters from the personal knowledge of the speaker." Hearing memories of actual events can be especially exciting when the person gathering the information obtains it firsthand from someone who actually lived through an important time in history. Children especially gain from exploring history with older relatives, senior citizens, and other older adults. These stories can help break down stereotypes of older people as young people see them as providers of information who are helping them make connections to the past.

Pros and Cons of Oral History

Many feel oral history offers important material that is otherwise unavailable through traditional forms of written history. The Duke Collection of American Indian Oral History provides a unique portrayal of the American Indian culture through interview typescripts from 1967 to 1972. Accounts of Indian ceremonies, customs, social conditions, philosophies, and standards of living are detailed as a window to a different time so future generations may relive the lives of their ancestors in full color.

In their book *The Oral History Manual,* Barbara W. Sommer and Mary Kay Quinlin (2002: 3) discuss the importance of oral history to underrepresented groups of people: "Oral history can help document previously undocumented information about communities, organizations, businesses, events, or the lives of individuals." When these oral histories are told, they are often perceived as being less biased than written historical accounts, as oral history is based on firsthand experience and is therefore not interpreted by a subjective source. However, memories fade and become distorted over the years, affecting accuracy.

Historians and others who have written about historical events are, at times, distrusted, and their perspectives on certain topics are perceived as biased because of their color and gender: over the years, historians have tended to be predominantly white males. On the other hand, others believe their accounts because they have been written by trained historians.

The Oral History Interview

Some important points must be kept in mind when conducting oral history interviews. The listener needs to request permission for the interview and to obtain a signed permission form; these are common ethical practice standards within the oral history profession. Interviewers should carefully plan their questions and present them to the interviewee ahead of time. During interviews, the interviewers should take notes unobtrusively, and if they want to record the interview, they should ask the interviewee for permission to do so. Exhibit 5-1 provides a sample permission form that can be used when conducting an oral history interview.

In a 1990 article in *Book Report,* media specialist Augie Beasley discusses some interview ground rules and other information about conducting an oral history interview. He also describes a role-play-

---

Exhibit 5-1. Permission Form for Oral History Interview

Oral History Interview Permission Agreement

_____ will make available
to scholars, teachers, students, the following oral history interview.
Oral History Interview
Participant (in print)

_____
Signature of Oral History Interview Participant granting permission

_____
Date: _____
Interviewer Name: _____
Date of Interview: _____

AGREEMENT

I,_____, the participant and narrator, grant permission to
_____ to publish,
duplicate, or use the recording or transcription obtained from me on
_____, _____. This includes transferring this recording to
other mediums.
I, _____, the
collector of this oral history interview, agree to preserve the product of this interview according to the professional standards of The Oral History Association.

---

ing activity for students to perform prior to conducting the interview. Following are some of Beasley's ground rules:

- Be punctual to demonstrate the interview is important to you.
- Establish rapport before the interview.
- Begin with prepared questions, expand with probe questions, and encourage spontaneity.
- Treat the interviewee with respect; do not patronize.
- Take caution so as not to show dissaproval or outward dis-agreement with the interviewee.
- Additional questions may be necessary to refocus if the inter-viewee begins to ramble.
- Expect pauses as the conversation progresses, and allow the interviewee time to process and expand on his or her experi-ences.

Oral history and life experience stories can overlap, and the StoryCorps project contains some tales that might fit into both categories. StoryCorps is a national oral history project that began in 2003 in New York City's Grand Central Station. Its goal is to celebrate one another's lives through listening. It was founded by David Isay, and it includes making recording equipment available throughout the country in its StoryBooths. People can find out where the booths are located and reserve one through www.storycorps.net and record their stories and those of friends and family members.

Participants leave with a CD copy of their story, and the interviews and copies of the stories are archived at the American Folklife Center at the Library of Congress. StoryCorps tales are broadcast weekly on National Public Radio (NPR), and Isay (2007) published some in his book *Listening Is an Act of Love*. The interview facilitators contribute ideas for stories to be broadcast on NPR. A podcast of the stories can be obtained with Apple iTunes.

Summary

Family tales, life experience tales, and reminiscences are important to our personal lives and to the cultures and values of our families, now and in the future. Telling, hearing, and collecting these tales can be an ongoing and exciting part of a person's life. They allow wonderful memories to be shared with family members and others across generations. Unlike oral history tales, family tales tend to focus on personal stories that aren't of real historical significance overall.

Oral history is an important part of storytelling and can serve an important role in providing new or valuable historical information. There has been some debate over the pros and cons of oral history in terms of its veracity, objectivity, and interpretation. A number of techniques are helpful in gathering oral history through interviews. Preparation is key, and it is very important to obtain a signed permission form from the person being interviewed.

Chapter 6 will look at the skills involved in telling legends and epics. Legends involve people, places, and events told locally and around the world. Epics are narrative poems telling remarkable deeds of leaders and warriors. Both legends and epics are entertaining, and they are often of great historical value.

Suggested Resources

Davis, Donald. 1993. *Telling Your Own Stories: For Family and Classroom Storytelling, Public Speaking, and Personal Journaling.* Little Rock, AR: August House. ISBNs: 0874832357; 9780874832358
This handbook explains the importance of family tales and why everyone should be aware of the stories told in their own family and be prepared to pass them on to future generations. Davis gives useful ideas to help family members get started talking about their memories and stories.

Myerhoff, Barbara. 1992. *Remembered Lives: The Work of Ritual, Storytelling, and Growing Older.* Ann Arbor: University of Michigan Press. ISBNs: 0472103172 (hardcover); 9780472103171 (hardcover); 0472081772 (softcover); 9780472081776 (softcover)
Myerhoff recounts the importance of storytelling among a group of Jewish people who had emigrated from Eastern Europe in the early twentieth century. They told stories of being old, living in the old country, being a Jew, and what their lives were like in America. She found that their reasons for recounting their lives were twofold: to share irreplaceable memories of their earlier life but also to share stories of the Holocaust. Many older Jewish people fear that the Holocaust will be forgotten once they are gone. However, others believe that by sharing their personal stories, they can ensure that their presence and their stories about the Holocaust will be remembered after they are gone.

The Oral History Association. www.oralhistory.org (accessed May 1, 2009).
Standards for oral historians are extremely important, and the Oral History Association develops and promotes professional models. Its initial goals and guidelines and subsequent versions state principles, rights, and obligations of practicing oral historians. It includes additional guidelines for educators and students.

Schneider, Keith. 2007. "Lives on the Record and on the Web." *New York Times,* April 10.
Schneider discusses the ability of elderly people to tell their stories electronically and describes "video legacy projects" that are produced by older people and broadcast on the Internet "to audiences of family members and well beyond that."

Sommer, Barbara W. and Mary Kay Quinlin. 2002. *The Oral History Manual.* Lanham, MD: AltaMira Press. ISBNs: 0759101000 (hardcover); 9780759101005 (hardcover); 0759101019 (softcover); 9780759101012 (softcover)

The key elements of oral history include legal and ethical issues; a structured interview format, with a controlled setting; and appropriate equipment, techniques, and provisions for an accessible repository. These elements are outlined and explained to help master the techniques of oral history.

Zousmer, Steve. 2007. *You Don't Have to Be Famous: How to Write Your Life Story.* Cincinnati, OH: Writer's Digest Books. ISBNs: 9781582974385; 1582974381

Zousmer has written a wonderful book about writing life stories. He explains why a person might want to write his or her life story, how to get started, strategies, the writing and rewriting, possible publishing options, and frequently asked questions. He includes extra ideas on adding photos, documents, letters, and scrapbook items and an appendix about "Profiling Yourself on Video."

Bibliography

Allen, Katherine R. 1987. "Promoting Family Awareness and Intergenerational Exchange: An Informal Life-History Program." *Educational Gerontology* 13, no. 1: 43–52.

Beasley, A.E. 1990. "Memories and Tape Recorders." *Book Report* 32–34.

Davis, Donald. 1993. *Telling Your Own Stories: For Family and Classroom Storytelling, Public Speaking, and Personal Journaling.* Little Rock, AR: August House.

Doris Duke Collection of American Indian Oral History. Western History Collections, The University of Oklahoma. Norman, Oklahoma. Available: http://digital.libraries.ou.edu/whc/duke/.

Family Genealogy and History Internet Education Directory. Available: www.academic-genealogy.com (accessed April 25, 2009).

Isay, David. 2007. *Listening Is an Act of Love: A Celebration of American Life from the StoryCorps Project.* New York: Penguin Press.

Lopukhin, Elisabeth. 1991. "Reminiscence." *Resource Handbook for Lay Ministries.* Syosset, NY: Orthodox Church in America. Available: www.oca.org/RHArticle.asp?SID=15&ArticleID=225 (accessed April 25, 2009).

Mooney, William and David Holt (eds.). 1996. *The Storytellers's Guide: Storytellers Share Advice for the Classroom, Boardroom, Showroom, Podium, Pulpit, and Center Stage.* Little Rock, AR: August House.

Oral History Association. Available: www.oralhistory.org/.
Oxford English Dictionary, 2nd ed., s.v. "oral history."
Sommer, Barbara W. and Mary Kay Quinlin. 2002. *The Oral History Manual*. Lanham, MD: AltaMira Press.
StoryCorps. Available: www.storycorps.net (accessed April 25, 2009).

Chapter 6

✳ Storytelling with Legends and Epics ✳

Legends and epics are part of folklore. Folklore includes traditional creations of all peoples throughout history. Folklore contains superstitions, customs, dances, riddles, legends, folktales, and so forth that are passed on in the oral tradition through word of mouth. Folklore becomes folk literature when it is gathered and written down. In this chapter we will explore the significance of legends and epics in the world of storytelling.

Legends

There are a number of definitions for the term *legend,* with the most common one being that a legend is almost always a story based on actual people or events and that has been handed down over time. Legends are believed to have a historical basis, although their veracity cannot be proven. In *Myths, Legends, and Folktales of America: An Anthology,* David Leeming and Jake Page (1999) make a good point regarding how and why groups of people carry on the legendary tradition. They note that legends "tend to be based on actual events and persons and, over time, are carefully tailored, often exaggerated, and serve to express some group aspiration" (p. 5). According to the book *Great Myths and Legends* (1984: 7), which includes myths and legends about heroes and heroines, legends were "told to glorify someone who had performed great deeds or caused marvelous things to happen." In some cases, it will be a verifiable fact that a certain person lived or an event occurred in a specific place; in other instances, while the truth hasn't been established, it is accepted as truth. Legends are always somewhat believable; the teller describing the person or event seemingly believes that it really happened and that the tale has a historical background that the listener believes is true. This distinguishes legends from *folktales,* which are wonderful stories but are seldom believed. Legends were told or passed on as a way to make certain that a tale so good or so outrageous would never be forgotten. Legends can be fun, exciting, and sometimes a little scary, and they are often used educationally.

People choose the events and people they think are worth remembering, and they tell the stories in hopes that others will continue the tales. Legends have been passed down from person to person and have changed along the way. Some have been altered in minor ways, while others have been exaggerated and changed significantly. These changes reflect the way a particular person or a group wants that event or person to be remembered.

In general, books that cover legends tend to divide them in similar ways, grouping them according to the following types:

- Personal legends (legends about specific people)
- Place names (geographically based legends)
- Supernatural legends
- Local legends
- Modern legends
- Urban legends

Legends about People

There are stories about people that a culture deems worth remembering. Legendary people can be plain, everyday folks or well-known people. This chapter covers saints, people whose lives reflected holy qualities; folk heroes and heroines, legendary men and women of great strength, ability, or achievement; and indigenous people, in this case, Native Americans.

Saints

Many early legends told stories of the lives of the saints (Cuddon, 1998: 451), including St. Christopher, the patron saint of travelers; St. Valentine, the patron saint of lovers, who is celebrated each year on February 14th; St. Patrick, the patron saint of Ireland, who is best known for driving the snakes from Ireland; and St. Nicholas, the patron saint of sailors, merchants, archers, children, and students. St. Nicholas is one of the most beloved figures to children who dream about or wait up for his visit on Christmas Eve. There are many stories and legends about his life and deeds, which are told, printed, and published in books, movies, and on the World Wide Web.

Folk Heroes and Heroines

Most tales of folk heroes or heroines grow taller, longer, more outrageous, and less believable as they are handed down from one generation to the next. The result is that these stories lie somewhere between myth and historical truth. They feature such heroes as King Arthur, Robin Hood, Molly Pitcher, and Johnny Appleseed. King Arthur is a legendary character in British history whose adventures represented the struggle between good and evil, right and wrong. Robin Hood is another British legend known for robbing the rich to give to the poor and for fighting against injustice. Molly Pitcher brought pitchers of cool spring water to the tired and thirsty Continental soldiers during the Battle of Monmouth on June 28, 1778. Johnny Appleseed, or John Chapman, was a legendary American who planted and supplied apple trees to much of the United States.

The Arthurian legends have appeared over time, as early as 63 AD, and others choose a later date of the sixth century for some stories of Celtic mythology. The tales are composed of many stories, and there are even more versions of these tales in England. There isn't a clear answer as to Arthur's actual identity, so dates and stories abound. It isn't even known if Arthur was a true historical hero or merely a legendary one. Many of the stories are told using the name of Arthur as an amazing legendary figure, but a lot of these just use the name Arthur and don't have any real connection to Arthur, the King of Camelot. The tales are popular, and many bibliographies of the tales are extensive.

Native American Legends

Native Americans have told and passed on legends that keep their culture, lessons, and teachings alive. Often, tribes have myths and legends that reflect their beliefs and customs and that relate historical events. Native American legends help people learn important lessons from the natural world around them.

Native American legends originate from the various tribes throughout the United States and are distinctive tales reflecting their special history, culture, or circumstances. The following tale is a Chumash Indian legend.

Chumash Indians Creation Myth

The Chumash myth tells of a great deluge which engulfed the earth, taking with it all living things save for the Spotted Woodpecker, the nephew of Kaqunupenawa, the Sun God.

Spotted Woodpecker survived the flood by perching itself atop the tallest tree in the world, but as he saw the water rise all the way to his feet, he cried out for his uncle's help. "Save me, I'm drowning!" he cried. The Sun God's daughters heard him and told Kaqunupenawa that his nephew was dying of cold and hunger. The Sun God lowered his torch, the one he used to light the world and create the stars, and he warmed the Spotted Woodpecker with its heat. He then tossed two acorns in the water at his feet, so that he would be able to pick them up and eat them. The Sun God fed more acorns to the Spotted Woodpecker, which now explains why they are its favorite food.

After the flood, the Sun God, Morning Star, the Moon, and Slo'w the Great Eagle were discussing the creation of new people to populate the earth with the Sky Coyote, trying to decide on their appearance. The Great Eagle and the Sky Coyote argued whether the humans should have hands like the Sky Coyote's, who believed that the new people should be made in his image. He won the argument, and the next day, all gathered around a white rock so that Sky Coyote could press his hand into it to make his hand print, but the Lizard, who had been a silent observer at the proceedings, leapt forward and pressed his own hand onto the rock. Lizard escaped the furious Sky Coyote, and the Sun and the Eagle approved of the hand print and this is why human hands are somewhat shaped like the Lizard's.

The first people were created from the seeds planted on Limuw (Santa Cruz Island) by Hutash, the Earth Goddess. Hutash was married to the Sky Snake (The Milky Way), who made lightning with his tongue and gave the people their first fire. The people kept the fire burning to stay warm and cook their food. Since the people were getting more comfortable, their population grew until the Island became too crowded.

They also made so much noise that Hutash could not get any sleep, so she decided it was time to allow some of the people to cross over to the mainland. Hutash made Wishtoyo, a Rainbow Bridge which extended from the tallest peak of the Island to the tallest inland mountain near Carpinteria. She told the people to cross carefully, and to never look down, but some did, and fell off the Rainbow Bridge and into the ocean, where they were turned into dolphins by Hutash to prevent them from drowning. This is why the Chumash Indians consider the dolphins to be their brothers. The Chumash honor Hutash every September with a great Harvest Festival named after her.

Source: The Indian Legend Web page. Available: www.indianlegend .com (accessed April 25, 2009).

The Indian Legend Web site has many more legends. All legends have been edited from historical documents and are believed to be in the public domain. Several other Web sites that offer Native American legends by tribe are included in the "Suggested Resources" section at the end of this chapter.

Legends with Geographical Connections

Because many legends have a historical background, they can serve as significant sources of information about the heritage or legacy of a specific geographical area. Such information is very important to the people who live there. Many such areas have books written about their legends.

Legends can be connected to specific towns, states, regions, and countries. They can provide an added dimension to our knowledge about a place—for example, about its history, values, and traditions. Some books about legends have special sections of interest to the author or to the people of that geographical area. For example, in *Legendary Connecticut: Traditional Tales of the Nutmeg State,* David Philips (1984) offers a special part titled "Colonial Legends about Indians." Philips states that the five Connecticut stories in this section are "the creations of whites" (p. 259) and that they "reveal the attitudes of the white settlers toward Native Americans" (p. 259). He points out that the Indian population was seldom friendly toward the Europeans who had settled on their land. This added section is somewhat unique in that many of these tales are not found in the standard reference books of folklore and folktales.

Books that focus on legends told in specific states or geographic areas of the United States or other countries include stories that are very similar in nature but appear in completely different locations. Legends travel from location to location, and as they become more well known in another area, they are told in a way that reflects that locality.

One especially striking personal legend from David Philips' book is "The Leatherman," a tale that has been told throughout Connecticut for years and has been covered in many other sources as well.

The Leatherman

The Leatherman appeared on a Connecticut path one day in the mid-1800s and walked throughout Connecticut and New York State for many years. He covered the same 365-mile route every 34 days with perfect regularity. People would mark their calendars and set out food for him or present him with a plate of food as he walked by.

There have never been any firm facts about who the Leatherman was or where he came from, but there are suppositions or guesses as to his history. He dressed all in leather from his hat to his boots, which suggested that he had a history concerning leather in some way. One theory was that the Leatherman was a man named Jules Bourglay, from France. Bourglay had been engaged to a lovely woman, who was the daughter of a leather merchant and the merchant sought confirmation that this man could provide for his daughter. The merchant let Jules Bourglay work in his leather business, and as the man did very well, the leather merchant let him take on more responsibilities of the business. Then the leather market fell, and the leather business started performing very poorly. The leather merchant blamed the demise of his business on Jules Bourglay and sent him away, telling him he would never be allowed to marry his daughter. It is said Bourglay left France on a boat to the United States, and with nowhere to go and no place to settle when he arrived in the United States, the man started walking, wearing the leather pieces he had on his back and feet, walking off his sorrow. Without proper financial means, Bourglay walked, all dressed in leather, and became known as The Leatherman. When he was approached by anyone, he opened his mouth and pointed, hoping for a bite to eat.

One enterprising teacher from Bristol gathered her students and had them form a line to be ready when the Leatherman appeared. She chose the "Student of the Month" to present a plate of food to the Leatherman as he walked past the line of children. No one spoke to the quiet man as he passed, and he didn't make any comments to them.

Another woman also kept a note about his schedule so she could leave a plate of food out for him every 34 days. He would come to her porch, and the food would be there for him to take. One day, the woman was away and her husband greeted the Leatherman heartily, asking questions about his life, his walking, and his history. It is reported that, at these words, the Leatherman turned about, walked away, and never stopped at that house again.

He slept by the side of the road or in local caves. He survived rattlesnakes, known to inhabit many of the caves he slept in, and the Blizzard of 1888 before he died in 1889 from injuries suffered in a fall.

Source: Adapted by Emily Chasse from Philips (1984).

It is not surprising that the people of the state of Connecticut, the "Land of Steady Habits," would choose to remember the Leatherman, a man who clearly lived his life in a steady way and exhibited consistency in that life. He exhibited qualities that many people in Connecticut strive to adopt and display in their own lives.

Exhibit 6-1. On a Personal Note: "Bride's Brook"

When I work with classrooms, I have noticed that teenagers like the idea that they share stories with adolescents in other states. Perhaps, when young people are forming their own identities, they appreciate having something in common with others in distant places. This is especially true, I have found, with romantic legends. Connecticut has a wonderful tale, "Bride's Brook," which is also found in Massachusetts' legends, legends from Wales, and, most likely, in more locations.

In the legend of "Bride's Brook," two young people were anxious to marry, but they needed to follow the law that required that one must wed in their home parish. The couple lived in New London in the Massachusetts Bay Colony, but the magistrate they needed to perform the nuptials was not available on the day they chose to wed. He might have been away on business or, possibly, bad weather had kept him elsewhere, but there was not any other possible local official to carry out the wedding ceremony. The groom heard that an official from a nearby location was available, but this man had no legal jurisdiction in the couple's township. However, the official, John Winthrop, agreed to stand on one side of the stream separating the couple's parish from his official jurisdiction and unite the couple in holy matrimony. From that day forward this small, bubbling stream was known as Bride's Brook. The legend had added historical significance, as Winthrop later became governor of the Massachusetts Bay Colony.

Tall Tales and Urban Legends

Although most legends are traditional stories or tales of historic events or people, other important types of legends include tall tales and urban legends. Tall tales tell special stories of people who are "larger than life" and who can accomplish amazing things. An urban legend is defined as "an often lurid story or anecdote that is based on hearsay and widely circulated as true" (*Merriam-Webster's Online Dictionary*).

Tall tales have been around for a long time. Examples include the tales of Paul Bunyan, Pecos Bill, and Mike Fink told by early settlers to North America. According to legend, Paul Bunyan was a giant lumberjack and was a frontier hero who completed amazing tasks with the help of Babe, his huge, incredibly strong, blue ox. Pecos Bill was a legendary American cowboy with amazing strength and courage. Mike Fink was a tough riverboatman who worked on the flatboats of the Ohio and Mississippi rivers. In many ways, such tall tales reflected the belief that early citizens of this country were the biggest, the best, and the most outrageous.

The urban legend is considered to be very American and usually involves ghastly and horrible events. Everyone wants to spread the word, so these tales are quickly accepted as true and passed on to the next person without checking the facts. These include stories such as "The Vanishing Hitchhiker," "The Rat Discovered in a Kentucky Fried Chicken Order," and "The Lady in Red."

One of the most well-known, "The Vanishing Hitchhiker," can be found in books of urban legends and on many Web sites. In this story, a driver picks up a female hitchhiker and tells her he'll take her to her destination. After driving awhile he notices she has disappeared from the backseat. Alarmed, the driver goes to the address the hitchhiker had given him and is told by residents that the girl he describes has been dead for many years.

Urban legends are generally told among friends, especially around Halloween and during other late-night gatherings. Tellers can include an urban legend in a performance if they feel the tale is appropriate for the setting, group, and event.

Epics

An epic is a very long narrative poem describing the amazing and heroic deeds of a leader or warrior. There are two kinds of epics. The first type, labeled as *primary,* was initially told orally, and the second type, *secondary,* was originally written. Epics can have a distinctive meter, which helps a storyteller learn the story. If epics are new to a teller, the teller should start with some short stanzas from epic poems, such as the following examples:

1. From Longfellow's "Hiawatha":

   By the shores of Gitche Gumee
   By the shining Big-Sea-Water,
   Stood the wigwam of Nokomis,
   Daughter of the Moon, Nokomis. . . .

2. From Aleksandr Pushkin's "The Tale of Tsar Saltan":

   Three fair maidens, late one night,
   Sat and spun by candlelight.
   "Were our tsar to marry me,"
   Said the eldest of the three,
   "I would cook and I would bake—
   Oh, what royal feasts I'd make. . . ."

3. From Edgar Allan Poe's "The Raven":

   Once upon a midnight dreary, while I pondered, weak
       and weary,
   Over many a quaint and curious volume of forgotten lore,
   While I nodded, nearly napping, suddenly there came a
       tapping,
   As of some one gently rapping, rapping at my chamber
       door.
   " 'Tis some visitor," I muttered, "tapping at my chamber
       door—
   Only this, and nothing more."

Normally, with oral storytelling, it is best not to memorize the story, but epics are different: a teller needs to memorize the words. The skills needed for epic poems would follow the ones described for memorizing Greek poems. Dolores Palomo (1974) speaks about Greek culture and memorization of Greek poems. She states, "Oral learning depends upon memorization, which in turn depends upon repetition not only of entire passages but of sounds and rhetorical units within the work" (p. 418).

Teachers or other adults working with children or adolescents can't be expected to memorize lengthy epics. However, memorizing an eight-line stanza from an epic poem to recite to young people can be useful—and fun. Children and adolescents appreciate the sound of the language contained in these epics, and even a short piece can provide an example. Once young people have heard the language and have gotten a sense of the story, they may be more likely to tackle reading the epic.

"The Tale of Tsar Saltan," by Aleksandr Pushkin, was written as a story-poem. In many ways, however, it resembles a mini-epic, reads like a legend, and has a pleasing rhythm.

When tellers use "The Tale of Tsar Saltan" with adolescents or adults, they can read an early section so the audience can hear the rhythm of the words, then tell the story, and then read the last section to finish the tale. Because it is an intriguing tale, the story is not especially difficult to learn. The distinctive meter and rhythm are captivating and make it fun to read aloud.

"The Tale of Tsar Saltan" has been published in two forms. The first simply contains the story, and the other contains the story with the words presented in metered form. The tale is very good, it has an especially nice flow, and the rhythm is wonderful when read in epic metered form.

Because this guidebook concerns the art of telling stories, this section is restricted to oral epics. It includes *The Epic of Gilgamesh*, from the Sumerians/Babylonians; Homer's *The Iliad* and *The Odyssey*; the Finnish epic *The Kalevala*; the English *Beowulf*; and India's *The Mahabharata* and *The Ramayana*. These epics, arranged in chronological order, are briefly summarized.

The Epic of Gilgamesh

The Epic of Gilgamesh is perhaps the oldest written story on earth. It was originally written on 12 clay tablets and tells a story dating from somewhere between 2750 and 2500 BCE. Gilgamesh was the best known of ancient Mesopotamian heroes. The epic is Sumerian, and its origin has been traced to preliterate days. Narrative poems, telling of heroic deeds of their kings, told the epic of Gilgamesh, a king who was part human, part divine, and who wanted to live forever.

A wild man named Enkidu lived with wild animals in a nearby region. He heard the stories of Gilgamesh and decided to challenge him. Enkidu went to Urak, where Gilgamesh lived, and the two fought. They were both very strong, but Gilgamesh won. When Enkidu admitted defeat, he reminded Gilgamesh that he had a duty to be fair to his people. Gilgamesh liked the words spoken by Enkidu, and, after that the two became the best of friends. Gilgamesh continued to pursue immortality.

Homer's The Iliad *and* The Odyssey

The two epics were composed and recited orally long before they were written down (Fleming, 1974: 17). *The Iliad* and *The Odyssey* were the epic poems attributed to the ancient Greek poet Homer around 1,000 BC, and they are considered to be the greatest works of Greek literature. They both deal with the war between the Trojans and the Greeks. As with many epics, they contain themes of strength, weaknesses, good, evil, conflict, and fate.

The Kalevala

The Kalevala is the national folk epic of the Finnish people. This epic poem comes from the oral tradition, and its written form is attributed to Elias Lonrot. Lonrot had edited other oral poems, and he wrote down the words to *The Kalevala* in the 1800s, including its many folktales, stories, and songs. *The Kalevala* was composed by folksingers in Finland over centuries, and it changed as it was sung by many different singers.

The beauty of the oral tradition stems from the fact that no one person can be considered to be the author; rather, many people have composed the epic by singing about those qualities they want their country to be known for. The original manuscript burned in the Fire of Turku, which also destroyed the University of Turku, in 1827. *The Kalevala* is composed of five books and is the longest epic in the world with 22,975 lines.

Beowulf

Beowulf, of unknown authorship, is an Old English epic poem, recorded between the eighth and early eleventh centuries. It was the first long narrative poem in English literature. Beowulf, the hero, has three battles to win. The first is against Grendel, a societal outcast who attacks the Danish people, including the warriors, while they slept in the Great Hall built by King Hroogar. The second is against Grendel's mother, who attacks the king's most trusted warrior to avenge Grendel's death. The third is against a dragon that is angry and destroys everything in his path after discovering that his favorite cup has been stolen. Beowulf and his warriors try to fight the dragon, but most of the warriors leave in fright. There is only one young warrior, Wiglaf, who is brave enough to stay and help Beowulf slay the dragon. Beowulf dies in that battle from wounds he received and is remembered to this day.

The Mahabharata *and* The Ramayana

These two Indian epics, the two longest epic poems in world literature, were composed around 500 BC and contain stories of heroes dealing with issues of family, loyalty, marriage, integrity, religion, life, and death.

In *The Ramayana,* a beloved story, Rama spends his life marching in search of human values. It contains stories of Rama's life with his wife and family.

The Mahabharata is part of Hindu history and is an important part of its mythology. It discusses human goals while explaining the connection between the individual and society.

Summary

Legends are stories that are usually about actual people or events and that have been handed down over time—and they have often changed in the process. Although they are *believed* to be historically based, their veracity can't really be proven. They are often grouped according to several familiar types: personal (about specific people or groups), geographically based, supernatural, local, modern, and urban. Because they have a historical basis, they can provide important information about the heritage or legacy of a specific geographical area and about the people who live there. Because legends travel and change over time to suit a given locality, similar stories enjoy a wide distribution around the world.

Studies of any region's legends and epics cannot be complete without an understanding of its history, and neither can a study of the region's history be thorough without taking into account the stories the people from the region remembered and retold to themselves and others.

Epics are long narrative poems that describe the amazing feats of heroes and other casts of characters. *The Epic of Gilgamesh* and *Beowulf* are two examples of the epics discussed in this chapter. Chapter 7 will look at telling a story through song.

Suggested Resources

About.com. "Urban Legends." http://urbanlegends.about.com (April 25, 2009).
    David Emery's Web site has a slide show, a blog, and information concerning the history of urban legends.

American Folklore. www.americanfolklore.net/ee.html (accessed April 25, 2009).
    This Web site contains a wealth of stories and information from Native American tribes throughout America, such as the tale "Crow Brings the Daylight," in which Crow flies south to bring daylight to the Inuit people, who live in darkness all year long.

Ausubel, Nathan. 1989. *A Treasury of Jewish Folklore: Stories, Traditions, Legends, Humor, Wisdom, and Folk Songs of the Jewish People.* New York: Crown. ISBNs: 0517502933; 9780517502938

Ausubel believes that "the stories and sayings we heard time and again from the lips of our parents are never really erased from our memory" (p. xvii). He also points out that rabbis and preachers employed old legends, parables, and tales for didactic ends. He sees folklore as a never-ending process and includes many wonderful stories and bits of wisdom from the Jewish tradition.

HyperEpos: Epic on the Internet. www.auburn.edu/~downejm/hyperepos .html (accessed April 25, 2009).
This Web site provides links to other sites focused on epic poetry.

Legends of America: A Travel Site for the Nostalgic & Historic Minded. www.legendsofamerica.com/NA-IndianMyths.html (accessed April 25, 2009).
Myths, legends, and stories from various tribes are given, with discussion about their cultures and customs. The Native American tribes believed that the universe was bound together by nature and spirits.

Native American Culture. www.ewebtribe.com/NACulture/stories.htm (accessed April 25, 2009).
Looking at Native American culture, this Web site provides creation myths, legends from tribes across American Indian prophecies, and other stories.

Perseus Digital Library. www.perseus.tufts.edu/hopper (accessed April 25, 2009).
Perseus is a wonderful and complete collection of resources for the study of the ancient world, including archaeology, atlases, texts and translations, text tools, and lexica. This digital library contains a database of art and archaeology images.

"Pushing Up the Sky." 2000. *Scholastic Scope* (Teacher's Edition) 49, no. 6 (November): T-3.
Joseph Bruchac's book of plays, *Pushing Up the Sky: Seven Native American Plays for Children* (Dial, 2000), can be used in combination with this *Scholastic Scope* article. This particular tale explains how the people from different tribes cooperated and worked together to change the height of the sky from low to higher, the height it is today. The article suggests that "it is a good way to start talking about what a legend is and why people create them" (p. T-3). Bruchac's book contains an accompanying guide that provides language arts activities to be used in a discussion about the book.

Bibliography

About.com. "Urban Legends." New York: The New York Times Company. Available: http://urbanlegends.about.com (accessed April 28, 2004).

American Folklore. Available: www.americanfolklore.net/ee.html (accessed April 25, 2009).

Baker, Ronald, ed. 1982. *Hoosier Folk Legends*. Bloomington: Indiana University Press.

Cuddon, J.A. [John Anthony]. 1998. *Dictionary of Literary Terms and Literary Theory,* 3rd ed. Cambridge, MA: Penguin Books.

Fleming, Margaret, editor. 1974. *Teaching the Epic*. Urbana, IL: National Council of Teachers of English.

Grant, Steve. 1996. "Series on the Leatherman." *Hartford Courant,* June 20–July 22.

Great Myths and Legends, the 1984 Childcraft Annual. 1984. Chicago: World Book

Honko, Lauri. 2002. *The Kalavela and the World's Traditional Epics.* Helsinki, Finland: Finnish Literature Society.

Leeming, David and Jake Page. 1999. *Myths, Legends, and Folktales of America: An Anthology.* New York: Oxford University Press.

Legends of America: A Travel Site for the Nostalgic & Historic Minded. Available: www.legendsofamerica.com/NA-IndianMyths.html (accessed April 28, 2009).

Merriam-Webster's Online Dictionary. s.v. "urban legend." Available: www.merriam-webster.com/dictionary/urban%20legend (accessed May 18, 2009).

Native American Culture. Available: www.ewebtribe.com/NACulture/stories.htm (accessed April 28, 2009).

Palomo, Dolores. 1974. "Homeric Epic, the Invention of Writing, and Literary Education." *College English* 36, no. 4 (December): 413–421.

Philips, David. 1984. *Legendary Connecticut: Traditional Tales of the Nutmeg State.* Hartford, CT: Spoonwood Press.

Pushkin, Aleksandr Sergeyevich. 1996. *The Tale of Tsar Saltan.* New York: Dial Books.

"Walker's Unusual Legend Is Told." 2005. *Hartford Courant* (New Haven edition), September 12, p. 3.

White, Glen E. 1977. *Folktales of Connecticut.* Meriden, CT: The Journal Press.

Chapter 7

✳ Ballads ✳

Ballads are excellent vehicles for sharing stories. According to the standard definition, a *ballad* is a song that tells a story. Additional definitions, presented in Exhibit 7-1, show the ballad to be a wonderfully multidimensional and complex type of tale.

Exhibit 7-1. Definitions of *Ballad*

- "The only commonly accepted answer to the question, 'What is a Ballad?' is 'a folksong that tells a story' where the folksong means a song that has been transmitted by word-of-mouth rather than by print" (Buchan, 1972: 1).
- "The ballad is a form of poetry or verse generally sung but sometimes recited" (Thursby, 2006: 47).
- "The tradition of composing story-songs about current events and personages has been common for a long time. Hardly an event of national interest escapes being made the subject of a so-called ballad" (Harmon, 2003: 50).
- "The ballad uses the same melody for each stanza and tells its story in short stanza and simple worlds [*sic*; words]. Most simply put, ballads are songs that tell stories" (Thursby, 2006: 48).
- A ballad is characterized by "[w]at a ballad singer's objective is (to tell a story) and how she or he accomplishes that objective (by singing)" (George and Jones, 1995: 105).
- "A ballad is usually a story that is sung" (Thursby, 2006: 103).
- "It is not easy to establish a definition of what we call nowadays the popular or traditional ballad" (Gerould, 1957: vii).
- The word *ballad* derives from the Latin and Italian *ballare*, "to dance." Fundamentally a ballad is a "song that tells a story and originally was a musical accompaniment to a dance" (Cuddon, 1998: 71).
- "Almost without exception, ballads were sung; often they were accompanied by instrumental music" (*Funk & Wagnalls Standard Dictionary of Folklore, Mythology, and Legend*, 1984: 106, c.v. "ballad").
- A ballad is a "folk-song that tells a story" (Gerould, 1957: 3).
- Bertrand Bronson's widely accepted definition of a ballad is "a song that tells a story" (Nicolaisen, 1992: 27).

A teller can perform a ballad with or without musical accompaniment. Often the ballad is complete without accompaniment, and ballads performed a cappella can be intriguing. Balladeers can perform their tale using various actions, gestures, sounds, and movements, along with varying voice levels, further enriching the storytelling experience. The terms *balladeer* and *ballad singer* are used interchangeably in this chapter.

There are three distinct types of ballads. The first is the *folk* or *traditional oral tale* spread by word of mouth. An example of a folk ballad, "My Bonnie Lies over the Ocean," a traditional Scottish folk song, may have its origin in the history of Charles Edward Stuart, commonly known as Bonnie Prince Charlie.

My Bonnie Lies over the Ocean

My Bonnie lies over the ocean
My Bonnie lies over the sea
My Bonnie lies over the ocean
Oh bring back my Bonnie to me
Bring back, bring back
Bring back my Bonnie to me, to me
Bring back, bring back
Bring back my Bonnie to me

A second type of ballad is the *literary tale* and these have often been printed and published. An example of a well-known literary ballad is Samuel Taylor Coleridge's (1927) "The Rime of the Ancient Mariner."

The third type, the *broadside* ballad, is substantially different from the first two. These were advertisements, stories, or news-type information published inexpensively on a sheet of paper and were never performed. They can be thought of as an early form of tabloid journalism and were often topical, funny, and sometimes subversive. Some of England's Robin Hood ballads appeared as broadsides.

Ballads have reflected social change and political action in both good and bad times by different individuals or groups of people. Ballads composed by individuals include melodies sung by young men and women singing to lost loves or by cowboys calming their nerves as they ended their day's work.

Ballads may change or expand into new formats. Today, some might ask if rap songs are a new kind of ballad. Rap songs can be a popular way to tell stories to others, but, in terms of meter and rhyme, they don't fit the ballad format that will be described here. However, they do have some things in common, such as the desire to tell a story.

Balladeers can select various types of instruments to play when they sing a ballad—for example, guitars, mandolins, harps, or drums. The accompaniment should do just that—accompany—and not overwhelm the story.

Francis James Child, a Harvard University professor, author, and collector of ballads, assembled the definitive collection of ballads, *The English and Scottish Popular Ballads* (Child, 1962). Child is considered the most significant writer on the subject of ballads. Other ballad scholars include such notable writers as H.M. Chadwick, W. Chappell, W.J. Entwistle, and G.H. Gerould. These writers provide information on ballads from particular time periods and geographic areas and that deal with specific topics.

Traditional folk ballads can be categorized into groups. In his *A Scottish Ballad Book,* David Buchan (1973: 5) organized them into three major groups:

- The magical and marvelous
- The romantic and tragic
- The historical and semi-historical

A fourth type, the comic ballad, is often Scottish.

Ballad Format

The most important elements of a ballad include the meter and rhyme, repetition, and refrain. Traditional ballads were set to Common Meter, described later, but modern ballads, including "Scarborough Fair" (Simon and Garfunkel) or "For the First Time" (Kenny Loggins) use a more contemporary meter.

Meter and Rhyme

Traditional ballads were typically composed of four-line stanzas, with the second and the fourth lines rhyming. A simple example would be:

> On top of spaghetti
> All covered with *cheese*
> I lost my poor meatball
> When somebody *sneezed.*

Followed by more verses:

> It rolled off the table
> And onto the floor
> And then my poor meatball
> It rolled out the door.

Special elements of a ballad include *meter* and *rhyme.* Meter refers to the pattern of stressed and unstressed syllables in a song. A ballad generally uses alternating four stress lines and simple repeating lines, often with a refrain. A typical ballad meter is a first and third line with four stresses (iambic tetrameter) and a second and fourth line with three stresses (iambic trimester).

The rhyme pattern ABCB is the most common type of rhyme found in the old ballads and is still commonly used. This pattern indicates the identity of the last stressed vowels.

The word sounds that repeat are often organized by letters to convey a pattern of repetition. For example, in the "On Top of Spaghetti" ballad, the word sound of a "long" letter e at the end of the second and fourth lines is repeated:

> A—On top of spaghetti
> B—All covered with *cheese*
> C—I lost my poor meatball
> B—When somebody *sneezed.*

Repetition

Repetition involves sounds and words being frequently said over and over. For example:

> John Henry was a little baby
> Sittin' on his papa's knee
> He picked up a little hammer and a little piece of steel
> Said "Hammer's gonna be the death of me, Lord, Lord!
> Hammer's gonna be the death of me."
>
> The captain said to John Henry
> "'Gonna bring that steam drill 'round
> Gonna bring that drill out on the job
> Gonna whop that steel on down, Lord, Lord!
> Gonna whop that steel on down."
>
> John Henry said to his Captain
> "A man ain't nothing but a man
> But, before I let your steam drill beat me down
> I'll die with a hammer in my hand, Lord, Lord!
> I'll die with a hammer in my hand."

Refrain

A refrain is a phrase, line, or lines repeated at intervals during a ballad and especially at the end of a stanza. For example:

> Ol' Dan Tucker was a fine old man
> Washed his face in a frying pan
> Combed his hair with a wagon wheel
> And died with a toothache in his heel.
>
> **Refrain:**
> Get out of the way for old Dan Tucker
> You're too late to get your supper
> Supper's over and dinner's a cookin'
> An' Old Dan Tucker's just standin' there lookin'.

Now old Dan Tucker is come to town
Riding a billy goat, leading a hound
Hound dog bark and the billy goat jump
Landed Dan Tucker on top of the stump.

Refrain:
Get out of the way for old Dan Tucker
You're too late to get your supper
Supper's over and dinner's a cookin'
An' Old Dan Tucker's just standin' there lookin'.

Major areas of focus in ballad literature are cowboy, geographical, historical, religious, tragic, and work and labor themes. The following material explores these themes and their particular ballads.

Types of Ballads

Types of ballads vary by topical areas. Although ballad literature focuses on many topics, the types outlined here are the most often cited and described in the literature: cowboy, historical, maritime, patriotic, political, religious, tragic, work related, and geographical. Ballads can be connected to hard times and good times, and they can concern prejudice or peace and freedom.

Cowboy Ballads

The original cowboy ballads were usually simple and often included repetition; they were composed of four-line verses with rhyming patterns. These ballads, written by the cowboys individually or as a group, consisted of songs they sang to their cattle as they rode or at the end of a long day as they sat by a campfire (Lomax and Lomax, 1938: 119). The cowboys themselves represented many different cultures—for example, African Americans, Mexicans, Scandinavians, Irish, and British. The West was the meeting ground of cultures and their resulting cowboy ballads (Pedersen, 1997: 135).

Other fictitious cowboy ballads sprang from the singing cowboy of the movie screen and are not valid reflections of the lives of real cowboys. In many ways cowboys were misunderstood. "Common

American workers' heroes like the cowboys were blown out of proportion and fake folk heroes like Pecos Bill were invented by writers trying to cash in on people's need for escapist fiction, stabilizing values, and national identities" (Pedersen, 1997: 136).

The traditional cowboy ballad "Bury Me Not on the Lone Prairie" may reflect the mixed feelings of the cowboys. They chose the life of a cowboy because it allowed them to roam and be free, but the prospect of being buried on the prairie with the wild coyotes and buzzards is not as appealing as being near "the little church on the green hillside."

Bury Me Not on the Lone Prairie

"O bury me not on the lone prairie"
These words came low and mournfully
From the pallid lips of the youth who lay
On his dying bed at the close of day
"O bury me not on the lone prairie

Where the wild coyote will howl o'er me
Where the buffalo roams the prairie sea
O bury me not on the lone prairie"

"It makes no difference, so I've been told
Where the body lies when life grows cold
But grant, I pray, one wish to me
O bury me not on the lone prairie"

"I've often wished to be laid when I die
By the little church on the green hillside
By my father's grave, there let mine be
O bury me not on the lone prairie"

The cowboys gathered all around the bed
To hear the last word that their comrade said
"O partners all, take a warning from me
Never leave your homes for the lone prairie"

"Don't listen to the enticing words
Of the men who own droves and herds
For if you do, you'll rue the day
That you left your homes for the lone prairie"

"O bury me not," but his voice failed there
But we paid no heed to his dying prayer
In a narrow grave, just six by three
We buried him there on the lone prairie

We buried him there on the lone prairie
Where the buzzards fly and the wind blows free
Where rattlesnakes rattle, and the tumbleweeds
Blow across his grave on the lone prairie

And the cowboys now as they cross the plains
Have marked the spot where his bones are lain
Fling a handful of roses on his grave
And pray to the Lord that his soul is saved

In a narrow grave, just six by three
We buried him there on the lone prairie

Historical Ballads

Many ballads were and are composed as a way to remember important events and people. In the Scottish ballad "Mary Hamilton," Mary is a young woman who, as lady in waiting, attends to the needs and care of the Queen of Scots. There are many versions and verses to the ballad, but in all versions of the song Mary Hamilton has an affair with "the highest steward of all." She bears a child and kills the baby, rolls it in a handkerchief, and throws it in a well or some other body of water. Hamilton is tried and condemned to die, not for her affair but rather for committing infanticide.

"The Night They Drove Ol' Dixie Down," by J. Robbie Robertson and made famous by Joan Baez among other singers, tells stories of the South after the Civil War. The line "the money's no good" refers to the Confederate bills being worthless.

Maritime or Sea Shanty Ballads

The sea shanty is a special kind of ballad and has distinctive rhythms. Some are active, fun, delightfully light, and full of energy. Many others are sad and at times mournful. The shanties were work songs with repeated refrains. Shanties were sung as an accompaniment to work being performed, and they had a rhythm that fit the work to be accomplished. For example, it may not feel like a song, but, the simple "Oh, Yo, Ho, Heave Ho. Oh, Yo, Ho, Heave Ho" tune could easily fit the job of pulling in an extremely heavy rope.

The word *shanty* comes from the French word *chanter*, "to sing," and, as William Cole (1967: 8) has noted, "[Shanties] were work songs and most do not come over well as poems." The refrains were sung while hard work was being done, and the rhythms reflected the strenuous work actions of hauling, pushing, pulling, and carrying. Harold Whates feels that if sea shanties are to be collected and preserved, it should be done carefully and truthfully. He gives the example of "a sailing ship squaring away and setting topsails after a week of strong headwinds . . . . The heavy topsail yard is hoisted in a series of long, vigorous pulls, for which an appropriate shanty would be 'Blow the Man Down'" (Whates, 1937: 262).

Sea shanties were passed on during times of work, and a sailor might introduce it to new shipmates after changing ships. This ensured that the song would last a long time, one of the requirements of a sea shanty.

Sea songs differ from the sea shanties. Sea songs were the ones sailors sang during times of relaxation, such as "Shenandoah."

Shenandoah

Oh Shenandoah,
I long to hear you,
Away you rolling river,
Oh Shenandoah,
I long to hear you,
Away, I'm bound away
'Cross the wide Missouri.

Oh Shenandoah,
I love your daughter,
Away you rolling river,
I'll take her 'cross
Your rollin' water,
Away, I'm bound away
'Cross the wide Missouri.

'Tis seven years,
I've been a rover,
Away you rolling river,
When I return,
I'll be your lover,
Away, I'm bound away
'Cross the wide Missouri.

Oh Shenandoah,
I'm bound to leave you.
Away you rolling river,
Oh Shenandoah,
I'll not deceive you.
Away, I'm bound away
'Cross the wide Missouri.

—Traditional

Recordings by the Clancy Brothers, Tommy Makem, Eddie Dillon, and others include sea songs and shanties such as "Finnegan's Wake" and "Go to Sea No More," among others.

On most occasions the singing of the sea shanties probably lacked fine musical quality. However, the songs usually began in an impromptu manner, and if they were repeated enough over time, they might become an unofficial sea shanty. When these songs were sung repeatedly over a long period of time, the sea shanties could be shared among a group of workers, or, because of their catchy tunes, could be adopted by members of other groups. The sea shanties were distinguished according to when and where they were sung.

Groups of sailors might sing them as they set sail, repaired fishing lines, mopped the deck, or performed other repetitive actions. Sea shanties and songs served two purposes. The first was that they were sung as a way to accomplish the work. Second, they were sung for pleasure.

Patriotic Ballads

Most countries have songs and ballads professing love of the country, songs that make people feel their country is special, setting them apart from other countries. The ballads may depict people and events from the birth of the nation, events that are sometimes hard, at times glorious, and never to be forgotten. These songs are learned by children and are sung throughout childhood, young adulthood and adulthood, and by older adults. Young children want to believe that their country is the greatest, and they enjoy singing proudly. One of the best ballads about the United States—and one many people like to sing—was written by Woody Guthrie. Guthrie was a life-long balladeer who composed at least a thousand songs about events and people he wanted the world to know about and remember. Studs Terkel, interviewer, actor, and writer, said Guthrie's song about America, "This Land Is Your Land, This Land Is My Land," "has nothing to do with bombs bursting in air, nor with sanctimonious blessing. It has to do with what this country is all about" (Cray, 2004: xvii). Guthrie's song makes Americans feel very proud of their country simply because of all it has to offer.

Ballads about Politics; Peace and Justice; Anti-war and Other Forms of Activism

Activism for peace and justice can feel stronger when people in the movement sing the same songs and ballads together—for example, "Study War No More," a traditional black spiritual; "Cruel War," a traditional song; "Where Have All the Flowers Gone?" by Pete Seeger; and "With God on Our Side" by Bob Dylan.

Some of the Mother Goose rhymes reflect the history and feelings of the British people. The nursery rhyme "Baa Baa Black

Sheep" is a lament about paying taxes to the government, and there is a sad message about the Black Plague in "Ring a Round a Rosie." The ring represents the round red rash that was a symptom of the disease.

> Ring a round a rosie,
> A pocket full of posies;
> Ashes! ashes!
> We all fall down.

Anti-war songs, such as Arlo Guthrie's "Alice's Restaurant," express anti-war sentiment, and many ballads by Woody Guthrie, including his songs "Pastures of Plenty" and "Deportee," refer to injustices and hardships suffered by workers and immigrants.

The collective group Riot-Folk is composed of young people who work for social change and use music as a tool to promote that change. They work together, share income from their music, and give their music away for free on their Web site (www.riotfolk.org). They write ballads that reflect their feelings about political situations and perform around the world at benefits, conferences, and political events. One of the Riot-Folk members, Evan Greer, wrote "The Ballad of Hurricane Katrina," which is covered later in this chapter. Other groups around the world also combine music and activism—for example, the South African-based Soweto Gospel Choir.

Religious Ballads

Early religious groups had songs and ballads that needed to be memorized because the organizations didn't have songbooks. In some cases, these songs predated the invention of the printing press. In other cases, the lack of songbooks was the result of inadequate funds to pay for their production or purchase. The songs needed to be memorized, so they had to be simple and somewhat repetitive, with occasional responses.

After the invention of the printing press, religious groups could obtain songbooks—if they could afford them. These books could include lyrics and musical notation for religious songs. But churches and religious groups could also have ballads everyone knew and that were taught beginning in childhood. "Joshua Fought the Battle of Jericho" might be used in religious lessons on spiritual strength.

Joshua Fought the Battle of Jericho

Joshua fought the battle of Jericho,
Jericho, Jericho,
Joshua fought the battle of Jericho,
And the walls came tumblin' down.

You may talk about your kings of Gideon,
You may talk about your men of Saul,
There's none like good old Joshua
At the battle of Jericho.

Up to the walls of Jericho,
He marched with spear in hand.
"Go blow those ram horns,"
Joshua cried,
"'Cause the battle is in my hand."

Then the lam'ram, sheep horns
Began to blow,
Trumpets began to sound,
Joshua commanded the children to shout,
And the walls came tumblin' down.

That morning
Joshua fought the battle of Jericho,
Jericho, Jericho,
Joshua fought the battle of Jericho,
And the walls came tumblin' down.

—Anonymous

Another religious ballad, less well-known but much loved by members of the Religious Society of Friends (commonly known as

Quakers), is "The George Fox Song." It is about the man who founded the religion in England in the 1600s. The song talks about the basis of the Quaker faith, that there is an "inner light" within each of us, no matter what religion or country a person belongs to. The chorus of the song speaks of walking in the Light.

George Fox had as a youth suffered great anguish as he sought an answer to his spiritual quest. His answer came, after much reading of the Scriptures and visits to many ministers and counselors, when he heard a voice within him say, "There is One, even Christ Jesus, that can speak to thy condition." "And when I heard it," he later reported, "my heart did leap for joy." George Fox had found God directly without the aid of ritual or clergy, and henceforth his distinctive message was that Christ speaks directly to each person who seeks Him, and people should listen to the teacher within; God placed His light within each person, and as people follow the way God directs them, they shall be led into life and Truth (New England Yearly Meeting Web page). George Fox wore leather clothing because it was very durable and fit the life he led, being often outdoors, riding horseback as he traveled, and speaking to people about God and the Quaker faith. People in England referred to George Fox as the "man in leather breeches."

The George Fox Song

There's a light that is shining in the heart of a man,
It's the light that was shining when the world began.
There's a light that is shining in the Turk and the Jew
And a light that is shining, friend, in me and in you.

Chorus:
Walk in the light, wherever you may be,
Walk in the light, wherever you may be!
"In my old leather breeches and my shaggy, shaggy, locks,
I am walking in the glory of the light," said Fox.

With a book and a steeple, with a bell and a key

They would bind it forever but they can't (said he).
Oh, the book it will perish and the steeple will fall
But the light will be shining at the end of it all.

Chorus

"If we give you a pistol, will you fight for the Lord?"
"But you can't kill the Devil with a gun or a sword!"
"Will you swear on the Bible?" "I will not!" said he,
"For the truth is more holy than the book to me."

Chorus

There's an ocean of darkness and I drown in the night.
Till I come through the darkness to the ocean of light,
For the light is forever and the light it is free
"And I walk in the glory of the light," said he.

Chorus

Source: Words and lyrics by Sydney Carter. ©1964 Stainer & Bell, Ltd. (Admin. Hope Publishing Company, Carol Stream, IL 60188). All rights reserved. Used by permission.

Tragic Ballads

Most ballads over time concern tragedy—about a lost love or a terrible event, possibly from a natural or a man-made disaster. "For two hundred years 'Barbara Allen' has been the best loved of all English ballads" (*Anglo-American Ballads*, 1999, Notes, p. 15). Most versions of "Barbara Allen" are told in this way: A young man is dying of unrequited love for Barbara Allen. They have split because of a misunderstanding, and she comes to his deathbed but shows no sorrow. When he dies, she is stricken with grief and dies soon after. "It encompasses both of the ideas most common in British and American ballads of love—that is, that love leads to death and that a proud lover always destroys himself and his loved one" (*Anglo-American Ballads*, 1999, Notes, p. 15).

Music is healing and can calm a broken heart or help an afflicted group of people. Many ballads were composed after Hurricane Katrina, including songs by well-known artists such as Bruce Springsteen, Nora Jones, and Michael Jackson. Many other heart-felt ballads were written by people such as Evan Greer of Riot-Folk, in Massachusetts.

The Ballad of Hurricane Katrina

The ticketseller's terrified
haunted by his dreams
of half-empty trains
rolling out from New Orleans
and the hundreds who came begging
but were harshly turned away
how many of them died
cuz they could not afford to pay?
three days warning
the suburbs turned to ghost towns
second cars left locked in driveways
while in the city people drowned
because they had no escape
from the fury of the sea
what happened here was murder
it was no simple tragedy.
good morning america
how did you get this way?
averted eyes and centuries of chains
here comes the story of the hurricane
and the thousands dead in the city by the sea
murdered by our greed in new orleans
if you're black then you're a looter
if you're white you're finding food
i ask myself what i'd have done in any of their shoes?
would i have thought about my neighbors in the other part of town

would i know any of their names? would i have dared to
stick around?
you can blame the president
or you can blame the sea
but they were murdered by the culture
of this economy
murdered by our fear
and our apathy
they were murdered by you
they were murdered by me

we lay in your bed naked and we watched it on tv
as the soldiers and the cops marched past the dead bodies
they were only there protecting private property
i felt sickened by the sight and sickened by my memory
of the miles that i'd driven and the gasoline i'd had
burned
of the love songs that i'd written, and the money that i'd
earned
how can we go on living our lives the same way?
how can we keep pretending that we are not part of their
game?

Source: Evan Greer, Riot-Folk! Collective, www.riotfolk.org. Reprinted by permission.

Greer's ballad represents the sadness felt by so many but also
feelings of anger because they saw discrimination and prejudice in
the aftermath of the storm. Raquel Aurilia, wife of Cincinnati Reds
second baseman Rich Aurilia, wrote a CD single, "The Need" (2004),
which she hoped would give comfort or provide the people of the
Gulf Coast with a sense of hope in the trying times after the
hurricane.

Work or Labor Ballads

Workers sing ballads either to motivate them to carry out their work or to motivate union members. Ballads can energize workers to band together to form a union. Fragments of the song "The Union Maid," "You can't scare me, I'm working for the union, working for the union, I'm working for the union, 'til the day I die . . . ," from Woody Guthrie's album Hard Travelin' (Guthrie, 1998), is a perfect example. So is "I Dreamed I Saw Joe Hill Last Night," a labor ballad written by Alfred Hayes, a radical songwriter, labor activist, and member of the Wobblies workers' union. Joe Hill was an itinerant worker who traveled from job to job. In 1914 he was accused of murdering a shopkeeper who had managed to shoot the intruder before he died. That night Joe Hill visited a local doctor for treatment of a bullet wound that, Hill said, was the result of an argument over a woman.

Four other people were treated for bullet wounds that same might, and 12 people were arrested in the case before Hill was arrested. He denied murdering the shopkeeper, and the location of his bullet wound supported his claim. But Joe Hill was put to death for the murder after a controversial trial and later memorialized by several folk songs.

I Dreamed I Saw Joe Hill Last Night

I dreamed I saw Joe Hill last night,
Alive as you or me.
Says I, "But Joe, you're ten years dead."
"I never died," says he,
"I never died," says he.

Source: www.sacredchao.net/iww/joehill.shtml. Maintained by Joe Wreschnig. This material is in the public domain.

Just as a country's values, history, and culture are reflected in their folk tales, their history and political activity are often found in the lyrics and choruses of their ballads.

Geographical Ballads

Geographical ballads can include stories of locations, boundaries, the climate, or physical features of a country or other area. Ballad singers compose music to highlight their favorite geographical regions or the history of a location.

"In the British Isles the border conflicts between the English and the Scots produced many splendid ballads" (Cuddon, 1998: 73). There are many other English and Scottish ballads from the sixteenth, seventeenth, and eighteenth centuries. "The finest of English and Scottish ballads are the tragic ballads" (*Funk & Wagnalls Standard Dictionary of Folklore, Mythology, and Legend*, 1984: 108). Examples include "Sir Patrick Spens," "Lord Randal," and "The Cruel Brother."

Other ballads relate the adventures of legendary figures and popular heroes. Many British ballads told of the exploits of Robin Hood, a legendary figure who was reportedly born in the mid-1300s and had many fine attributes. It is said that he lived a life of freedom, that he was kind, warm-hearted, and merry, and that he had incredible archery skills.

Scottish ballads include traditional tales, sometimes tragic. Some include stories about the marital relationship, precarious at times, and about humorous courting incidents. But, all in all, they "know how to smile, smirk, laugh, and even guffaw, and come out much the better for it" (Nicolaisen, 1992: 39). One humorous tale, "Get Up and Bar the Door," shows how stubborn both members of a couple can be when faced with the need to get out of a warm bed to close the door against the wind.

Danish ballads, on the other hand, are generally "somber in tone and intense in their recital of action" (*Funk & Wagnalls Standard Dictionary of Folklore, Mythology, and Legend*, 1984: 109). Danish ballads tend to focus on tragedies, terrible feuds, and misfortune. Very few of them are light or humorous. One, "Ribold and Guldborg," tells of what happens when an eloping couple is overtaken by the girl's father and brothers. Her brother mortally stabs Ribold, and Guldborg, slaying herself, dies in his arms.

Books that provide information about ballad singers are tribute to the people who wrote, or are described in, the thousands of songs and ballads composed throughout time. Many books and articles describe the rich musical history of the peoples of the world in their work, their loves, in revolution, war, politics, religions, and as they struggled for workers' rights, personal growth, dignity, and peace.

Singers, Players, and Composers of Ballads

A discussion of ballad composers and ballad material would not be complete without mentioning works by singers such as Pete Seeger, Woody Guthrie, Malvina Reynolds, Harry Chapin, Bob Dylan, Joan Baez, and Bill Harley or groups like The Weavers. Books that contain ballads or information about the ballads that have had an impact on history include *Rise Up Singing: The Group Singing Songbook,* by Peter Blood and Annie Patterson (2004); *Songs That Changed the World,* by Wanda Whitman (1989); and *The Coffee House Songbook,* compiled by Jay Edwards (1966).

Bill Harley entertains children and adults all across the country with songs and ballads. His song "The Ballad of Dirty Joe" makes children squeal with delight or cringe in horror as they hear of Joe's scummy boat, one eye, and dirty socks. Amidst Joe's filthy habits, children all cheer when Stinky Annie arrives. "It's Stinky Annie," someone said, "and her band of smelly varmints. She captures every boat she can and takes their undergarments" (Harley, 2005). Bill Harley has won multiple Emmy awards, and his delightful songs capture children's hearts. Children are thrilled with his characters and their escapades. Another song, "The Skunk in the Middle," from Harley's 1999 CD *Play It Again,* has such a captivating tune that children learn it without trying and repeat the story often to anyone willing to listen.

Pete Seeger's life is documented in a biography by David King Dunaway (1981), *How Can I Keep from Singing: Pete Seeger,* and in a film, *Pete Seeger: The Power of Song* (2008), written and directed by filmmaker Jim Brown and

> Tom Callinan, a balladeer from Connecticut, performs an original ballad about his grandmother, "I Never Knew Her Name," on the DVD that accompanies this book. His wife, Ann Shapiro, Director of the Connecticut Storytelling Center, accompanies Tom on a harp while Tom plays guitar and they both sing the ballad.

produced by Bill Eigen. Brown was able to blend archival footage, interviews, and home movies to project a portrait of Seeger through his long life as an activist working for social change while playing consciousness-raising music (*Tribeca Film Guide,* 2007). Seeger was never one to seek undue credit for positive changes made by the peace movement or environmental causes, but he inspired people in those movements with his singing and activism, and he helped those causes considerably.

Summary

A ballad is basically a song that tells a story. It can be performed with or without music. As is true for any performer telling a tale, the use of gestures, sounds, movements, varying voice levels, and so forth can enrich the experience.

There are three basic types of ballads. *Folk* or *traditional oral tales* are spread by word of mouth. The example used here is "My Bonnie Lies over the Ocean," known to most school children. *Literary ballads* have often been printed and published. Coleridge's (1927) "The Rime of the Ancient Mariner" is one example.

Meter and rhyme, repetition, and refrain are important elements of a ballad. Whereas traditional ballads use common meter, modern ballads are written in a more contemporary meter. The term *meter* refers to the pattern of stressed and unstressed syllables. In terms of rhyme, ABCB is the most common type used in traditional ballads, and it is still common in contemporary ones. *Repetition* involves using the same sounds and words over and over, while *refrain* refers to a phrase or line(s) that are repeated intermittently, especially at the end of a stanza.

Ballads vary by geography, history, and topical area. Ballads can be patriotic and political (e.g., promoting activism, revolution, peace, justice), work or labor related, religious, tragic, or maritime, just to name a few common topics. Ballads continue to be written and performed. Singers such as Pete Seeger, Woody Guthrie, Bob Dylan, and Joan Baez are well known for their ballads. A tragic ballad of recent vintage included here is Evan Greer's "The Ballad of Hurricane Katrina."

Suggested Resources

Adams, Cindy. "A Ballad Study Guide." http://studyguide.org (accessed April 29, 2009).

Adams works with students as they write a ballad about their experiences and helps them by offering ballad-writing tips, explaining ballad structure, and providing examples of ballads. This site has been named a Web English Teacher Outstanding Resource.

Blood, Peter and Annie Patterson. 2004. *Rise Up Singing: The Group Singing Songbook.* Bethlehem, PA: A Sing Out Publication. ISBNs: 0962670499 (softcover); 9780962670497 (softcover); 0962670472 (spiral); 9780962670473 (spiral); 0962670480 (library); 9780962670480 (library)

Blood and Patterson make it easy for people to find the right song for certain occasions. They provide thorough indexing by subject, title, artist, culture, holiday, and musicals. This book contains words, guitar chords, and sources for 1,200 songs. If you are looking for a song, you will find it here!

Clancy Brothers. 1990. *Presenting the Clancy Bros. & Tommy Makem.* Century City, CA: Everest. Audiocassette.

Contents include "Brennan on the Moor," "The Work of the Weavers," "The Stuttering Lovers," "Paddy Doyle's Boots," "The Maid of Fife-e-o," "The Bard of Armagh," "The Jug of Punch," "Roddy McCorley," "The Barnyards of Delgaty," "The Castle of Dromore," "The Bold Tenant Farmer," "Ballinderry," "Bungle Rye," "Eileen Aroon," and "Johnny, I Hardly Knew You."

Dzuris, Linda. 2003. "Using Folk Songs and Ballads in an Interdisciplinary Approach to American History." *The History Teacher* 36, no. 3 (May): 331–342.

An experience in a higher education setting involved students in the author's American history classes at Clemson University. Students had a fascinating learning experience with ballads, comparing the written history in their textbooks to folk songs and ballads from the same time period.

Lichtmann, Curtis and Barbara Lewis. 1985. "A Composer Teams with Student Lyricists to Make History Come Alive." *Music Educators Journal* 72, no. 2 (October): 37–38.

After hearing and reading information about ballads and lyric writing, students selected a historical event and then created ballad lyrics describing that incident. The students "experienced a more personal involvement than a written report could ever provide" (p. 37).

Livo, Norma J. 1996. *Troubadour's Storybag: Musical Folktales of the World.* Golden, CO: Fulcrum. ISBNs: 1555919537; 9781555919535
Livo shares stories that have been collected from around the world that celebrate music. It is organized by theme and includes activities.

Makem, Tommy. 2002. *The Best of the Clancy Brothers & Tommy Makem.* New York: Columbia Records. Compact Disc. Digital, stereo; 4 3/4 in.
Contents include "The Rising of the Moon," "The Bold Fenian Men," "Johnson's Motor Car," "Irish Rover," "A Nation Once Again," "The Jug of Punch," "Whiskey," "You're the Devil," "Isn't It Grand, Boys," "The Patriot Game," "I'm a Free Born Man of the Traveling People," "Mr. Moses Ri-Tooral-I ay," "Gallant Forty Twa," "The Old Orange Flute," "Royal Canal," "Whiskey Is the Life of Man," and "Paddy West."

Place, Jeffrey. 2004. *Classic Maritime Music from Smithsonian Folkways Recordings.* Washington, DC: Smithsonian Folkways. Compact Disc.
Contents include "Roll, Alabama, Roll," "The Alabama," "Shenandoah," "Greenland Whale Fisheries," "Paddy Doyle's Boots," "Haul Away Joe," "Homeward Bound," and many others.

Scott, John and Laurence Seidman. 2008. "Folksong in the Classroom. Volume VI. 1985–86." *Folksong in the Classroom* 6 (nos. 1–3): 1986. Available through EbscoHost (accessed August 7, 2008).
John Scott and Laurence Seidman provide a wonderful collection of ideas focusing on the railroads and the farmers and their cultural ties with Europe in "Folksong in the Classroom," an ERIC document. One section of this lengthy document describes a unique language arts class for eighth graders writing ballads for incoming fifth graders. The songs cover topics such as changing classes, lockers, showers, the cafeteria, and getting lost. Another section contains many stories of life on the railway and life on the farm in the Midwest, with ballads to accompany the stories as well as other follow-up activities for use with students.

Singer, Alan. 1997. "Using Songs to Teach Labor History." *OAH Magazine of History* 11, no. 2(Winter): 13–16.
Singer found that through songs his high school students gained an understanding of the ideas that helped form the labor movement. He believes that by reading and analyzing the lyrics to many of the labor songs students can gain insight into the ideas that drove the workers to organize unions. He used the "Miner's Lifeguard" song to help his students see the trials and deprivation that led miners to see that "Hard work and individual effort were not enough to improve someone's life. The only hope for miners was collective action through the union" (p. 14).

Whitman, Wanda. 1969. *Songs That Changed the World.* New York: Crown. No ISBN available.

This is a wonderfully complete book about songs and ballads that have had an impact regarding history. Songs are classified into the following categories: revolution, patriotism, war, work, hard times, escape, religion, politics, Empire, peace, anti-prejudice, social significance, and songs for a moving world. Within each category, Whitman discusses the importance of the songs to various social and political movements and to religious and ethnic groups. Each section (with 15 to 50 songs for each) includes a short description by area, with words and music for the verses. Whitman also includes indexes to song titles and an index of first lines that make songs easy to locate.

Bibliography

Adams, Cindy. 1999. "Ballad Writing." Available: www.studyguide.org/ballads.htm (accessed April 29, 2009).

Anglo-American Ballads, vol. 1. Cambridge, MA: Rounder. Compact Disc.

Aurilia, Raquel. 2004. "The Need." *Finding My Way.* Los Angeles: Shea Records. Compact Disc.

Baily, James. 1998. *An Anthology of Russian Folk Epics.* Armonk, NY: M.E. Sharpe.

Blood, Peter and Annie Patterson. 2004. *Rise Up Singing: The Group Singing Song Book.* Bethlehem, PA: A Sing Out Publication.

Brown, Jim et al. 2008. Pete Seeger: *The Power of Song.* New York: Weinstein Company Home Entertainment. DVD.

Buchan, David. 1972. *The Ballad and the Folk.* Boston: Routledge & Kegan Paul.

———. 1973. *A Scottish Ballad Book.* Boston: Routledge & Kegan Paul.

Chadwick, H. Munro and Nora K Chadwick. 1936. *The Growth of Literature.* Cambridge, England: The University Press.

Chappell, W. 1965. *The Ballad Literature and Popular Music of the Olden Time; A History of the Ancient Songs, Ballads, and of the Dance Tunes of England, with Numerous Anecdotes and Entire Ballads; also a Short Account of the Minstrels,* vols.1 and 2. New York: Dover Publications.

Child, Francis James. 1962. *The English and Scottish Popular Ballads.* New York: Cooper Square.

Childs, Peter and Roger Fowler, eds. 2006. *The Routledge Dictionary of Literary Terms.* New York: Routledge.

Clancey Brothers. 1990. *Presenting the Clancy Brothers & Tommy Makem.* Century City, CA: Everest. Audiocassette.

Cole, William. 1967. *The Sea, Ships and Sailors; Poems, Songs and Shanties.* New York: Viking.

Coleridge, Samuel Taylor. 1927. "The Rime of the Ancient Mariner." Yellow Springs, OH: Antioch Press.

Cray, Ed. 2004. *Ramblin' Man: The Life and Times of Woody Guthrie.* New York: W.W. Norton.

Cuddon, J.A. 1998. *The Penguin Dictionary of Literary Terms and Literary Theory.* London: Penguin Books.

Dunaway, David King. 1981. *How Can I Keep from Singing: Pete Seeger.* New York: McGraw-Hill.

Dylan, Bob. 1963. "With God on Our Side." *The Freewheelin' Bob Dylan.* Sony Music Entertainment. Available: www.dailykos.com/story/2008/9/10/83255/2774/695/593235 (accessed April 29, 2009).

Dzurias, Linda. 2003. "Using Folk Songs and Ballads in an Interdisciplinary Approach to American History." *History Teacher* 36, no. 3: 331–342.

Edwards, Jay. 1966. *The Coffee House Songbook.* New York: Oak Publications.

Entwhistle, W.J. 1939. *European Balladry.* Oxford: The Clarendon Press.

Funk & Wagnalls Standard Dictionary of Folklore, Mythology, and Legend. San Francisco: Harper & Row, 1984.

George, Robert A. and Michael Owen Jones. 1995. *Folkloreistics: An Introduction.* Bloomington, IN: Indiana University Press.

Gerould, Gordon Hall. 1957. *The Ballad of Tradition.* New York: Oxford University Press.

Greer, Evan. 2005. "The Ballad of Hurricane Katrina." Available: www.last.fm/music/Evan+Greer/_/Ballad+of+Hurricane+Katrina (accessed April 29, 2009).

Guthrie, Woody. 1998. *Hard Travelin'.* Washington, DC: Smithsonian Folkways.

Harley, Bill. 1999. *Play It Again: Favorite Songs (& One New Story).* Seekonk, MA: Round River Records. Compact disc. 1 sound disc (ca. 53 min.): digital; 4¾ in.

Harley, Bill. 2005. "The Ballad of Dirty Joe." *Blah, Blah, Blah: Stories about Clams, Swamp Monster, Pirates and Dog.* Seekonk, MA: Round River Records. Compact Disc.

Harmon, William. 2003. *A Handbook to Literature.* Upper Saddle River, NJ: Prentice Hall

Lomax, Alan and Ralph D. Cohen. 2003. *Alan Lomax: Selected Writing, 1934–1997.* New York: Routledge.

Lomax, John Avery and Alan Lomax. 1938. *Cowboy Songs and Other Frontier Ballads.* New York: Macmillan.

New England Yearly Meeting. 1985. *Faith & Practice of New England Yearly Meeting.* Cambridge, MA: New England Yearly Meeting.

Nicolaisen, W.F.H. 1992. "Humour in Traditional Ballads (Mainly Scottish)." *Folklore* 103, no. 1: 27–39.

Pedersen, E. Martin. 1997. "The Dreary Life of the Cowboy." *Social Education* 61, no. 3: 131–138.

Place, Jeffrey. 2004. *Classic Maritime Music from Smithsonian Folkways Recordings.* Washington, DC: Smithsonian Folkways. Compact Disc.

Pound, Louise. 1921. *Poetic Origins and the Ballad.* New York: Macmillan.

Ralston, William Ralston Shedden. 1970. *The Songs of the Russian People, as Illustrative of Slavonic Mythology and Russian Social Life,* 2nd ed. New York: Haskell House (1st ed., 1872).

Richmond, W. Edson. 1989. *Ballad Scholarship: An Annotated Bibliography.* New York: Garland.

Scott, John and Laurence Seidman. 1986. *Folksong in the Classroom,* vol. VI (1–3) (1985–86):1–107.

Sudol, David. 1980. "On Teaching Narrative Poetry: My Collective Ballad Bard." *English Journal* 69, no. 7 (October): 19–21.

Thursby, Jacqueline S. 2006. *Story: A Handbook.* Westport, CT: Greenwood Press.

Tribeca Film Guide. 2007. "Pete Seeger: The Power of Song." Available: www.tribecafilm.com/filmguide/archive/Pete_Seeger_The Power_of_Song.html.

Whates, Harold. 1937. "The Background of Sea Shanties." *Music & Letters* 18, no. 3: 259–264.

Whitman, Wanda, ed. 1989. *Songs That Changed the World.* New York: Crown.

Chapter 8

✳ Folktale Country Studies ✳

Folktales reflect the beliefs, customs, practices, and other traditions about a country. Learning about a country through its history and culture is enhanced by exploring the folktales told by members of that culture. Presentations of and about folktales from other countries or regions, or from different ethnic groups can be made before classes, associations, clubs, or other groups for instructional or informational purposes or for entertainment. Presentations of folktales can be especially appropriate when celebrating various holidays and other special occasions.

Folklore and Folktales

Folktales or folk stories are the most common type of folklore. Folklore includes beliefs, practices, traditions, superstitions, games, stories, songs, and customs of a group of people that are handed down from one generation to the next. Folklore can give us insights into a group or a country and its culture and can help us develop an understanding of and sensitivity to others. It thus promotes goodwill and helpfulness among diverse groups of people.

Folktale is a general term for numerous varieties of traditional literature, usually a characteristically anonymous, timeless, and placeless tale circulated orally among a people. Folktales are stories of the common folk and often start with "Once upon a time, in a land far, far away. . . ." Examples of folktales would include "Goldilocks and the Three Bears," "The Three Billy Goats Gruff," and "Why the Bear Is Stumpy Tailed."

Fairy tales are a special type of folktale. Like folktales, fairy tales are spread by word of mouth among the common folk. They are stories told by a fairy or a narrative of adventures involving fairies, witches, dwarves, goblins, and so forth. Examples of fairy tales would include "Cinderella," "Sleeping Beauty," and "The Elves and the Shoemaker." There is a great amount of overlap between these two terms.

Geographical, Historical, Social, and Cultural Connections to Tales

> "Why the Sea Is Salty" is performed on the accompanying DVD.

Tellers and teachers can find historical connections to a country's past through its tales. For example, any of the world's cultures have stories explaining why the sea is salty, such as the one below, "Why the Sea Is Salty," which is based on a story from China. The following version is adapted from "How the Sea Became Salty" by Kuo and Kuo (1976).

The Szechwan provinces of China held sizable salt mines, and wars were fought to control the land that contained them. Heavy salt taxes were collected, and policies were set to benefit the Szechwan government or those who owned the mines. The Szechwan people knew the value and importance of salt. "Why the Sea Is Salty" shows how salt affected one government official.

Why the Sea Is Salty

A young man was given a precious stone that produced salt because he acted so generously and selflessly. His brother, a greedy town official, stole that magical stone from the brother and his mother and tried to sell the salt it produced to make himself wealthy. But, the official was in such a hurry that he only listened to the words that made the salt start pouring forth: "Come, salt, come out salt," but didn't wait to hear the magical words that would make the stone *stop* producing the salt: "Stop, salt. Stop grinding salt." The brother booked a ship and crew and set sail for other lands to sell the salt. The ship's crew watched the greedy brother as his stone produced buckets and buckets of salt, but when they saw he couldn't get the stone to stop, they jumped ship and swam for shore. The greedy brother wouldn't leave his salt stone and was buried under the sea in his boat with the stone still producing the salt. The stone still produces salt at the bottom of the sea, and that is how the sea became salty.

Source: Adapted by Emily Chasse from Kuo and Kuo (1976).

Preparing a Country/Folktale Presentation

Many librarians, community workers, teachers, and tellers already use folktales when they speak with groups of children or adults. As was discussed in Chapter 3, storytelling is most effective when the story is told without having the book in hand. However, if tellers don't want to or don't feel comfortable doing so, reading a version of the tale is still useful. Or, they could locate a DVD, videotape, CD, or cassette tape version through their library and have their audiences watch or listen to it. Rabbit Ears Productions, Fairytale Theatre, and Weston Woods are several producers of folktale media. Finding a local storyteller would also be an option, but generally that would require paying a fee.

Including information about the connections between folktales and the countries and/or ethnic groups that originated them invigorates a performance of those tales. Initially, the leader or teller

Exhibit 8-1. On a Personal Note: Telling Chinese Tales to Older People

When I became aware that a group from the Elderhostel program on the campus where I worked would be spending a week studying China, I volunteered to tell them stories about China. I had enjoyed learning Chinese tales and had learned something about the importance of these stories to Chinese culture and history. The person coordinating the group's stay on-campus didn't understand why I thought these elderly participants would want to hear stories. After I gave her the example of the tale "How the Sea Became Salty" and told her of its importance to the history and culture of China, she happily welcomed me to the program. I gave an hour-long presentation that combined folktales from China with notes on the connections of the tales to the country's history and culture. My presentation met with great success, and I was invited back to present at other Elderhostel programs on Japan and Russia.

should investigate the country or group and read or listen to as many of its folktales as possible. To prepare a presentation, a teller can use library reference sources, books, or media resources about the particular country or group, books and media resources about the folktales from that country or group, folktale collections, and online sites. *Funk & Wagnalls The Standard Dictionary of Folklore, Mythology, and Legend* would be a good source to begin with, along with other "Suggested Resources" at the end of this chapter.

If leaders of projects or presentations have difficulty locating material that directly discusses a folktale connection, they can consult the following resources:

- Introductions to books of tales on that country, group, or topic may give useful information that will help a teller connect history and culture to the tales.
- Books of tales from that country, group, or topic may also include information on the book covers that will be helpful.
- Reference books on folktelling, storytelling, legends, etc., often have important information about individual countries, regions, and groups.

At times you may feel like a detective as you discover clues and associations. Note that folklore includes not only folktales, but also folksongs, games, beliefs, and so forth. All of these elements may be useful for this type of presentation.

Folklore in the Classroom

Studying folklore from different countries and ethnic groups can be useful and fun, especially considering the current emphasis on multicultural education. It is a wonderful opportunity for teachers to expose young people to social and cultural information from other countries. Elementary, secondary, and higher education instructors can integrate tales from other countries into their classroom curriculum.

The disciplines of social sciences and humanities can explore the history and cultural aspects of a country and how they could relate to certain folktales. The story of "Why the Sea Is Salty," presented earlier in this chapter, is a good example.

Connections are made in folktales to mathematical systems and scientific information. "The White-Hair Waterfall," a folktale from China, mentions the

> 🔊 "The White-Hair Waterfall" is performed on the accompanying DVD.

mathematical measure of a "li." A li is equal to approximately one-third of a mile. In the story, the people from a village had to walk seven li to obtain water. The tale tells how a young woman from that village was willing to give her life to reveal a special source of water to the people of her village (Jagendorf and Weng, 1980).

The areas of fine and performing arts have many connections to folk and fairy tales from various countries. The dragon is prevalent in Japanese art and often appears in Japanese folktales. In a Japanese tale, a monk flees from the unwanted advances of the girl Kiyohime. He hides under a huge bell in the temple. The girl follows, turns into a dragon, and curls around the bell, melting it and killing both the monk and herself.

Country/Folktale Presentations

Material for a program on a specific country or groups of people (e.g., an ethnic group) could be organized into the following sections:

1. Background information would be gathered from the wealth of nonfiction and reference sources that connect folktales to the people of various countries. This would include information from encyclopedias, atlases, and guides on folklore, holidays, cultures, religion, and so forth. Photos and relevant documents are also informative—and add a visual dimension.

2. Maps should be included to locate the country and show where a particular group of people lives. In addition to a *geographical* map, a *geological* map of the country might be included—for example, showing topographical information and important mineral, water, and agricultural resources.

3. Artifacts and articles from the country or group could be obtained and shared with members of the audience. This is an entertaining and informative way for the audience to connect with the people. Examples of household items might include kitchen utensils, dishes, and pans, toys, handicrafts, books and picture books, musical instruments, clothing, games, etc.

The presentation would proceed as follows:

• Introduce the country with an entertaining tale that uses elements of importance to the area. Additional tales would be dispersed throughout the program, as appropriate.
• Present an overview of the country, its people, and its history. You might include a timeline of the country's history and discuss its various rulers. Use maps, photos, and other documents that you have gathered. Interesting stories about the country's geography, history, and culture make an important connection for the listeners.
• Explain any of the country's symbols, motifs, and elements and show how they are important to the folktale(s).
• Intersperse activities or games that relate to the country, if they are useful and if the audience would be receptive.
• Conclude with any additional relevant points—and a closing folktale.

Most presentations of this type will last an hour or two, depending on the age and type of audience. Following is an example of a folktale presentation on China.

Folktale Country Study: China

A presentation on China might open with a story such as "The White-Hair Waterfall" (Jagendorf and Weng, 1980). This story is performed on the accompanying DVD. As mentioned earlier in this chapter, folktales are a people's way of explaining why things happen and of relating important events and people in their lives. Chinese tales certainly do this, and, in some ways, go beyond that. They seem to reflect the Chinese people's moral and ethical beliefs. They appear to be philosophical and ethical without seeming to be preachy or sermonizing. Chinese tales also tend to show the social conditions, manners, customs, and thoughts of a people during particular eras. With the rise and fall of the dynasties, living conditions differed, as did viewpoints toward life. The connection between the tales of the Chinese people and their history is fascinating. The tale "How the Sea Became Salty" (Kuo and Kuo, 1976) is a good example.

It's especially important to learn about the culture of the Chinese people and their history. It has special significance because China's folklore is made very complex by geographical variations and an extraordinarily long and complete written record. Chinese tales have themes and motifs that show up repeatedly in different stories. Exhibit 8-2 presents some Chinese symbols and their meanings. The symbols may appear individually or multiple times in a tale. The symbols of red, the mulberry, and the dragon play an important role in understanding the underlying symbolism of the story "The Golden Sheng."

End with a performance of the story "The Golden Sheng," from *Chinese Folk Tales*, by Louise and Yuan-Hsi Kuo (1976).

> 🎯 "The Golden Sheng" is performed on the accompanying DVD.

Storytelling for Special Occasions

As was noted at the beginning of this chapter, telling folktales is especially useful when commemorating country celebrations or holidays. Following are examples of occasions when Chinese folktales could be showcased.

Chinese New Year

The Chinese New Year starts with the new moon on the first day of the new year and ends on the full moon 15 days later. The Chinese New Year is the biggest holiday celebrated by Chinese people. It is often referred to as the spring festival because it signals the beginning of spring. (To learn more about the Chinese New Year, visit www.educ.uvic.ca/faculty/mroth/438/CHINA/chinese_new_year .html.) Key elements of the holiday include the following:

Exhibit 8-2. Chinese Symbols and Their Meanings

- **banyan tree:** In many countries this fig-bearing tree is considered the tree of knowledge and thought to be benevolent. This symbol plays an important role in "The White-Hair Waterfall," from *The Magic Boat and Other Chinese Folk Stories*, by M.A. Jagendorf and Virginia Weng (1980), or select another version.
- **crane:** The crane, much used in decorative art in China, is a symbol of longevity in some tales.
- **dragons:** The dragon, the oldest symbol in China, represents fertility and rebirth and was regarded as a benevolent creature to the Han people, the national majority. It was thought to be the supreme creature during the Han dynasty but other tribes, including the Miao people considered it to be evil and cruel. To them it stood as a symbol of the hated Han officials with whom they had so many problems and conflicts.
- **fox:** The fox is common to many Chinese tales. In many tales the fox can transform itself into anything or anyone. At the age of 50 a fox supposedly can turn into a woman and at the age of 100 it can take the form of a young and beautiful girl or wizard.
- **mountains:** This element occurs in "The White-Hair Waterfall." Mountains are regarded with great appreciation by the Chinese who hold some of them sacred.
- **mulberry:** This was thought to be a possible cause of pregnancy if eaten by a woman.
- **posters:** The custom of posting signs on doors, often red in color was used to announce happy occasions such as marriages, births, etc. This symbol appears in the tale "The Clever Wife," found in *Chinese Folk Tales* by Louise and Yuan-Hsi Kuo (1976). The posters announcing birth of a child also served as a subtle cue to keep quiet so the baby and parents could sleep.
- **red:** Red is the Chinese symbol of joy that was employed for most festive occasions. This symbol occurs in the tales "The Clever Wife" and "The Golden Sheng."
- **salt:** Salt has been a precious commodity since ancient times. The early Chinese used coins made out of salt for currency. Wars were fought for possession of land which contained salt mines in China, especially in the Szechuan province. Perform the story, "How the Sea Became Salty," from *Chinese Folk Tales*, by Louise and Yuan-Hsi Kuo (1976), or another version.
- **tiger:** Just as the dragon is chief of all aquatic animals, the tiger is lord to all land animals.

- Red paper wishes: On pieces of red paper celebrants write wishes of good luck, prosperity, wealth, happiness, good fortune, and longevity for the New Year.
- Special foods: Special foods include hot pot meal, shrimp balls, and noodles.
- Lanterns: According to Chinese tradition, at the very start of a new year, the presence of thousands of colorful lanterns hung out will make people cheerful.
- Incense: There is an incense stick race at many temples and the winner will be very lucky in the coming year.

Dragon Boat Festival

- The Dragon Boat Festival is a lunar holiday, occurring on the fifth day of the fifth lunar month.
- Celebrate with boat races in the shape of dragons.
- This is a time for protection from evil and disease for the rest of the year. It is fulfilled by different practices, such as hanging health-promoting herbs on the front door, drinking nutritious concoctions, and displaying portraits of Chung Kuei, the Protector Against Evil Spirits and Illness (Fang, 2006).

Kitchen God Festival

- The Kitchen God's Day falls on the twenty-third day of the last month in the Chinese lunar calendar.
- In one of the most distinctive traditions of Spring Festival, a paper image of the Kitchen God is burnt on Little New Year, dispatching the god's spirit to Heaven to report on the family's conduct over the past year. (To learn more about the Kitchen God's day, visit www.chinaculture.org.)

Folktale Country Study: Poland—Legends, Folktales, Fables, and Other Stories

The following presentation was compiled by Renata C. Vickrey, a student in the graduate folktelling course at Central Connecticut

State University. It is included here with her permission, and she retains the copyright.

    We are brought into the land of unknown and to places beyond seven mountains and seven forests by legends, fables, folktales, and other stories. . . .

    From ancient times people had dreams and told legends and folktales. Some of the legends and myths are placed in magical lands where one can escape from everyday duties and difficulties. Some legends take place in actual places that can be visited today. Folktales take place nowhere and everywhere at the same time. Place is not as important as the story it tells.

    Poland is no different, and like every other nation, has its own traditions, and an integral part of these traditions are countless legends, myths, and folktales. These stories of kings and queens and princesses, and dragons convey an important aspect of national heritage. Initially oral, then written stories have been handed down from generation to generation. Many of these legends have been around for a thousand years or more. They recount the meaning behind Poland's national symbols, and reveal stories of several of its early rulers and first kings.

    Legends were told by family members or folktellers who traveled from village to village. Some legends would mix historical facts with local elements and the teller's own imagination; some would add magical elements. One needs to believe in fairy tales, legends, and stories and have imagination. These stories present kings who are valiant, knights who are gallant, and princesses who are lovely; horses are swift and brave; swords are made of the finest steel, and the good always conquers the evil.

    Legends contain historical facts and some are included in old chronicles. The first known chronicler of Poland was Gallus Anonymous. He was a foreign monk who was invited to Poland by a king. He wrote the earliest chronicles of Poland from the beginning to his time, which was the beginning of the thirteenth century. Anonymus is first to mention the story of Popiel and Piast. Popiel and Piast were slaves; they both lived near Gniezno, which means nest, the first capitol of Poland. Gniezno was situated near the Goplo Lake, which was a home to many mermaids, water spirits, and fairies. Gniezno was also near the area where German tribes lived.

Germans are present in many legends, usually with a negative image. Germans are the invaders and they are valiant and evil. A very good example is in the legend of Popiel. Popiel's wife is a German woman who is very beautiful but wicked and cunning. Nobody mentions her name; instead the term German wife is used. By using the words "German wife," the teller already conveys to the listener the negative and evil character of her. All the bad fortunes happened to Popiel because of his bad behavior but mostly because of the bad influence of the German woman.

Another legend is about Lech and the town of Gniezno. Again there are historical elements in it. Gniezno was the first capitol of Poland, and one of the first dukes who is mentioned in Anonymous chronicles is the Duke Lech.

Perform "The Legend of Lech and Gniezno."

Because of the Polish history, with frequent invasions and partitions, legends were used as an important history lesson, especially taught to children. For about 123 years Poland was not on the map; it was under partition of three neighboring countries, Russia, Prussia, and Austria. The Polish language was not used in schools and it had to be preserved in homes. One of the ways to keep the language and beautiful and rich history alive was by telling legends and stories, which contained historical facts and referred to well-known geographical places.

Polish folktales, fairy tales, and stories originate from two sources. From the West came the troubadour lessons, and from the East, earthy and sometimes barbaric themes. These two trends blend into one and present a rich and smooth aspect of the oral history culture.

Folktales mirrored everyday lives and expressions of natural longing for happiness and justice. Everyday lives of villagers were full of hard work with very little reward for it. Most of the harvests had to be given back to the nobleman. Therefore there was natural longing for better life and social justice. Folktales gave examples of different situations and people's characteristics. People were good and evil and the poor, hard-working man not too bright, not too witty, but with deep conviction for justice, would go against the noble person, who was educated and intelligent but also selfish and very ineffective. In folktales, the poor countryman would be smart enough to defeat the enemy and as a result would win the king's daughter for his wife and later on, the whole kingdom.

One of the examples is in a story called "About the Hedgehog Who Becomes Prince." An ugly hedgehog who had done a good deed for the king received the king's daughter in marriage. The king's daughter refuses at first to marry, and then eventually she gives in and agrees with the king's command. There are two important lessons. First, one must stick to the promise, otherwise the punishment is even greater; second, the child must always listen to a parent if it means to fulfill a promise. In folktales, justice must be done and no crime can be unpunished. If crimes are committed by the poor man or by the nobleman or done to animals the guilty one always gets punishment.

Polish folktales are full of witches, devils, and ghosts. The most famous devil is Boruta, who lives in the area of Upper Silesia, where the coal mines are. Boruta is powerful and mischievous, but he is conquered by the hard-working miner. Witches are usually old women who live in forests or on the outskirts of villages. They are greedy, mean, and look for ways to make poor peoples' lives miserable. But they too are conquered by the poor countryman. All these elements are in the tale about "The Poor Countryman and the Greedy Hag."

Perform the story "The Poor Countryman and the Greedy Hag."

In this story jealousy brings theft, and of course such action must be punished. Each tale must provide a moral lesson. Folktales take place somewhere in an unreal world, but the situations and characters are very real and they convey the truth.

For centuries Polish folktales belonged to oral history; they were part of folklore and lower-class culture. However, in the eighteenth and nineteenth centuries, peasant and folk literature was discovered by professional writers. Suddenly the stories told by country women become well known and loved by many, and with the publication of the Brothers Grimm folktales, such literature becomes also important in Poland. The icons of Polish national literature such as Adam Mickiewicz and Juliusz Slowacki or Jozef Ignacy Kraszewski included folktales, legends, and other stories in their writings. Wojcicki Kazimierz is considered the father of Polish literary folktales. For many years he visited small villages in the most remote places in Poland and would write down all the stories that he had heard and named them *Klechdy,* which means folktales.

A special chapter in Polish folktales belongs to the region of the Tatra Mountains and its habitants—the mountaineers. The most famous character is Janosik, who takes from the rich to give it back to the poor. Janosik doesn't take anything for himself or for his comrades; he just wants to bring justice to the hardworking mountain people. These stories bring also description of a beautiful Tatra landscape and its people, who work hard and have deep respect for the nature that surrounds them.

Fables or short stories are an integral part of Polish oral tradition. They were made popular by Polish writer and poet Ignacy Krasicki. In his writings Krasicki presented human relations in contemporary events. He wanted to show a human behavior in different situations in which reason is valued over sentiment. His fables have rhymes that make them sound funny and light, but they convey the bitter lesson that the strong take constant advantage over the poor. Many fables were written in the time of Poland's partition and they contain characters of Poland's invaders, Russia, Prussia, and Austria, who took advantage of a weak Poland.

Perform the short fable "Birds in a Cage."

The folktales, legends, fables, and other stories have a mission to fulfill. Legends bring a lesson of history and heroism of our ancestors whereas folktales and fables bring important lessons of justice and morals.

Summary

Knowledge about the folklore and folktales of a country or group of people can add much to our understanding of others. Such knowledge provides insights into other cultures. In this chapter, the tale of "How the Sea Became Salty" provides such insight into the history, culture, and heritage of China.

When preparing a presentation about a particular country or people, a teller should read or learn important stories told in that country, making connections to the country's history by looking for elements that occur frequently in the tales, and finding stories that reflect the importance of that country's special holidays or celebrations. It is important to remember that folktales are but one type of folklore. It is also important to research other aspects of the country, including its history and culture—its songs, games, beliefs, customs, superstitions, and so forth. Being well briefed and prepared goes a long way in ensuring that the presentation will be both entertaining and instructive for people of all ages. With the current emphasis on multicultural education, country folktale presentations provide a great opportunity to expose young people to the social, cultural, and historical legacy of other countries and their peoples.

Chapter 9 looks at a type of tale that uses innovative aspects of technology: digital storytelling.

Suggested Resources

Print Resources

Ember, Melvin and Carol R., ed. 2001. *Countries and Their Cultures.* New York: Macmillan. ISBNs: 0028649508 (hardcover set); 9780028649504; 0028649478 (vol. 1); 9780028649474; 0028649486 (vol. 2); 9780028649481; 0028649494 (vol. 3); 9780028649498; 002864946X (vol. 4); 9780028649467

Ember focuses on the distinctive cultures of countries around the world. He includes beliefs, attitudes, values, and practices shared by the majority of the people in that country.

Green, Thomas A. *Folklore: An Encyclopedia of Beliefs, Customs, Tales, and Music.* Denver, CO: ABC-CLIO. ISBNs: 087436986X; 9780874369861

A team of renowned folklorists compile an extensive collection of folklore information, which includes information on the major types of folklore, including ballad, dance, myth, riddle, and legend. It provides a cross-cultural and interdisciplinary perspective on these traditional and modern topics.

Jones, Alison. 1995. *Larousse Dictionary of World Folklore.* Edinburgh: Larousse. ISBNs: 0752300121; 9780752300122

Jones covers central themes of folklore throughout the world, including traditional beliefs, customs, and celebrations. She includes the folk arts of ballads, blues, dances, superstitions, and more.

Leach, Maria and Jerome Fried. 1972. *Funk & Wagnalls Standard Dictionary of Folklore, Mythology, and Legend.* San Francisco: Harper & Row. [No ISBN number available]

This covers folk and culture heroes, tricksters, numbskulls, and folklore of plants and animals, stars, minerals, etc., with added information on dances, rituals, food customs, games, rhymes, and folklore information by country. It includes traditional information as well as unique and obscure material.

MacDonald, Margaret Read. 1992. *The Folklore of World Holidays.* Detroit: Gale Research. ISBNs: 081037577X ; 9780810375772

MacDonald gives people an inside look at holiday celebrations in many cultures, providing a wealth of information never gathered before in one source.

Mossman, Jennifer. 1990. *Holidays and Anniversaries of the World.* New York: Gale Research. ISBNs: 0810348705; 9780810348707

Mossman includes celebrations of holidays, birthdays, historical events of significance, saints' days, and more. This is a convenient resource for each date of the year, covering all periods, ancient and modern, with arrangement based on the Gregorian calendar. Also, each month is given a special entry with any added information and notes about special celebrations.

Thompson, Stith. 1989. *Motif-Index of Folk-Literature: A Classification of Narrative Elements in Folktales, Ballads, Myths, Fables, Mediaeval Romances, Exempla, Fabliaux, Jestbooks, and Local Legends, 1885–1976.* Bloomington: Indiana University Press. ISBNs: 0253338816 (vol. 1); 9780253338815; 0253338875 (set); 9780253338877

Tales are made up of a number of specific elements, and these elements are known as motifs. The element needs to be an identifiable part of the tale's makeup. The motif needs to be separate and give a single motif worth remembering. A country's tales may have themes and motifs that show up repeatedly in different tales.

Zipes, Jack. 1989. *Don't Bet on the Prince: Contemporary Feminist Fairy Tales in North America and England.* New York: Routledge. ISBNs: 0415902630; 9780415902632

Zipes has also published new and innovative tales for storytellers in books and other media talking about using storytelling with young people. *Don't Bet on the Prince* documents the ascent of contemporary feminist fairy tales and includes wonderful tales where women, young women, and girls stand up for themselves creatively and with grace.

Online Resources

Cheek, Patricia. Cinderella: A Mirror of a Culture.
http://cte.jhu.edu/techacademy/fellows/cheek/webquest/pcindex .html (accessed May 1, 2009).

On her Web site, Cheek discusses the importance of tales to understanding the culture of a people. She notes that "fairy tales are based on the social, moral, and intellectual beliefs of a particular group." She asks small groups of students to analyze one of the many versions of the Cinderella fairy tale from a country of their choice. They research the country or ethnic group that claims the version they've chosen and look for relationships between the people's lives and their tales.

Classical Myth: The Ancient Sources.
http://web.uvic.ca/grs/bowman/myth (accessed May 1, 2009).

Laurel Bowman includes links to texts and images of a timeline of Greek history and literature, the Olympian gods, and other links to classical mythology. This is primarily intended for use of Greek and Roman Mythology students at the University of Victoria, but everyone is welcome to use the site.

Connecticut Storytelling Center.
www.storycenter.org (accessed May 1, 2009).

Local groups in your state may be helpful for state or town stories. An example would be the site at the Connecticut Storytelling Center, located in New London, Connecticut. It was founded in 1984 with a mission to promote the art of storytelling in all its forms and to serve storytellers and story listeners throughout the state.

National Storytelling Network (NSN).
www.storynet.org (accessed May 1, 2009).

The NSN offers information on the art of storytelling, opportunities for training, networking, a calendar of events, a directory of tellers, and publishes *Storytelling* magazine.

Storyfest.
www.storyfest.com (accessed May 1, 2009).

Bob and Kelly Wilhelm lead monthly storytelling adventures around the world, including Maryland and Arizona. Other seminars are conducted online. Seminar topics include basic skills, master classes, or specialized topics, such as biblical, spiritual, or therapeutic storytelling.

Media Resources for Chinese Tales: Cassette Tapes, CDs, Videotapes, and DVDs

Close, Glenn and Mark Isham. 1995, 1988. *The Emperor and the Nightingale.* Rowayton, CT: Rabbit Ears Production. VHS tape 1 videocassette (40 min.) ISBNs: 0791200124; 9780791200124.

The emperor prefers a mechanical nightingale over the real one. The little bird stays true to the emperor and returns when the emperor is near death and the little nightingale is the only one that can help him.

***Magical Tales from Other Lands.* 1987.** Long Branch, NJ: Kimbo VHS tape 1 videocassette (27 min.) : sd.; ½ in. + 1 guide.

Three wonderful tales, "Why Monkeys Live in Trees," "The Magic Paint Brush," and "The Mountains of Love," appear on this video.

Sporn, Michael, H.C. Andersen, and Maxine Fisher. 1992. *The Nightingale.* Westport, CT: Weston Woods. 1 VHS tape videocassette (25 min.) ISBNs: 0788209574; 9780788209574.

This tale is set in the court of the emperor of China where he learns the difference between noise from a mechanical bird and the beautiful music of a real nightingale. The Hans Christian Andersen tale "The Nightingale" is adapted here, but it is based in feudal Japan rather than China.

Bibliography

Chasse, Emily. 1992. "Chinese Folktales: A Librarian's Contribution to the Elderhostel." *Activities, Adaptation & Aging* 16, no. 4: 1–6.

Cheek, Patricia. *Cinderella: A Mirror of a Culture.* Available: http://cte.jhu.edu/techacademy/fellows/cheek/webquest/pcindex.html (accessed October 18, 2008).

Eastman, Mary Huse, ed. 1915. *Index to Fairy Tales, Myths & Legends.* Boston: Boston Book.

Fang, Alex, 2006. "The Chinese Dragon Boat Festival." Available: www.ncsu.edu/midlink/dec97/holiday/boatz.html (accessed May 15, 2009).

Hare, M. 1968. *Polish Fairy Tales.* Chicago: Follett.

Haviland, V. 1963. *Favorite Fairy Tales Told in Poland.* Boston: Little, Brown.

Ireland, Norma Olin, ed. 1973. *Index to Fairy Tales, 1949–1972: Including Folklore, Legends & Myths, in Collections.* Metuchen, NJ: Scarecrow Press.

———. 1985. *Index to Fairy Tales, 1973–1977: Including Folklore, Legends & Myths, in Collections.* Metuchen, NJ: Scarecrow Press.

Jagendorf, M.A. [Moritz Adolph] and Virginia Weng. 1980. *The Magic Boat and Other Chinese Folk Stories.* New York: Vanguard Press.

Jobes, Gertrude. 1961. *Dictionary of Mythology, Folklore & Symbols.* New York: Scarecrow Press.

Jodelka-Burzecki, T. 1986. *Basnie polskie: wybór i opracowanie.* Warszawa: Ludowa Spóldzielnia Wydawnicza.

Kostyrko, H. 1960. *Klechdy domowe : podania i legendy polskie.* Warszawa: Nasza Ksiegarnia.

Krasicki, I. 1997. *Polish Fables: Bilingual Edition.* New York: Hippocrene Books.

Kuniczak, W.S. 1992. *The Glass Mountain: Twenty-six Ancient Polish Folktales and Fables.* NY: Hippocrene Books.

Kuo, Louise and Yuan-Hsi Kuo. 1976. *Chinese Folk Tales.* Millbrae, CA: Celestial Arts.

MacDonald, Margaret Read. 1992. *The Folklore of World Holidays.* Detroit: Gale Research.

Orlon, M. and Tyszkiewicz J. 1986. *Legendy i podania polskie.* Warszawa: Wydawn, PTTK "Kraj."

Roth, Rita. 2006. *The Story Road to Literacy.* Westport, CT: Teacher Ideas Press.

Santino, Betsy H. 1991. "Improving Multicultural Awareness and Story Comprehension with Folktale." *Reading Teacher* 45 (September): 77–79.

Schumacher, Mark. 2007. A-to-Z Photo Dictionary. "Japanese Buddhist Statuary." Available: www.onmarkproductions.com/html/shoki.shtml (accessed May 1, 2009).

Sprug, Joseph W. 1994. *Index to Fairy Tales, 1987–1992: Including 310 Collections of Fairy Tales, Folktales, Myths, and Legends: With Significant Pre-1987 Titles Not Previously Indexed.* Metuchen, NJ: Scarecrow Press.

Thompson, Stith. 1989. *Motif-Index of Folk-Literature: A Classification of Narrative Elements in Folktales, Ballads, Myths, Fables, Mediaeval Romances, Exempla, Fabliaux, Jestbooks, and Local Legends.* Revised and enlarged edition. Bloomington: Indiana University Press.

Williams, C.A.S. 1960. *New Encyclopedia of Chinese Symbolism and Art Motives.* New York: Julian Press.

Wójcicki, K.W. 1981. *Klechdy: staroztyne podanie i powiesci ludowe.* Warszawa: Panstwowy Instytut Wydawniczy.

Yolen, Jane. 1988. *Favorite Folktales from Around the World.* New York: Pantheon Books.

Chapter 9

✳ Digital Storytelling ✳

The phrase *digital storytelling* covers tales told through an exciting collection of images, music, and words designed to tell a personal story. Digital stories are short—three- to five-minute—compelling tales of emotional importance to the teller. These stories incorporate electronic content, including digital still photos, video clips, images, sound effects, recorded voices, and/or music to enhance the telling.

Joe Lambert (2007: 25), an early proponent, defined digital storytelling in a 2007 article in *The Futurist* as "short media pieces that combine a spoken narrative, still images and design elements using digital photo manipulation and digital video editing tools." Sheng Kuan Chung (2007: 17), an assistant professor of art education, states that "digital storytelling refers to the practice of incorporating digital text, imagery, video and audio into the presentation of a computer-mediated, multimedia story." Chung (2007: 17) also notes that the Digital Storytelling Association has stated that digital storytelling is "the modern expression of the ancient art of storytelling."

Digital stories can be posted on the World Wide Web for viewing. It should be noted that traditional storytelling is interactive and involves two-way interaction between a storyteller and one or more listeners. So, the expression *digital storytelling* is somewhat misleading, because at this point (in 2009) there isn't a venue for on-line, interactive storytelling. The only interaction that comes from digital production can happen after someone has viewed a digital story and wants to register a response or ask for more information. This may change with new technology, and there may come a time when the teller will be able to see and be seen by another person or group and connect in real time.

An accepted definition of storytelling, found on the National Storytelling Network's homepage (www.storynet.org), states, "Storytelling is the interactive art of using words and actions to reveal the elements and images of a story while encouraging the listener's imagination." The word *interactive* is of utmost importance to the storytelling experience from the viewpoint of the teller and any member of the audience.

It may be as subtle as simple eye contact or as obvious as direct participation by joining with the teller in song, rhyme, or other forms of sharing in the story. The storyteller creates the telling in the moment, with input from the audience. The input or interaction can change the way tellers put the tale together, including their emphasis on certain words, the way they change their facial expression, or the tone of their voice. The storytellers and their audience create the story together. At this point, this cannot happen with digital storytelling. In the future, however, there may be a "virtual" online path to digital storytelling.

Options for Digital Storytelling

Some great choices are available for storytellers to offer their performances online through community and student Web sites. Some Web sites allow visitors to post their performances and notes about upcoming appearances. Second Life, described later, allows tellers to post storytelling performances and also respond to reactions and questions submitted by someone who has seen one of their performances.

Center for Digital Storytelling

The Center for Digital Storytelling (www.storycenter.org) promotes the art of digital storytelling and offers instruction in digital storytelling to people with or without digital literacy skills. It offers basic workshops for those getting started, as well as specialized workshops focusing on training in more advanced educational, business, or artistic areas, as needed.

This site is full of examples of digital stories, opportunities for digital story training, and numerous programs benefiting community, educational, and business organizations developing special digital storytelling projects. The Center works with children, adults, teachers, and organizers involved with oral and local history, English as a second language (ESL), Spanish language, violence prevention, community arts, marketing, and much, much more. This site also includes the "Digital Storytelling Cookbook," general information on digital storytelling, a few digital tales, and other resources.

Second Life

Second Life is a three-dimensional virtual world where members investigate "arts and culture," "music," "education and non-profit," "photos and machinima," and other exciting areas. Members can create personal or business opportunities within these options.

Philip Rosedale dreamed of creating a world called Second Life in 1991 and began testing his concept, originally called Linden World, in 2002. Six months later the beta testing of Second Life opened to the public, and it went live in June 2003. Second Life imitates our real world, containing regions of land, water, and sky, and it allows visitors to see the Second Life space and participate according to their membership options.

Membership has various levels, including a basic membership, which allows a person to adopt an avatar character and investigate Second Life by visiting various showcases. After viewing the options within each area, basic members may choose to increase their membership to allow the purchase of land within Second Life. Once land has been purchased, members can build a house on their land, start a business on their property, and begin to create objects. A person, at a certain membership level, can start to buy, sell, or trade with other avatars. Millions of Second Life members from all around the globe often stop in to participate.

Digital Storytelling Production

Producing a successful digital story involves completing some basic steps. Using the following steps as guidelines, a person can produce a three- to five-minute digital story.

Exhibit 9-1. On a Personal Note: Second Life

After I registered for Second Life, selected my avatar, and chose a name for myself, I began exploring my options. I conducted a search with the word "storytelling" and visited a space it suggested called "Apollo's Garden." While there, I saw other residents lounging in swings, walking among the flowers, and speaking words. I wanted more, so I visited the SHOWCASE options and found, within Education, a STORYTELLERS GUILD. This group includes storytellers and their performances. One storyteller, Dale Jarvis, has his stories available for viewing and includes announcements of his past and upcoming storytelling events. Options for storytelling presentations and activities on Second Life are still being explored by its members.

The Story

The first steps are the most important, as they involve your personal story, told in the first person, about a significant event, person, place, or item that affected your life in a meaningful way. The story is the most important part of the process. Take your time creating this story and write, rewrite, and rewrite until you have a complete and well-composed tale. It should be a personal story that others can relate to as they watch it unfold. As your story is created, you will see opportunities to include various pieces of multimedia.

The story writing will be followed by creating a script and a storyboard. Relax and enjoy putting together the first parts of the process, and you will be ready to complete the technical part of your digital story when the first steps are finished.

The Script

After creating your story, you will develop a script based on your story, which includes the various pieces of multimedia that seem to fit with the story and feel useful. These may be photos, film clips, objects located on the World Wide Web, or other electronic items. Make certain these multimedia pieces add to the story and are not just included to shock or surprise your audience. This accompanying script will be approximately one to two pages long.

The Storyboard

Once the story and script are composed, construct a storyboard. The storyboard is a series of sketches, drawings, or illustrated screens that tell your story. It will look like a comic book version of the story or a filmstrip or a piece of the film from a movie. The author fills in the boxes or screens on the storyboard with drawings of the events and media in the tale. The storyboard can be created on any piece of paper or poster board using a pen or marker. It can also be designed using Microsoft Word or Microsoft PowerPoint.

The storyboard lets you see the progression of your digital story, with the media woven into the tale. You do not need to be an artist; you can fill in the screen with words or stick figures. These screens show the order of events in the story. If there will be a title screen or screens of explanatory material, include them as screens on the storyboard.

The storyboard shown in Exhibit 9-2 was designed in Microsoft Word using the following commands: INSERT, TEXT BOX, and DRAW TEXT BOX. You can plan the storyboard boxes and add notes about your recorded voice, music, or other sound effects. This helps keep track of the different types of media used in the story and will serve as a guide for the person filming the digital story. Adding short notes to the storyboard will be beneficial to the filming person or crew. Think of the storyboard as a map explaining the order of events in your digital story. The technical pieces of digital storytelling production may change frequently, but the storyboard will serve as a basic outline of necessary equipment and software.

Record Your Voice-Over

Garage Band or Pro Voiceover software is available for tellers to record their scripts as voice-overs for their digital story. Try to perform your script by telling the story rather than by reading or memorizing it so that it sounds natural. If you choose to read from the script, it helps to mark pauses so your voice sounds smoother and more natural.

Exhibit 9-2. Sample Storyboard

| **My Digital Story**

ADD CLIP ART

ADD FAIRY TALE TYPE MUSIC | Family of Tellers:

Grandmother
—Folk and fairy tales
—Family stories
Mother
—Folk and fairy tales
Father
—Family stories

ADD PHOTOS OF ROXIE, MOM & DAD | I started telling tales when I babysat or worked as a camp coun-selor.

ADD CLIP ART | After library school, I worked as a children's li-brarian and told tales in the elementary schools.

ADD CLIP ART |
| Now, I'm a librarian at Central Connecticut State University and teach storytelling courses.

ADD PHOTO OF CCSU | My book/DVD will be published this year:

ADD COVER IMAGE | | |

Gather Your Media Resources

You have selected photos, recordings, and other multimedia pieces. Prepare the photos in a JPEG format. Video clips can also be used, but be aware that they require a more complex set of steps.

Create Your Digital Story

Assemble your digital components and follow the directions for your movie-making software. If you are using an iMAC, follow the steps for iMovie. Those with PC platforms will use Movie Maker 2. Production equipment to create digital stories includes the following:

    Hardware
        Computer
        The Internet
        Cameras

Scanners

Microphone/speakers

Software

Apple iLife (iMovie, iPhoto, iDVD, iWeb, GarageBand)

Photoshop, QuickTime Pro, SmartSound, Final Cut Pro, Adobe Premiere, Movie Maker 2

Other software, as needed, to tell your story digitally

There are a variety of reasons for using digital stories with young people and adults. Those who want to learn the process of creating an engaging digital story can follow the steps necessary to write their personal tale, produce the script and the storyboard, and combine them with their choice of media to build their digital story.

Schools, libraries, community groups, and others train and educate members to produce quality digital stories. There are also Web sites that outline, explore, and offer training in digital storytelling production techniques, some of which are listed in the "Suggested Resources" section at the end of this chapter.

Uses of Digital Storytelling

In his book *Digital Storytelling in the Classroom: New Media Pathways to Literacy, Learning, and Creativity,* Jason Ohler (2008) has written a thorough discussion and outline of how to use digital storytelling in the classroom, describing how the technology can be especially effective with children and young adults. The introduction, by David Thornburg, an award-winning futurist, author, and consultant, describes Ohler's book as a map that readers can use to chart their own course with digital storytelling.

Anne Fields and Karen Diaz (2008), librarians working within their own community, designed and produced a digital story project that focused on telling stories about academic libraries. This is a unique work that discusses the process of creating a personal story about the lives of a community of people who work in an academic library and the wonderful tale of the library and discovering its unique gifts. Fields and Diaz truly built community, as they found transforming power in telling their story about the librarians, staff, students, and the entire campus community.

Jennifer LaFontaine, a community-based artist, helps diverse groups tell the stories of their communities and work for social change. She describes the Digital Storytelling Program leaders as creating "their own 3- to 5-minute video, using images, video clips, music, and, most importantly, their own voice" (LaFontaine, 2006: 78). She has worked to help groups design and produce media programs to tell their stories. She wants to "empower communities to tell their stories through media-based arts" (p. 77).

With the advent of digital storytelling in the 1990s, many of these groups have been able and encouraged to learn the skills involved in creating digital stories. This can involve training in digital media, such as digital still cameras, digital film cameras, and computer editing software. These skills and the accompanying equipment may be obtained through community-based organizations.

In England, the BBC has one of the largest collections of two-minute digital stories that have been produced by participants in workshops throughout the country. The BBC has a Web page (www.bbc.co.uk/tellinglives) that gives access to these tales. The site not only provides the tales but also gives general information on digital storytelling and tells folks how to produce short programs.

These examples show the exciting and remarkable ways that the new technology is affecting people around the globe. Proponents of digital storytelling have found their own, often unique, ways to use the technology to further educational curriculums, classroom presentations, oral histories, and community. These are noteworthy in describing this new form of storytelling and its many uses in the classroom and throughout our world.

Summary

Digital storytelling has been an electronic form of storytelling since the 1990s. It presents adults and young people with an area ripe for creative activities in cultural, ethnic, human interest, and other social groups, as well as with elementary, middle, high school, and higher education classrooms.

Digital story production involves the creation of a personal tale and a script and the construction of a storyboard. The storyboard will guide the progress of the digital story; it includes still or moving electronic images, a recorded narrative, and any other design elements.

Chapter 10 will discuss museums, traveling displays, exhibits, and other places where tellers might find story ideas and materials for composing a story.

Suggested Resources

Online Resources

The Center for Digital Storytelling.
www.storycenter.org (accessed May 2, 2009).
This site describes the workshops the Center offers to new and advanced participants, the schedules and locations of the workshops, and the programs and services available to community, business, and educational organizations. The site includes "The Digital Storytelling Cookbook" at www.storycenter.org/cookbook.html.

Digital School Collection: Teacher Resources.
www.adobe.com/education/digkids/storytelling/sevensteps.html (accessed May 2, 2009).
This site provides an in-depth explanation of the steps required to produce digital stories, from Step One: "Getting started" to Step Seven: "The applause you will receive when you finish."

"Digital Storytelling: A Tutorial in 10 Easy Steps."
www.techsoup.org/learningcenter/techplan/page5897.cfm (accessed May 2, 2009).
J.D. Lasica lists and outlines the steps involved in creating and producing a digital video. These steps come from workshops, books, and personal observations.

iLife Training Using Apple Technology.
http://edcommunity.apple.com/ali/story.php?itemID=9552 (accessed May 2, 2009).
iLife comes from the offices of Educational Technology in the Charter School of Education at Berry College, Mount Berry, Georgia, and the Apple Distinguished Educator program. This Web site gives steps to follow to create a digital story using Apple technology.

"Capturing Stories, Capturing Lives: An Introduction to Digital Storytelling."
www.jakesonline.org/dst_techforum.pdf (accessed May 2, 2009).

David S. Jakes, the instructional technology coordinator at Downer's Grove Community High School in Illinois, explains the process of producing a digital story and explores what students can learn from producing digital stories and why he feels it is so important.

Print Resources

Howell, Dusti D. and Deanne K. Howell. 2003. *Digital Storytelling: Creating an eStory.* Worthington, OH: Linworth. ISBNs: 1586830805; 9781586830809
Howell and Howell describe the steps involved when creating a digital story. They explain how to plan the storyboard and to select the correct equipment and software, and they answer a lot of basic questions about scanning, adding text, capturing video, working with slides, etc. This step-by-step guide will be extremely useful to beginners as well as to experienced digital story producers.

Bibliography

British Broadcasting System. *Telling Lives: Your Digital Story.* Available: www.bbc.co.uk/tellinglives (accessed May 3, 2009).
Chung, Sheng Kuan. 2007. Art Education Technology: Digital Storytelling. *Art Education* 60, no. 2: 17–22.
Fields, Anne M. and Karen R. Diaz. 2008. *Fostering Community through Digital Storytelling: A Guide for Academic Libraries.* Westport, CT: Libraries Unlimited.
Howell, Dusti D. and Deanne K. 2003. *Digital Storytelling: Creating an eStory.* Worthington, OH: Linworth.
LaFontaine, Jennifer. 2006. "From the Story Circle to Cyberspace." *Women & Environments International Magazine* 72/73 (Fall/Winter): 77–81.
Lambert, Joe. 2007. Digital Storytelling: How Media Help Preserve Cultures. *The Futurist* 41, no. 2: 25.
McClean, Shilo T. 2007. *Digital Storytelling: The Narrative Power of Visual Effects in Film.* Cambridge, MA: MIT Press.
Ohler, Jason. 2007. "Art, Storytelling, and the Digital Economy." *School Arts* 107, no. 2: 58–59.
———. 2008. *Digital Storytelling in the Classroom: New Media Pathways to Literacy, Learning, and Creativity.* Thousand Oaks, CA: Corwin Press.
Rowland, Craig. 2007. "The Art of Digital Storytelling." *School Arts* 107, 2: 42.

Chapter 10

❋ Other Resources for Locating Tales ❋

As discussed in previous chapters, stories come to us in various forms from many different sources. Originally stories were told orally and passed on by word of mouth. We still obtain many tales orally, but we can also access tales in print and digital formats and from historical institutions, works of art, museums of various types, and traveling displays or exhibits, to name just a few sources. With the World Wide Web (covered in Chapter 9), the wealth of available sources is exponential!

Some tales are ready for storytellers to retell, but others require minor changes or additional material to personalize the tale. Composing new types of tales can be especially fun, because storytellers can be creative and design stories based on what they know but then add to it. When presented, these tales will be a teller's own stories, although credit must be given to the original authors.

This chapter will provide suggestions for places to find stories and story ideas from new sources. There are countless stories waiting to be told, including those about events or persons the teller has experienced or encountered. The following areas are covered in this chapter:

- Tales from news sources
- Stories from cultural institutions, museums, traveling exhibits, and displays
- Fables, old and new

Tales from News Sources

Newspapers and online news sources offer a wealth of stories and information about people, events, and places that can be repurposed into tales. For example, a storyteller from Connecticut researched the baseball legend Jackie Robinson and composed a story about his life. She presented her story to groups of middle school students who reportedly enjoyed hearing about this legendary star. Much of her material for the story came from newspaper articles published during Robinson's years as a young baseball star.

To develop a story from news sources, a teller first needs to research the person or event using newspaper and magazine articles and online sources. News articles are excellent sources of information because they are told by someone who was present at the time the person or event was being covered.

Tales about Real People

Tales about real people might be about local, state, or national politicians; local officials; musicians; authors; sports figures; or town characters, just to name a few examples. Often these are people who have led unusual, sometimes eccentric, lives or experienced important or exceptional circumstances, incidents, or conditions. They could also be perfectly ordinary folks who have typical, customary, or familiar things happen to them.

Newspapers often place local interest stories in the "Town" or "Local News" sections. These sections have special appeal, because some of their readers will recognize the featured persons.

When stories are about real people, there are important considerations to be made regarding the facts. There should not be a lot of embellishment; the facts need to reflect the person's life accurately.

Some political leaders, especially those with unique personalities, would be prime examples of "real characters" who would provide the essentials of a good story. For example, Representative Bella Abzug (1920–1998) led an amazing life that contained certain aspects that would make her story notable.

Representative Bella Abzug

Bella Abzug was a U.S. Representative from New York State (1970–1976). She was recognized as a "unique character" and would serve as a good example of a person of integrity who lived her life honorably and who should be remembered with affection and respect. A student could undertake a research project about Abzug's life, which could be compiled and included in a portrayal of her for a lesson in history or social studies.

A teller (or teacher) could appear dressed as Bella Abzug, wearing one of the many bold hats that she usually sported, and then begin telling her life story:

My name is Ms. Bella Abzug. I was born in 1920, a daughter of Russian immigrants, and I grew up pretty poor in the Bronx. By the age of 13, I started giving speeches in my synagogue and went on to want to serve in Congress. Now, I represent New York State in the U.S. Congress.

I have some areas where I feel very strongly that we need to pay attention and watch these topics carefully. I believe our civil liberties need to be protected and expanded, and, with that in mind, I helped write the Freedom of Information Act, The Right to Privacy Act, and The Sunshine Act.

The Sunshine Act states that, with some exceptions, "every portion of every meeting of an agency shall be open to public observation." Doesn't it make sense that we should be able to find out what happened at meetings that we weren't able to attend? And, the Right to Privacy Act makes the government disclose any agency's records if we request to see a copy of them. If the FBI has a file on me, I want us to be able to see it. Wouldn't you? I want to make certain if they DO have a file on me, that everything is CORRECT!

The Freedom of Information Act is also important. This act allows for the full or partial disclosure of previously unreleased information and documents controlled by the United States Government. Once again, if there is information kept hidden, I want to be able to get hold of it, when needed! We need to keep activities and information about our agencies open to the public.

Abzug left us with a story that might be a useful and fun teaching tool. Bella Abzug was a bright and exceptional woman, an outspoken champion of women's rights, the peace movement, and civil rights. In her *Time* magazine eulogy to Ms. Abzug, actress Shirley

MacLaine (1998: 43) applauded her as one of the few people she knew who was "always right about character," and she stated that the "courage she displayed in acting on her convictions sometimes stunned people."

A dramatization could also be prepared telling the story of Ms. Abzug's court appearance in which she argued to have the sentence reversed for a man from Mississippi, Willie McGee, who had been unfairly convicted of raping a Caucasian woman. Abzug worked tirelessly for this man while white supremacists, not pleased with Abzug as she tried to get the case reversed, threatened her and refused to allow her to stay in a local hotel. At that point, she was eight months pregnant and was forced to sleep at the bus station (Bosworth, 2003: 21).

Willie McGee, a 36-year-old black veteran and father of four children, was a truck driver in Laurel, Mississippi. Troy Hawkins, a Caucasian woman, claimed she was raped by a man with "kinky hair." McGee was arrested and held incommunicado for 32 days until he signed a confession that he later retracted. The all-white jury in the first trial found him guilty after two minutes of deliberating, while a lynch mob waited outside. The Civil Rights Congress (CRC) defended McGee through several trials, organized worldwide protests, and led extensive media campaigns. The CRC held mass protests in 1950 in Jackson, Mississippi, demanding a new trial and a stay of execution. The Supreme Court issued three stays of execution but refused to dismiss or review the case despite new evidence that Hawkins had forced McGee to have sexual relations with her for years by threatening to accuse him of rape. In March 1951, McGee was put to death in the electric chair.

Abzug had a vision of women, minorities, young people, and the poor, elderly, and unemployed people forming a coalition that would provide help for the millions of people whose needs are not met. Gloria Steinem, writer, feminist, and women's rights reformer, remembered Abzug as the author of many laws that concerned women's needs. Steinem recalled Abzug's work helping to pass a law to ban discrimination against women who wanted to obtain credit cards, loans, and mortgages (Cowern, 1998: 19). Abzug was also the author of numerous books, some of which are included at the end of this chapter.

Senator Harold Hughes

There are other U.S. congressional leaders who could be the subject of stories worth telling to a group of young people or adults. One example would be Iowa Senator Harold Hughes.

> There are some people whose stories require careful treatment reflecting their lives of integrity and understanding. Harold Hughes (1922–1996) had difficult early years spent in rural poverty, followed by alcohol dependence in later years. He also served in World War II.
>
> Depressed and ready to commit suicide, Hughes had a religious conversion and realized he could work with God and devote himself to religious life. He had planned to kill himself in the bathtub to avoid creating a mess. As Hughes considered raising the gun to his head, he had his religious conversion.
>
> He imagined God telling him to put the gun down, take God as his savior, and live a life of peace. He did just that, stood up, stepped out of the bathtub, left the bathroom, and placed a call to his minister. After relating the events he had just lived through, he told the minister of his conversion and volunteered to help teach Bible studies to the congregation.
>
> A truck driver by trade, he was able to stop drinking in 1954, with assistance from Alcoholics Anonymous. In the ensuing years, Hughes moved toward public service in government, and he served as governor of Iowa in the 1960s. As their Senator from 1969 to 1975, he was able to get alcohol treatment legislation passed, and, assured of reelection as a liberal Democrat, Hughes said he could not reconcile serving in a government he felt wasted so much money on the military and war. He devoted the rest of his life to spiritual ministry and died in 1996, leaving a legacy of peace, religious work, and better availablility of positive alcohol treatment programs.

News Stories with Unverifiable Facts

A second category of story developed from news sources is one that is designed to tell a good story but for which the facts may not be verifiable. A tale about a young woman and her violin is such a story. It was reported in the *Hartford Courant* newspaper in the 1980s, but the article is no longer available. When storytellers tell tales of people and events that aren't based on facts, they can embellish as they want. It is understood that tales are made up of "universal truths," but they are accompanied by improvisation and embellishment. Storytellers can make note of this to their audiences, but it is not required.

Anne Ryland's Guadanucci Violin

A famous Italian violin instrument maker in the 1600s made gorgeous violins. Those that have survived and remain in good condition today may be worth hundreds of thousands of dollars. One of the Guadanucci violins was given to a promising teenage musician in 1960 by a relative who recognized his talent. This young man took it with him when he married and moved to the United States. He and his wife had three daughters, but Anne, the youngest, was the only one to express an interest in his violin. She learned to play and, as a child, become quite skilled. Her father gave her the instrument when she was a teenager. He died soon after, but she continued to display her dedication to the violin.

Sadly, Anne had a problem with alcohol and went into treatment in her late twenties. Before she left, she begged her mother and sisters to guard the violin for her until she returned. But there came a time when her mother and sisters sold it to a neighbor so they could indulge in various extravagances. The buyer questioned the small price for an instrument of that quality.

When Anne returned home, she happily anticipated her reunion with her violin. But, her mother and sisters said they had sold it only because Anne hadn't been there to help out when they were near starvation. They insisted that their father had considered it a family treasure for all their use. Anne was furious, located a temporary, but inferior, violin, and proceeded to take her mother and sisters to court. The judge asked all of them for their stories, and after they finished he asked if any of them could play the violin. Each sister wanted to show her connection to the violin and scratched out a tune before abandoning it to Anne. When Anne started to play, everyone in attendance shed tears, as her music was so beautiful.

"Anne," the judge said, "That is clearly your violin and I'm sorry it wasn't ready for you upon your return." Looking at the mother and sisters, he directed them to repay the neighbor, with interest, and told Anne to take her violin home and enjoy it. The neighbor nodded to Anne, wished her well, and said he had always wondered about the circumstances and hoped she'd get years of happiness from her violin.

Source: Adapted by Emily Chasse.

Stories from Cultural Institutions, Traveling Exhibits, and Other Displays

Cultural institutions such as museums and historical societies, traveling exhibits, and other displays lend themselves well to developing tales to tell. Their collections and displays contain stories waiting to be told, and tellers can enhance and expand information about each one, weaving stories from the historical, geographical, or social aspects of the art, artifact, and so forth. Embellishing the facts can make the item or object appealing in new ways, and both children and adults will find the displays fascinating in ways they might not have experienced without the highlighting storytellers can give them.

Museums

Museums contain a wealth of information. Many museums house artifacts and objects from the past as well as the present. In their exhibits and on their Web pages, they explore the backgrounds of particular subjects and topics and may include tales based on the collection and on the objects contained there. Museums in other countries also contain information for storytelling involving their own national artifacts, and, because of the World Wide Web, this information is very accessible.

There are many types of museums—too numerous to list. Some have general appeal for a broad audience, while others cater to specialized audiences—for example, those with special interests (e.g., art, history, natural history, science, ethnic studies, the environment, sports, religion, politics). Some museums focus on specific geographic areas (e.g., particular cities, regions, states, countries).

Museums will often schedule storytelling performances focusing on tales related to their collections. These events are especially entertaining, because you can observe various performance styles and see how the tellers use gestures, voice, movements, and other paralinguistic effects. Museum exhibits change throughout the year, and the ones listed here may no longer be available.

State historical societies and libraries also offer much information on artifacts, tales, legends, and more. They may schedule folk or fairy tale telling performances. For example, the Connecticut Historical Society, in Hartford (www.chs.org), has offered stories of immigrants, Native Americans, African Americans, and West Indian tales of Anansi (a clever, cunning, and often mischievous trickster figure), as well as tales of Hartford in general and its historical figures. Their educational programs focus on the political, social, and economic history. Among tales of the area is the following "Legend of the Charter Oak."

Legend of the Charter Oak

The Charter Oak stood in Hartford at the time of the struggle for Independence from England in the 1700s. In 1662, Connecticut received its Royal Charter from England's Charles II and later had to defend it against those same people. The ruling British considered splitting the state between Massachusetts and New York.

In 1687, Sir Edmund Andros, representing the King of England, demanded the Charter be returned to England. Connecticut leaders managed to secure the document and hide it in the branches of an oak tree outside the room in a tavern where the leaders and the representative of the King were meeting. No one will ever know for certain how it happened, but the room where they were meeting was plunged into darkness. While everyone was scrambling in the dark, it is said that someone passed the charter to Captain Joseph Wadsworth, who was outside one of the windows of the tavern, and he hid the charter in the oak tree for safekeeping.

The tree was a majestic 500-year-old white oak and Wadsworth's bold move allowed Connecticut to preserve not only the document, but the rights of the colonists. The tree has held the nickname "Charter Oak" from that date until its fall during a storm in 1856. The Charter Oak is Connecticut's official State Tree and an image of it was selected to emblazon the back of Connecticut's state quarter.

Sources: Adapted by Emily Chasse. This tale can be found in books and on the World Wide Web at: http://digital.library.upenn.edu/women/marshall/country/country-III-33.html.

The Smithsonian Institution's Web site (http://www.smithsonian.org) features areas for educators that include lesson plans and study units on a wide range of topics. The activities focus on figures, historical artifacts, and cultural events, and highlight science and technology issues of interest. Many of the lesson plans contain stories and storytelling activities.

Children's Museums

Museums focusing on objects, activities, events, and fun for children often offer storytelling support in various forms. They may present workshops for children and adults who want to learn storytelling, as well as provide time and space for anyone to share their own stories.

Art Museums

Art museums, such as the Museum of Modern Art (MoMA) in New York City (www.moma.org), have links to hundreds of Web pages that include information on various areas of art. Many of these pages provide stories, legends, and tales. For example, a 2007 MoMA Web page told about an installation by Elaine Reichek that contained information on weaving as well as stories about weaving and weavers. One segment dealt with a program on the story of embroidery, knitting, and weaving as it relates to art and relations between the sexes. This exhibit used the ancient story of Arachne to illustrate a point about the skill of weaving. This Greek myth tells the story of Arachne and Athena.

Arachne

Arachne was a mortal and a very skilled and fine weaver. She was so good that she became arrogant and said she was as good as Athena, the Goddess of Weaving. Athena heard about Arachne's boast and challenged her to a contest where they would each create a tapestry. Arachne's piece rivaled Athena's, which made Athena so angry she hit Arachne repeatedly on the head. Arachne realized she should never have compared herself to a goddess and hung herself from a tree branch in shame. She died, ending her life with a large, swollen body and head and with thin dangling arms. Athena felt sorry for Arachne and brought her back to life as a spider, and Arachne has been weaving her beautiful webs ever since.

Sources: Adapted by Emily Chasse. "The Story of Arachne" can be found in books and on the World Wide Web at www.hse.k12.in .us/staff/DBROVIAK/Page%20files/Mythology/Stories/Arachne % 20and%20Athena.htm.

The Metropolitan Museum of Art (www.metmuseum.org) in New York City also weaves stories through its collections and special exhibitions. The focus is on art, but the displays cover archeology, history, and culture, among other areas.

The J. Paul Getty Museum (www.getty.edu/museum) in Los Angeles collects works of art in the areas of European paintings, drawings, sculpture, illuminated manuscripts, decorative arts, and photographs. The museum offers numerous programs for teachers and children, including school visits, teacher programs and resources, lesson plans, puzzles, and games. It also hosts a Family Storytelling Series.

There are also museums that highlight ethnic, cultural, social, racial, and religious groups. They often include stories about their collection or about specific objects in their collection. Examples of such museums include Native American museums.

Native American Museums

Native American museums are located throughout the United States and Canada. They offer programs and exhibits that often contain information about Native American tales and storytellers.

The National Museum of the American Indian (NMAI) has a presence in Washington, DC, New York, and Maryland. NMAI offers tours, family resources, and materials to use in the classroom, as well as educational activities at the museum and resources for teachers and students.

The Four Directions Institute has built a California Indian Museum and Cultural Center in Santa Rosa, California. It represents the major Indian cultures of the United States and offers information on the customs and religious practices; the cultures of the peoples, including food production, housing, tools, and clothing; and maps of the regions in which they lived. It also gives examples of their stories, myths, and legends and discusses some of their important people, including their leaders, and events. Exhibits include posters, PowerPoint displays, recordings, and artifacts.

The Mashantucket Pequot Museum and Research Center (www .pequotmuseum.org) in Mashantucket, Connecticut, contains Native American materials; artifacts such as a dugout canoe, wigwams, clothing, and food; and information on the histories and cultures of all Native peoples in the United States and Canada. The museum hosts a celebration of winter solstice with activities and age-old tales told by Native American storytellers.

The Institute for American Indian Studies (www.birdstone.org) in Washington, Connecticut, offers storytelling events such as a "Haunted Trail Walk" and an annual "Storytelling Festival," where the Native American art of oral tradition can be experienced. Many of the displays contain artifacts and stories about Native American folklore, which can be useful when introducing and using Native American tales.

Traveling Exhibits and Displays

Exhibits and displays from a museum or other institution often travel in order to expand the viewing audience. People who are unable to travel a long distance to the home location are happy to make a short trip to view an exhibition.

Thomas Hart Benton Murals

In the fall of 2007, a traveling display of Thomas Hart Benton murals appeared at the Museum of American Art in New Britain, Connecticut, along with Benton murals owned by the museum, which reflect social and work scenes during the 1930s in America. This exhibition sparked numerous tales from faculty and students from Central Connecticut State University (CCSU) about certain pieces of the artwork. Faculty told stories about some of the events portrayed in the murals, based on their knowledge of those specific works. A CCSU art history professor told about the Benton murals located on campus and in New Britain, and others told about certain pieces of artwork at the museum. These stories were captivating to many of us and will be retold in the future.

Students at CCSU had been asked to contribute a piece of artwork, an essay, a performance, or other display on the topic "What would one or more of the people painted in one of the Benton murals look like or be doing in that mural if it were today?" Students submitted their projects, which included art, poetry, video, journalistic writing, performance, theater, music, and multimedia works in response to the Benton murals. They told stories through their artwork, writings, and plays that were presented at the museum and were on display the night of the museum tour. In essence, they were creating new stories with their creative works.

The CCSU Night at the Museum event was an overwhelming success, according to many of the faculty and students who participated. It is just one example of a way to incorporate tales into art, literature, and dramatic activities. College students have a level of sophistication that allows them to help fully plan and participate in such activities, but similar events could also be planned for elementary and secondary education students, as well as for senior citizens, art groups, various clubs, community organizations, and so forth.

Slave Quilts

An especially significant traveling display and exhibit involving storytelling concerns slave quilts. Slave quilts are quilts, dating from the 1800s, that were said to have secret codes embedded in them that could help slaves find a path to freedom. Information about these codes was passed between family members and other slaves to explain how to recognize the special features of the quilt squares and understand the coded information. These secret codes provided clues that were used, in combination with the Underground Railroad, to guide slaves north to the free states and then to safety in Canada. Numerous displays, exhibits, books, articles, Web sites, and video and DVD productions discuss these slave quilts, the secret codes, and the stories surrounding them.

The quilts have been passed down through families for years. They have been displayed in exhibits and as traveling collections, and they have been viewed in the owners' homes. The stories and the secret codes sewn into them are discussed at each showing.

The topic of secret codes in slave quilts has been controversial among some academics and scholars. Information about the secret codes was primarily passed on by word of mouth, through stories and oral instruction, not by written documentation. Some historians don't consider oral history to be reliable or valid. It has been pointed out that African-American slaves were not allowed to receive an education, so most were unable to read or write. Therefore, it should not be a surprise that they didn't keep written records of the secret quilt codes. The field of African-American quilt history is relatively new, and more information will be discovered as the topic is further researched (Tobin and Dobard, 1999: 26).

World Wide Web sites, articles, and books in the "Suggested Resources" section at the end of this chapter present information on the secret codes and slave quilts. Some of these resources explain the quilt patterns and show examples of the secret codes. The debate over the validity and truth of secret quilt codes won't be settled anytime soon.

A storyteller could describe the slave quilts and codes and tell a story involving slaves and the quilts. They could address the controversy for their listeners, and a discussion could follow. The video version of the story "Follow the Drinking Gourd: A Story of the Underground Railroad" (Rabbit Ears Productions) is based on one of the fictionalized accounts and could be used to create a story. Other sources of information about the story can be found in the "Suggested Resources" and the "Bibliography" at the end of this chapter.

Fables

Fables are short tales designed to communicate a truth or a lesson about life. Usually they are in the form of a story expressing practical wisdom featuring animals behaving as people. Fables often tell stories, but they are not considered to be in the same category as folk and fairy tales. Fables communicate a moral and have an inherent teaching or learning aspect to them, whereas folk and fairy tales are told primarily for entertainment and enjoyment.

Early fables by Aesop, a Greek slave who lived in the mid-sixth century BC, were told to point out a moral lesson to adults. These fables provided a harmless way to criticize superiors or people in charge without suffering the consequences of punishment for belittling people of a higher rank. "We cannot be certain which of the hundreds of fables attributed to him (Aesop) he actually told" (Bader, 1991: 5). Many of the fables we attribute to Aesop resemble those told in the Hitopadesa stories, a collection of Indian fables in sixth century AD, and in the *Panchatantra*, which consists of five books of animal fables and magic tales that were compiled in India between the third and fifth centuries AD.

Other collections of fables were compiled by French poet Jean de la Fontaine (1621–1695), French poet and writer Jean Pierre Claris de Florian (1755–1794), and Russian writer Ivan Kriloff (1760–1844), among others. More currently, Arnold Lobel published new collection of fables in the 1980, and another book of fables was translated by Susan Ouriou, retold by Veronica Uribe, and published in 2004. Many other new books of individual fables are published each year.

Using fables with children may or may not prove useful. Many people maintain that most young children do not really get the point of fables. Both Jean Piaget and Lawrence Kohlberg, two noted psychologists who have written about the stages of moral development in children (Piaget wrote about children from infancy through ten years of age; Kohlberg expanded the ages through adolescence and early adulthood), don't believe the morals of fables make sense to young children (Pillar, 1983: 5). Other research has suggested that older elementary school–aged or gifted students can appreciate fables and that older young adults can appreciate the moral or point of a fable.

Arlene Pillar, a teacher of elementary school children, has found that many basal readers contained fables. She also notes that the early McGuffey basal readers placed importance on the teaching of morals and moral behavior (Pillar, 1983: 3–4). Pillar (1980) conducted a study with children in grades two, four, and six in two suburban schools and found that fables were inappropriate for moral instruction in the early elementary grades but that older children had a higher level of moral judgment. She felt that if fables are presented at developmentally appropriate times, they can generate values.

Summary

Storytellers should always be aware of their surroundings and on the lookout for interesting news stories, events, exhibits, fictional accounts (including fables), and accounts of real people that might lend themselves to the creation of a new story. There are so many stories waiting to be told. New tales—and older stories as well—will emerge. A teller just needs to look for them.

New stories can, of course, be gleaned from newspapers, magazines, television, radio, Web sites, and blogs. Cultural institutions of all types, traveling exhibits, and other displays offer abundant sources of material. A teller doesn't even have to visit a museum for material. Museum Web sites worldwide offer an exponential amount of information to glean. And there are a multitude of types of museums, from art to science to Native American to natural history, just to name a few.

Traveling exhibits and displays from museums and other institutions bring material from the home institution(s) to a teller's own neighborhood. For example, this chapter described a local display of Thomas Hart Benton murals that was informative and inspired many attendees to engage in their own creative endeavors. The long and short of it is that there is an abundance of material out there.

Chapter 11 presents ways to share stories with children and help guide young people in their storytelling journeys.

Suggested Resources

Print Resources

The Book of Fables: Including Fables by La Fontaine, John Gay, Robert Dodsley, Christian Gellert, Gotthold Lessing, Claris de Florian, Ivan Kriloff, and Others. 1962. New York: F. Warne & Co.
This book includes fables from many lands and authors, from Aesop (about 620–560 BC) to Kriloff (1768–844), and more.

Coan, Peter Morton. 1997. *Ellis Island Interviews: Immigrants Tell Their Stories in Their Own Words.* New York: Facts on File. ISBNs: 0816034141 (hardcover); 9780816034147 (hardcover); 0816035482 (softcover); 9780816035489 (softcover)
This unique collection contains stories from Ellis Island immigrants telling about their journeys to freedom from Europe, the Middle East, and elsewhere.

Cohen, Noam. "In Douglass Tribute, Slave Folklore and Fact Collide." *New York Times* (East Coast Late Edition), January 23, 2007, p. A.1.

Noam Cohen's 2007 *New York Times* article describes two plaques, located under a statue of Frederick Douglass, that explain the secret codes sewn into family quilts that helped slaves on their journey north to freedom. Cohen reports that some historians feel the codes are a hoax and feel the plaques should not be displayed near the Douglass memorial statue.

"Follow the Drinking Gourd: A Story of the Underground Railroad." 1992. Rowayton, CT: Rabbit Ears Production. VHS videocassette.

Taj Mahal plays the music of this traditional folksong, as it flows through an appealing story of one family's escape from slavery via the Underground Railroad.

Ives, Sarah. "Did Quilts Hold Codes to the Underground Railroad?" *National Geographic News,* February 5, 2004. http://news.nationalgeographic.com.au/news/2004/02/0205_040205_slavequilts.html (accessed February 26, 2009).

Ives presents background information on slave quilts and includes some of the quilt patterns, named "wagon wheel," "tumbling blocks," and "bear's paw," which appear to have contained secret messages guiding slaves to their freedom. She cites the book by Jacqueline Tobin and Raymond Dobard (1999), *Hidden in Plain View: A Secret Story of Quilts and the Underground Railroad,* which describes a sampler quilt that contained the different quilt patterns. Slaves would use the sampler to memorize the code.

Pillar, Arlene. 1980. "Look Before You Leap: Fables for the Elementary Level." Paper presented at the Annual Meeting of the National Council of Teachers of English, November 16–21, 1980." ERIC Documents, ED196028. EBSCOhost (accessed January 19, 2009).

Arlene Pillar believes fables are not appropriate for early elementary-aged children. She believes they are more suited to children older than second grade.

Tobin, Jacqueline and Raymond Dobard. 1999. *Hidden in Plain View: A Secret Story of Quilts and the Underground Railroad.* New York: Doubleday. ISBNs: 0385491379; 9780385491372

Tobin and Dobard discuss the transmission of secret codes in the slave quilts, and Tobin and African-American quilter Ozella McDaniel Williams talk about the evidence that there were secret codes sewn into quilts. In her foreword to Tobin and Dobard's book, Maude Southwell Wahlman notes, "Quilts were one of many media used to encode cultural knowledge" (p. 8).

Video Resources

Baker, Sharon K. 2004. *Whispers of Angels: A Story of the Underground Railroad.* Wilmington, DC: Teleduction, Inc. Videorecording: DVD video (60 min.). ISBNs: 1568391390; 9781568391397

Burton, LeVar , Mark Mannucci, and Jeanette Winter. 2007. *Follow the Drinking Gourd.* **Baltimore, MD: GPN Educational Media. Videorecording: DVD video, 1 videodisc (30 min.).**
Runaway slaves journey north along the Underground Railroad by following directions in a song "The Drinking Gourd". Based on the book *Follow the Drinking Gourd* by Jeanette Winter.

"Follow the Drinking Gourd: A Story of the Underground Railroad." 1992. Rowayton, CT: Rabbit Ears Production. VHS Videocassette.

Online Resources

"Follow the Drinking Gourd: A Cultural History." www.followthedrinking gourd.org (accessed February 26, 2009).
The song "Follow the Drinking Gourd" was first published in 1928. It is believed that the song helped slaves escape. A drinking gourd typically referred to something hollowed out to serve as a cup, but in the song the drinking gourd refers to the Big Dipper constellation, which points north and helped the slaves go north to freedom.

"The HistoryMakers® Video Oral History Interview with Serena Strother Wilson." www.thehistorymakers.com/programs/dvl/files/Wilson_Serenab.html (accessed January 3, 2008).
In this Video Oral History Interview (tapes 1–5, March 16, May 16, 2005; in the archives of the HistoryMakers, Chicago), Serena Strother Wilson discusses the code she learned about that was hidden in the patterns of quilt blocks that had been handed down through five generations of her family.

The Institute for American Indian Studies (Washington, Connecticut). www.birdstone.org (accessed May 2, 2009).
Visitors to the institute will discover much about Native American Indians and their storytelling connection.

Ives, Sarah. "Did Quilts Hold Codes to the Underground Railroad?" *National Geographic News,* February 5, 2004.
http://news.nationalgeographic.com.au/news/2004/02/0205_040205_slavequilts.html (accessed February 26, 2009).

Ives presents background information on slave quilts and includes some of the quilt patterns, named "wagon wheel," "tumbling blocks," and "bear's paw," which appear to have contained secret messages guiding slaves to their freedom. She cites the book by Jacqueline Tobin and Raymond Dobard (1999), *Hidden in Plain View: A Secret Story of Quilts and the Underground Railroad,* which describes a sampler quilt that contained the different quilt patterns. Slaves would use the sampler to memorize the code.

The Metropolitan Museum of Art (New York City).
www.metmuseum.org (accessed May 2, 2009).
On the "Explore and Learn" section of its Web site, the museum offers activities in different areas of the curriculum. In "The Art of Ancient Egypt: A Web Resource," students are encouraged to write a creation myth from a certain region or about a particular temple. Students may wish to dramatize their myths and present them to the class. This could be done in a variety of ways, through music and dance, dramatic readings, pantomime, or skits. The museum also hosts electronic versions of teacher resources, including objects, a timeline, curriculum connections, and more.

Quilter's Muse Virtual Museum.
www.quiltersmuse.com/the_secret_quilt_code_2007.htm (accessed May 2, 2009).
Cummings' diverse Web site features much information about quilt history, including information on the Underground Railroad "secret quilt code" quilts.

Seven Quilts for Seven Sisters.
www.einet.net/review/946733-419242 (accessed May 2, 2009).
This is a group of performers who present a program designed to educate the public about the slaves, their quilt making, and the communications to be found in quilts, including hidden messages to help slaves escape.

"African American Quilting Traditions." University of Virginia.
http://xroads.virginia.edu/~UG97/quilt/atrads.html (accessed May 2, 2009).
This World Wide Web site contain essays, articles, and photographs about the textile traditions of Africa and the connections among slavery, quilting, and the Underground Railroad. The University of Virginia's Web site also includes photos of quilts, textiles, and plantation weaving houses.

Women of Color Quilters Network.
www.wcqn.org/quiltsources.html (accessed May 2, 2009).

The Women of Color Quilters Network is a nonprofit group founded to foster and preserve the art of quilt making among women of color and documents African-American quilt making.

Bibliography

Bader, Barbara. 1991. *Aesop & Company: With Scenes from His Legendary Life*. Boston: Houghton Mifflin Company.

The Book of Fables: Including Fables by La Fontaine, John Gay, Robert Dodsley, Christian Gellert, Gotthold Lessing, Claris de Florian, Ivan Kriloff, and others. 1963. London: F. Warne & Co.

Bosworth, Patricia. 2003. "Bella Abzug." *The Nation* 277, no. 3: 20–21.

Cowern, Christine. 1998. "Gloria Steinem Remembers Bella Abzug." *WE International* (Spring/Summer): 44–45.

Florian, Jeanne Pierre Claris. 1888. *The Fables of Florian*. New York: J.B. Alden.

"Follow the Drinking Gourd: A Cultural History." Available: www.followthedrinkinggourd.org (accessed February 26, 2009).

"Follow the Drinking Gourd: A Story of the Underground Railroad." 1992. Rowayton, CT: Rabbit Ears Production. Videorecording.

Ives, Sarah. "Did Quilts Hold Codes to the Underground Railroad?" *National Geographic News,* February 5, 2004. Available: http://news.nationalgeographic.com.au/news/2004/02/0205_040205_slavequilts.html (accessed January 3, 2008).

J. Paul Getty Museum. Available: www.getty.edu/education (accessed May 2, 2009).

Krylov, Ivan Andreevich. 1827. *Favole Russe*. Perugia, Italy: Presso Bartelli e Costantini.

La Fontaine, Jean de. 2007. *Fables*. Urbana: University of Illinois Press.

Livo, Norma. 1986. *Storytelling: Process and Practice*. Littleton, CO: Libraries Unlimited.

Lobel, Arnold. 1980. *Fables*. New York: Scholastic.

MacLaine, Shirley. "Eulogy." *Time,* April 13, 1998, p. 43.

Mashantucket (CT) Pequot Museum and Research Center. Available: www.pequotmuseum.org (accessed May 2, 2009).

Monjo, F.N. 1970. *The Drinking Gourd*. New York: Harper & Row.

National Geographic XPEDITIONS: Geography Standards in Your Classroom. "Quilting: The Story of the Underground Railroad." Available: www.nationalgeographic.com/xpeditions/lessons/matrix.html (accessed December 3, 2008).

Pillar, Arlene M. 1980. "Look Before You Leap: Fables for the Elementary Level." Paper presented at the Annual Meeting of the National Council of Teachers of English, November 16–21, 1980. ERIC Documents, ED196028. EBSCOhost (accessed January 19, 2009).

————. 1983. "Aspects of Moral Judgment in Response to Fables." *Journal of Research and Development in Education* 16, no. 3: 39–46.

Ryder, Arthur W., trans. 1925. *Panchatantra.* Chicago: University of Chicago Press.

"Slave Quilt Exhibit." Available: www.nsa.gov/museum/museu00033.cfm.

Tobin, Jacqueline and Raymond Dobard. 1999. *Hidden in Plain View: A Secret Story of Quilts and the Underground Railroad.* New York: Doubleday.

"Underground Railroad Quilt Code." Available: http://educ.queensu.ca/~fmc/may2004/Underground.html (accessed May 2, 2009).

Uribe, Veronica. 2004. *Little Book of Fables.* Toronto: Groundwood Book.

Ventura, Cynthia L. and Lori M. Carlson. 1990. *Where Angels Glide at Dawn: New Stories from Latin America.* New York: Harper Trophy.

Williams, Jay. 1969. *The Practical Princess and Other Liberating Fairytales.* New York: Parents' Magazine Press.

Winter, Jeanette. 1988. *Follow the Drinking Gourd.* New York: Knopf.

Zipes, Jack David. 1986. *Don't Bet on the Prince.* New York: Methuen.

Chapter 11

✳ Telling Tales with Young People in the Community and Classroom ✳

Young people are ready to experience folktales, fairy tales, myths, legends, and stories of all types. They enjoy watching them being told, telling them themselves, and participating in storytelling activities and events of all kinds. This chapter will explain how to engage young people with tales in their school curriculums, clubs, outside events, and other activities. It will provide suggestions for ways to help them with stories and will explore the many storytelling resources available to teachers, librarians, and anyone who works with young people.

Storytelling with Young People

Librarians, teachers, and other storytellers have a wonderful audience waiting for them in the classrooms of local schools. One of the most important ways they can interact with children in the classroom is through storytelling.

Many books and articles discuss successful and enjoyable storytelling projects with children and adolescents. These programs encourage teachers, librarians, and other tellers to tell or read tales to young people and inspire them to tell stories to classmates, friends, parents, and adults. Some of these resources are listed in the "Suggested Resources" section at the end of this chapter.

Historically, children's librarians have appreciated the benefits of stories for young people. Effie Louise Power, who in the early twentieth century was one of the first librarians to hold a professional position dedicated exclusively to working with children, recognized the value of folktales in developing the "culture, physical repose and spiritual vision" of children (Power, 1969: 13). She en-

> **Exhibit 11-1. On a Personal Note: My Daughter as Storyteller**
>
> I told stories to my daughter from the time she was born, and early on she developed the ability to tell a story. "Brer Rabbit and the Tar Baby" was an early favorite of hers, and she loved to hear my husband and I laughing while she told the tale.
>
> My daughter would regularly appear in my "Folktelling: Art & Technique" class offered in the graduate program of Reading & Language Arts at Central Connecticut State University. I was proud to ask her to perform as an example of children telling tales. It seems that children who are exposed to tales from an early age are likely to develop a skill in the area.

sured that children would have access to folktales by editing many important collections of tales herself.

Hearing folk and fairy tales being performed provides many benefits to children. By experiencing the same tale simultaneously, teachers, tellers, students, and librarians share important feelings and emotions. This creates a common bond that promotes positive future encounters. This common bond helps everyone realize that we are all human beings and that we can enjoy feelings of kindness, pride, and hope while seeing our mistakes as we are all also susceptible to feelings of anger, violence, envy, and greed.

Gail De Vos (2003) discusses the importance of telling tales with adolescents. She finds that telling stories with teens helps fulfill their special need to belong, establish a sense of self, develop a value system, and enjoy being part of a group. It also satisfies the everpresent desire to be entertained. Hearing tales told by an adult creates a significant bond between the adult and child and can lead to later positive interactions.

De Vos also finds that while teens enjoy performing tales in front of younger audiences, it is also important and fun for them to tell to their peers. While it is often more difficult for people of the same age group to perform in front of their peers, it can be very rewarding. Developing the ability to speak in front of peers will prove beneficial to teenagers when they are called upon to make presentations in the future, whether stories or other types of material.

De Vos discusses the criteria for selection of tales. It is of the utmost importance that the teller choose appropriate tales, be comfortable with the audience, and find stories that can hold teenagers' interest, as well as be a story the teller enjoys. In addition to providing information for getting started and for ways to be most effective with the stories, De Vos provides great ideas for stories to tell. She has found that adolescents have enjoyed and appreciated the following story:

Final Exam

There were two college students of junior standing taking a difficult chemistry course and they both had earned "A's" so far that semester. These two friends were so confident that, the weekend before finals, they decided to visit some friends and have a big party. They had a great time, but after the late night spent partying, they slept all day Sunday and didn't make it back to college until early Monday morning.

They both felt pretty miserable so, rather than taking the final that morning, they decided to skip it and tell their chemistry professor they had missed the final because of a flat tire. The professor agreed they could make up the final the next day.

The young men were excited and relieved. They studied that night for the exam. The professor placed them in separate rooms and gave them a test booklet. They quickly answered the first problem worth 5 points. Cool, they thought! Each one in separate rooms, thinking this was going to be easy. . . then they turned the page.

On the second page was written . . .

For 95 points:

Which tire? _____

Source: Adapted by Emily Chasse from De Vos (2003).

It is a good story with a fun ending that could take someone by surprise. It is perfect for teenagers. De Vos's book will help a teller choose the best stories for a presentation. Anyone ready to begin telling to youth would do well to read her annotated bibliography of tales.

Performing Before Children in Schools

When performing before a large group or an entire school, tellers should use a lapel microphone to allow appropriate physical movement. They should also view the performance space ahead of time and plan accordingly. They should be mindful of students' ages and sophistication in order to select appropriate tales.

Tellers can also volunteer to assist teachers with appropriate curriculum-specific activities. As mentioned earlier, children from other countries or whose parents are immigrants enjoy hearing stories told from their countries of origin. It can provide these children with a sense of pride to hear and watch others listen to and enjoy a story from their mother country. Tellers could offer to work with teachers in the following areas: language arts, history, social studies, geography, art, drama, math, and science.

Language Arts

Reading stories and writing about tales can be a fun and engaging activity within the language arts curriculum at any age. After telling tales with fantastic creatures and characters, writing exercises could focus on magic characters—for example, genies ("Joshua and the Genie"), witches ("The Black Geese of Baba Yaga"), princesses ("Cinderella"), or mystical objects (lanterns and lamps, such as in "Aladdin"), stones ("Stone Soup"), and mirrors ("Sleeping Beauty").

History, Social Studies, and Geography

After telling local, national, or worldwide legends (e.g., about the Loch Ness Monster, Paul Bunyan, or the ghosts of California's Mojave Desert), there could be activities focusing on the geography and topography of the area, historical timelines of the area, biographical information on local characters, etc.

Art

Art activities with stories are abundant and include the following:

- Discussing magical characters found in tales (genies, jenns, pixies, elves, giants, etc.)
- Imagining what the character would look like and produce paintings, drawings, or computer graphics of the characters
- Discussing the colors they would associate with different stories or with various characters, settings, or actions
- Creating folktale objects from clay and collages or computer-generated displays of characters or magic objects from the stories

Drama

Librarians or storytellers could tell a tale that would be appropriate as a play. After hearing a tale such as "The Three Billy Goats Gruff," students could be asked to retell the story and create scripts, select student actors, and design settings for a performance in the classroom or for the school.

Mathematics

Younger students could be told nursery rhyme tales that involve numbers or counting—for example, "One-two, buckle my shoe," "One for the money," or "Ten Little Monkeys bouncing on the bed." Older students could be told the tale of "The White-Hair Waterfall." One part of this Chinese story tells about a journey that must be made by villagers to obtain water. The journey entails traveling seven li. A li is equal to approximately one-third of a mile; thus, seven li would equal approximately two and a half miles. Students could be given an exercise requiring them to measure things in the classroom, school building, or town to determine the length in terms of the number of li (Jagendorf and Weng, 1980: 101).

"The Leatherman," a Connecticut legend from the 1800s, tells of a man who walked through New York and Connecticut for years in all seasons. Students could be asked to determine how many miles the Leatherman walked each week, each month, each year, or during his lifetime. One version of "The Leatherman" is told in

Chapter 6. The legend can also be located in *Legendary Connecticut: Tales of the Nutmeg State,* by David Philips (1984: 100), and in articles in the *Hartford (CT) Courant* newspaper (e.g., Grant, 1993: A1).

Science

Greek mythology can be incorporated into an astronomy curriculum for any age level. There are so many myths to choose from (see Chapter 4). Activities could involve stargazing and writing original stories about how a certain star or constellation came to be. A fascinating and very helpful book, *Star Myths of the Greeks and Romans* (1997), provides a thorough list of the constellations, their stories, an appendix with star maps, and pictures of the constellations.

Jim Cronin, a middle school teacher in Aurora, Colorado, wrote an article in *Science Scope,* "Teaching Astronomy with Multicultural Mythology." Mr. Cronin wanted to emphasize multicultural education so he decided to incorporate stories about the night sky from other cultures into his astronomy unit. Mr. Cronin started reading a few classical myths each week to his students and he found they listened quietly and attentively. StarLab, an inflatable planetarium, was available in Mr. Cronin's school district and his students were able to view the constellations as he read the accompanying stories. After the students had heard a number of stories, he challenged them to invent a constellation and create their own myth to accompany it. Of these, the following tale, "The Sky Lizard," seems especially creative.

The Sky Lizard

Long ago in a far away land, Lizard lived in a village with his two best friends. Lizard was happy that he had these friends because he was selfish and not very friendly. His favorite thing to do was to get attention. The village in which the animals lived was full of people and almost all of them loved animals. Every animal was loved and got lots of attention, all except lizard that is. The village people thought he was slimy and disgusting. The more the fuzzy, cuddly animals came, the less and less attention Lizard got. Even when Lizard was hated, he still got attention one way or another. Lizard got a marvelous idea: he would get (steal) the great diamonds from the High Emperor! If he dressed in these fine jewels he would certainly get lots of attention!

Lizard spent many, many hours planning and plotting his whole scheme. Because Lizard was not the brightest of all animals, he naturally did not think of the Great Emperor's magic wizard. As soon as the emperor noticed that his jewels were gone, he called on his great wizard. "Wizard," he said, "find me the thief that stole my diamonds!" So it was done, and the next command was, "Wizard, send Lizard to the sky where he will never steal again."

This was done immediately and Lizard never stole again. Even now we can still see Lizard in the night sky, still dressed in his fine diamonds.

—*Brett Anderson*

Source: Cronin, Jim. 1996. "Teaching Astronomy with Multicultural Mythology." *Science Scope* (Nov/Dec): 15–17. Reprinted by permission.

Because the names of numerous Greek and Roman gods and goddesses have been used in product trade names, students could be asked to take a field trip to a grocery or clothing store or read newspaper advertisements to find names of various gods and goddesses—and mortals. They will quickly recognize such brands as Nike (Goddess of Victory) shoes, Poseidon (God of the Sea) swim tattoos, Venus (Goddess of Beauty) hair products, and so forth. Adrian Room, author of *Dictionary of Trade Name Origins* (1982), lists many brand names whose provenance is classical mythology—for example, Ajax, Atlas, Hercules, Jupiter, Mars, Mercury, and Vulcan (p. 5).

Children Telling Tales

After children hear many tales told by teachers, librarians, and other tellers, they will start to understand the world of storytelling. At that point, it is not very difficult to energize them to begin telling tales to others.

Children who tell tales make incredible gains in many discipline areas, especially in language arts, listening, vocabulary, speaking, and organizing. They also develop confidence, poise, and self-esteem, as well as the ability to think on their feet. In addition to benefiting from all of these pluses, they also have an amazing amount of fun! Some children and young people are natural storytellers; others pick up the skill very easily with minimal guidance.

One exercise could involve a storyteller performing a simple folk or fairy tale. After the storyteller completes the tale, the young people could form small groups, and, within those small groups, the young people could try retelling parts of the tale. Augusta Baker and Ellin Greene, in *Storytelling: Art & Technique*, have a section on "Children and Young Adults as Storytellers." They describe programs the adults can use to introduce young people to storytelling. They cover the importance of gestures, movement, voice levels, and sounds to the story (Baker and Greene, 1987: 31).

One simple but effective technique, known as story circles or circle telling, is an effective way to help get children started. Heather Forest, storyteller and author, outlines this method in her books and on her Web site (www.storyarts.org/lessonplans/lessonideas/index.html): "One person begins a tale and stops after a few sentences. The next person picks up the story thread and continues it, then stops. Next person adds to it and so on until the tale comes to a resolution. The story could begin with a pre-selected title or subject to guide the improvisation. Try recording the story circle on a tape recorder for later listening." Forest's Web site and books discuss storytelling activities to use in language arts lesson plans that contribute to children's speaking, listening, reading, and writing skills.

There are aids and games anyone can make or purchase to help children as they explore telling tales. Young people will enjoy reading, listening to, and watching a wide variety of tales. The 398 section of the Dewey Decimal collection in the school or public library will contain books, videos, cassette tapes, and DVDs of wonderful tales and collections of stories. The students can read until they find a tale they really love and want to share with others.

Initially, they should read the story for sheer pleasure and re-read it until they feel like they have a sense of the story, characters, setting, mood, and action. They shouldn't try to memorize the story, but, as they retell it to themselves, they will gain a sense of how they will perform it using different voice levels, volumes, and emphasis. They will start to plan their actions, gestures, and kinesthetic movements and paralinguistic effects. Teachers and/or librarians should help students discover the best stories for them, and they should practice telling them with gestures and movements and varying voice levels and emphasis, to themselves, again and again. The students should write the key points or an outline onto small index cards that can be reviewed before any performance.

Teachers, tellers, and/or librarians can help students choose a friend or family member for their first performance. Encourage listeners to make positive comments only, in the beginning. As students work with their story, the teacher or another teller can give them more direction for changes to the story.

When the librarian/teacher/teller feels that the student is ready for a larger audience, he or she can help facilitate other performances. The student may be ready for a public performance to the class or a larger group. Many of the books listed earlier in this chapter include sections that describe how to help children learn to tell stories.

Storytelling groups can be an especially good way to introduce young people to the art of storytelling. The children and adolescents can experience storytelling with others who are learning at the same time, being able to share their apprehensions and nervousness, when necessary. They will often bond together as they hear, see, and experience the positive outcomes of everyone's new knowledge of storytelling.

There are also an incredible number of other excellent articles and books describing ways to include storytelling in the classroom. Some of these are listed in the "Suggested Resources" section at the end of this chapter.

Helping Children with Tales

Tellers may have a positive influence on children's lives and experiences. The stories contain messages of inner strength, courage, and wisdom that can transfer to children's understanding of life, values, beliefs, and challenges. Folk and fairy tales can offer children positive messages and have been told for centuries among individuals and groups of people. These tales pass on their messages subtly and without a sense of moralizing or preaching.

Bruno Bettleheim believes folk and fairy tales can help children understand themselves and their feelings. In his book *The Uses of Enchantment: The Meaning and Importance of Fairy Tales* (1977), he discusses the importance of helping children find meaning in life, which he feels can be terribly hard and takes a lot of growth to be able to achieve. Bettleheim believes children need to learn to understand themselves in order to better understand others. His book explains the ways he believes folk and fairy tales can do this for younger children. He feels that fairy tales allow children to experience fear and danger through the actions of the intrepid heroes in the fairy tales. By enjoying a safe edge of fear when the heroes undertake scary actions, children realize they can come through the storytelling experience safely.

Alison Davies, a professional storyteller, writer, and poet from Nottingham, England, feels storytelling is of the utmost importance to children's development in the classroom both educationally and socially, and she describes many of the reasons in her book *Storytelling in the Classroom: Enhancing Traditional Oral Skills for Teachers and Pupils* (2007). One reason is that "Storytelling stretches the imagination. It encourages children to escape into a fantasy world, and supports their daydreams, which has positive benefits on mental health and clarity leaving them better able to cope with day-to-day situations (fairy tales are ideally suited for this purpose)" (Davies, 2007: 6).

Librarians, teachers, and tellers can offer tales to children and hope they gain insight from the stories, but unless an adult has professional training in clinical therapy, it would be unprofessional and inappropriate to attempt to indoctrinate or influence a child using stories. Adults might be tempted to try and use stories to change a child or young person's behavior, but no one can predict how a child might be affected by a tale. However, an adult who works closely with young people should be prepared to suggest a favorite tale if asked by a child or another adult or parent.

Telling Tales to Children with Special Needs

Sharing tales with special needs children does not have to be terribly different from telling stories to children without such needs. However, a teller should take special care to connect with these children and let the teller's warmth and sensitivity to their special needs guide the time spent with them. There are some basic guidelines, outlined below, that a teller should remember to use when planning these types of programs. Baker and Greene (1987: 80–85) discuss these ideas in detail and encourage the use of clear facial expressions and body movements.

Blind—Tellers need to remember the importance of words and the sound of the teller's voice. Visually impaired children will also make vivid mental images in their minds.

Emotionally disturbed—Emotionally disturbed children may have short attention spans and could be hyperactive. Select shorter tales with vivid, colorful words. If possible, involve the children in the telling of the story.

Hearing impaired—The tellers' faces should be in the light, not hidden by shadows. They should use clear facial expressions and active body movements and gestures. They should speak slowly. If they know sign language, that would be best.

Learning disabled—The thought processes of learning disabled children may not work as well as they do in other children, and these children may have short attention spans and be easily distracted. They do best with short tales that include vibrant actions and words.

Mentally challenged—Tellers should choose tales based on strong, simple plots, with obvious humor and concrete language, without abstract ideas. Cumulative stories with repetition are fun and useful.

Summary

Storytelling with, for, and by children is a fun, interactive, and fulfilling endeavor. Folktales, fairy tales, myths, and legends find an eager audience among young people. Young people love to hear stories, and, as they grow older, they find that telling tales can also be rewarding. They enhance young people's language, listening, vocabulary, speaking, and organizing abilities and help them gain confidence and self-esteem—and have fun.

Many storytelling ideas are available for teachers, librarians, and other adults who want to share tales and help guide young people as they embark on their own storytelling journey. Tales and related activities are useful in many disciplinary areas, including language arts, history, social studies, geography, art, drama—and even science and math.

Chapter 12 discusses tandem tales, drama, and puppetry.

Suggested Resources

De Vos, Gail. 2003. *Storytelling for Young Adults: A Guide to Tales for Teens.* Westport, CT: Libraries Unlimited. ISBNs: 1563089033; 9781563089039
De Vos feels teens can tell stories to younger children but encourages them to tell to peers. It can be fun for them and beneficial to their self-esteem. De Vos gives guidance for adults helping teens select stories and advice about working with adolescents through storytelling.

Dey, Denny and Gary Grimm. 1979. *Storytelling . . . To Develop Creative Thinking and Listening Skills.* Carthage, IL: Good Apple. ISBNs: 0916456463; 9780916456467
Dey and Grimm provide a wonderful explanation of how, when, and why to offer tales to students. The benefits of storytelling they discuss include enjoyment, improving listening skills, increasing communication skills, sparking children's imaginations, and nurturing the connections between teachers and students. Dey and Grimm provide original stories and suggest how other tellers might alter and adapt them. They also suggest activities to use with the tales.

Dubrovin, Vivian. 1997. *Storytelling Adventures: Stories Kids Can Tell.* Masonville, CO: Storycraft. ISBNs: 0963833928; 9780963833921
This book is fun for children who are just getting started telling stories. The tales are simple (but not too simple), and the author gives ideas for possible props and activities to accompany the stories.

Dubrovin, Vivian and Bobbi Shupe, eds. 1994. *Storytelling for the Fun of It: A Handbook for Children.* Masonville, CO: Storycraft. ISBNs: 0963833936; 9780963833938

Dubrovin and Shupe offer suggestions for helping children create their own stories, as well as how to find, select, adapt, and learn folktales, fairy tales, legends, family stories, and tall tales. They discuss how to learn a tale without memorizing it and how to use voices, body movements, facial expressions, and gestures. They also describe ways to add props or costumes and the possibilities of including crafts, puppets, masks, and music.

Gillard, Marni. 2003. *Storyteller, Storyteacher: Discovering the Power of Storytelling for Teaching and Living.* Portland, ME: Stenhouse. ISBNs: 1571100148; 9781571100146

Gillard's multifaceted book encourages teachers to look at family tales, anecdotes, songs, poems, and other stories for lessons that she feels can have significant impact on ourselves and our children. She also covers ways to find, choose, and tell stories, and for not only sharing the tales, but also learning from the experience. This book will help teachers incorporate stories into their lesson plans, learn how to compose their own tales, and help children find the power that comes from their own storytelling.

Gordh, Bill. 2006. *Stories in Action: Interactive Tales and Learning Activities to Promote Early Literacy.* Westport, CT: Libraries Unlimited. ISBNs: 1591583381; 9781591583387

Gordh suggests ideas for fun activities that will capture the imaginations of children from early childhood through early elementary grades. The material engages children through participation in early literacy activities with stories, games, puppetry, finger plays, and more.

Grugeon, Elizabeth and Paul Gardner. 2000. *The Art of Storytelling for Teachers and Pupils: Using Stories to Develop Literacy in Primary Classrooms.* London: David Fulton. ISBNs: 1853466174; 9781853466175

In this practical handbook, Grugeon and Gardner encourage teachers to use storytelling in their classrooms, discover how telling stories can improve literacy levels in children, and incorporate it in their teaching. They also encourage helping children develop their own storytelling abilities.

Haven, Kendall. 2000. *Super Simple Storytelling: A Can-Do Guide for Every Classroom, Every Day.* Englewood, CO: Teacher Ideas Press. ISBNs: 1563086816; 9781563086816

Haven provides storytelling exercises and a step-by-step introduction to learning to tell tales.

Kraus, Anne Marie. 1998. *Folktale Themes and Activities for Children, vol. 1: Pourquoi Tales.* Englewood, CO: Teacher Ideas Press. ISBNs: 1563085216; 9781563085215

————. 1999. *Folktale Themes and Activities for Children*, vol. 2: *Trickster and Transformation Tales.* Englewood, CO: Teacher Ideas Press. ISBNs: 1563086085; 9781563086083

Kraus's two volumes of resource guides are full of folktale ideas and activities for elementary school teachers. She provides background on the tales, explains activities and teaching plans for the stories, and includes related information and bibliographies. She discusses how to choose and present tales that are full of wisdom and humor for all involved.

Lehrman, Betty. *Telling Stories to Children: A National Storytelling Guide.* Jonesborough, TN: National Storytelling Press. ISBNs: 1879991349; 9781879991347

This guide gives basic information on finding tales and learning to tell them. It looks at different types of tales; various techniques for telling and adding movement and sound to the tales; elements of planning successful storytelling programs; and many additional elements of storytelling fun. It is a small but compact volume, and it's available from the National Storytelling Network for a very reasonable price.

MacDonald, Margaret Read. 2005. *Twenty Tellable Tales: Audience Participation Folktales for the Beginning Storyteller.* Chicago: American Library Association. ISBNs: 0838908934; 9780838908938

A list of storytelling books wouldn't be complete without this resource by Master Storyteller Margaret Read MacDonald. Here she shares twenty tales from all over the world that are easy for beginners to learn. She offers advice on learning, rehearsing, and presenting the tales as each teller builds a collection of his or her own stories.

Mooney, William. 1996. *The Storyteller's Guide: Storytellers Share Advice for the Classroom, Boardroom, Showroom, Podium, Pulpit and Center Stage.* Little Rock, AR: August House. ISBNs: 0874834821; 9780874834826

Mooney believes that it is through stories that we learn and that we all tell stories. This book covers how to find the right tales, shape and customize them, create original stories, practice performance techniques, and many other aspects of storytelling performance.

Santa Clara County, California Department of Education. 2001. *Where Do I Start? A School Library Handbook.* Worthington, OH: Linworth. ISBNs: 1586830430; 9781586830434

This is a wonderful book of general library information providing an overview of storytelling in the "Library Services" chapter. After a terrific introduction to the field of storytelling, the book summarizes information on locating stories, selecting tales, and basic steps to begin storytelling performances.

Schimmel, Nancy. 1992. *Just Enough to Make a Story: A Sourcebook for Storytelling.* Berkeley, CA: Sisters' Choice Books and Recordings. ISBNs: 093216403X ; 9780932164032

Schimmel, a professional storyteller, offers wonderful advice to teachers, librarians, community leaders, and anyone else who wants to tell stories to children or adults. She offers help with choosing, learning, and telling stories, as well as advice on choosing the appropriate medium to use when telling tales.

Sierra, Judy. 1996. *The Storytellers' Research Guide.* Eugene, OR: Folkprint. ISBNs: 0963608940; 9780963608949

Sierra's guide is extremely useful for beginning or advanced tellers. She includes research basics, gives ideas on ways to select stories, and explains copyright in a clear manner.

Sima, Judy and Kevin Condi. 2003. *Raising Voices: Creating Youth Storytelling Groups and Troupes.* Westport, CT: Libraries Unlimited. ISBNs: 156308919X ; 9781563089190

Sima and Condi have written a fun and useful work to consult when considering creating storytelling groups for children and adolescents. They describe their own experiences with storytelling groups and report on the benefits that storytelling provides in terms of literacy; conflict resolution; artistic and cultural development; personal and spiritual development; and creative imagination. They offer numerous activities to help plan the start-up, including setting goals and objectives, recruiting members, possible meeting spaces, and more. Their suggestions will help the group establish rules, work toward a positive environment, plan the meeting structure and agendas, and more. These groups provide a fun and exciting way for children and adolescents to experience the positive aspects of storytelling with and for their peers and others.

Smith, Cindy and Judy Kay Thurston. 2007. **"Cross-Generational Storytelling."** *School Arts* 107, no. 2 (October): 40–41.

A program could be held with teachers, librarians, storytellers, and senior citizens to create books of shared stories from childhood adventures. This type of activity was carried out and is described in this article. Third and fourth grade students shared memorable times, telling stories of a favorite birthday or of their worst day ever. The Central Michigan University pre-service art teachers served as scribes and illustrators.

Star Myths of the Greeks and Romans: A Sourcebook Containing the Constellations of Pseudo-Eratosthenes and the Poetic Astronomy of Hyginus. **1997.** Grand Rapids, MI: Phanes Press. ISBNs: 1890482927 (hardcover);

9781890482923 (hardcover)   1890482935 (softcover)   9781890482930 (softcover)
This comprehensive resource for classical constellations gives detailed commentaries on the constellation myths, with woodcut illustrations. It includes the corresponding Greek and Latin names.

Bibliography

Baker, Augusta and Ellin Greene. 1987. *Storytelling: Art & Technique.* New York: Bowker.

Bettleheim, Bruno. 1977. *The Uses of Enchantment: The Meaning and Importance of Fairy Tales.* New York: Vintage Books.

Bruchac, Joseph and Thersa Flavin. 2000. *Pushing Up the Sky: Seven Native American Plays for Children.* New York: Dial Books for Young Readers.

Davies, Alison. 2007. *Storytelling in the Classroom: Enhancing Traditional Oral Skills for Teachers and Pupils.* London: Paul Chapman.

De Vos, Gail. 2003. *Storytelling for Young Adults: A Guide to Tales for Teens.* Westport, CT: Libraries Unlimited.

Grant, Steve. "On the Road, Retracing the Leatherman's Path." *Hartford (CT) Courant,* June 20, 1993, p. A1.

Harrison, J. 1988. *Making Life Books with Foster and Adoptive Children and Adolescent Therapy* (pp. 377–399). Oxford, England: John Wiley & Sons.

Jagendorf, M.A. and Virginia Weng. 1980. *The Magic Boat and Other Chinese Folk Stories.* New York: Vanguard Press.

Kuo, Louise and Yuan-Hsi Kuo. 1976. *Chinese Folk Tales.* Milbrae, CA: Celestial Arts.

Lehrman, Betty, ed. 2005. *Telling Stories to Children: A National Storytelling Guide.* Jonesborough, TN: National Storytelling Press.

Myers, John and Robert Hilliard. 2001. *Storytelling for Middle Grade Students.* Bloomington, IN: Phi Delta Kappa Educational Foundation.

"Once Upon a Time: The Storytelling Card Game." Available: www.atlas-games.com/onceuponatime/index.php (accessed May 3, 2009).

Polette, Nancy. 2000. *Gifted Books, Gifted Readers: Literature Activities to Excite Young Minds.* Englewood, CO: Libraries Unlimited.

———. 2006. *Books Every Child Should Know: The Literature Quiz Book.* Westport, CT: Libraries Unlimited.

Philips, David E. 1984. *Legendary Connecticut: Traditional Tales from the Nutmeg State.* Hartford, CT: Spoonwood Press.

Power, Effie. 1969. *Bag O'Tales: 63 Famous Stories for Storytellers.* New York: Dover Publications.

Room, Adrian. 1982. *Dictionary of Trade Name Origins*. Boston: Routledge & Kegan Paul.

Santa Clara County, California Department of Education. 2001. *Where Do I Start? A School Library Handbook*. Worthington, OH: Linworth.

Schiro, Michael Stephen. 2004. *Oral Storytelling & Teaching Mathematics: Pedagogical and Multicultural Perspectives*. Thousand Oaks, CA: Sage.

Sima, Judy and Kevin Condi. 2003. *Raising Voices: Creating Youth Storytelling Groups and Troupes*. Westport, CT: Libraries Unlimited.

Star Myths of the Greeks and Romans: A Sourcebook Containing the Constellation of Pseudo-Eratosthenes and the Poetic Astronomy of Hyginus. 1997. Grand Rapids, MI: Phanes Press.

Yolen, Jane. 2008. "Use Your 'Creative Memory.'" *Writer* 121, no. 1: 22–23.

Zipes, Jack David. 1995. *Creative Storytelling: Building Community, Changing Lives*. New York: Routledge.

Chapter 12

✳ More Fun! Tandem Telling, Plays, and Puppetry ✳

This chapter covers other forms of storytelling for tellers who would like to broaden their technique and repertoire. It will also examine and consider drama with folk or fairy tale presentations and activities. Tellers may discover new formats for telling and new ways to incorporate theatre or acting with young people through folk or fairy tales.

Tandem Tales

Two storytellers can perform a story in tandem, each agreeing to learn one or more parts of the tale. They need to split the parts, including (1) the introduction, (2) the beginning of the story, (3) each character, (4) any supplemental description or information given in the tale, and (5) the ending. One of the tellers needs to take the lead in opening the tale and throughout the performance.

Tandem telling of tales is a wonderful skill to have in storytelling. It can be a fun and exciting activity for adults, young adults, and children. Performances of this type of tale will be enjoyed simply for the entertainment they give. Tandem telling can be performed by adults or young people. Although the discussion in this chapter involves tandem tales told by two people, tellers could attempt a tale with more than two characters, if it felt appropriate. Again, designing the separation of parts and lines would be of the utmost importance, and allowing time for sufficient practice would be the key to a smooth production.

Advice for Tandem Telling

Tellers wishing to attempt tandem telling should be aware of some of the special requirements involved. Ellie Toy (2008), a Connecticut storyteller, performs tandem tales and offers some advice:

- The two tellers must know the tale very well. Both tellers must understand and remember their parts and be ready to continue the story when their turn comes.
- It can be hard to locate stories that make good tandem presentations. The tale must be divided, but it requires more than just splitting the lines between two or more people. The decision to divide the parts between the tellers can be challenging, but a suitable and appropriate division of parts is vital to the tandem tale's success.
- Tandem tellers must be able to trust and rely on their partner(s).
- Tandem telling takes much more time and may require many more rehearsals than is true for individual tellers.

Other useful notes for tandem telling, according to Toy, include the following:

- Listening skills are vital to recognizing lines for the next teller to join in with his or her section of the tale. This response must be automatic or else the flow of the story will be jeopardized.
- Clear, strong speaking skills are important in any folk or fairy tale performance, but they are especially important and necessary for tandem telling. The second teller can't miss a line because of poor or unclear speech.
- Tellers must be able to organize the story in a tandem structure that is fitting, clear, concise, and easily understood by all involved. There can't be any rambling or bantering during a tandem tale, or the other teller could be easily confused.

People, young or old, attempting to tell a tandem story can increase many language arts, communication, and social skills:

- Listening is vital when performing a tandem tale, as the tellers are expected to recognize the lines leading to their parts of the performance. The response must be automatic so that the natural flow of the story will be maintained.
- Tellers must organize their thoughts and carry out a complex plan to successfully perform a tandem tale.

- Writing skills—Tandem tales require a student teller to write out the plan for the tandem performance, including the script, props, and staging.
- Organizational skills—A tandem tale takes a significant amount of planning, including dividing the story, assigning speaking parts, and announcing background information.
- Self-esteem—When telling stories of any kind, the teller gains confidence, and this leads to increased pride in one's actions and abilities. Tandem telling will provide this self-confidence for the teller as well as instill self-assurance and self-respect.

Two of the tandem tales Ellie Toy and her partner, Sharon Lynch, have used include the following:

- **"Clancy's Coat"**—This story is about a tailor named Tippett who has trouble getting around to returning an old winter coat to Clancy, the farmer. However, he takes advantage of the opportunity to mend a broken friendship.
- **"The Tailor"**—In this well-traveled tale, a tailor is finally able to save enough pennies to buy material to make a wonderful overcoat for himself. Once his coat is ready, he loves it and wears it everywhere. He even wears it to bed, sometimes, because it is so cozy! Finally, it gets all worn out. Or, at least, he thought it was all worn out. But, every time he thinks it is worn out, he discovers a way to remake it into another favorite piece of clothing. In the end, we realize that, over the years, he has made and re-made it into a touching story that will continue to be told forever.

> Toy and Lynch perform their wonderful and unique tandem version of "The Tailor" on the accompanying DVD. This shows the best of tandem telling when you watch how skillfully they manage to combine their talents in the telling of this tale.

Ann Shapiro, from the Connecticut Storytelling Center, stresses the importance of timing and pacing when performing a tandem tale. The tellers need to know their parts very well and to have an understanding of the timing for each part. They need to know how quickly or slowly they should respond to the other teller with their lines and the speed they should use to deliver those lines.

The two tellers will decide on the pace for the entire story and on any movements or gestures they will use with each other or as part of the story. They will decide ahead about their voice levels and will plan any added bursts, cries, or exclamations.

Shapiro stresses the importance of choosing a story each tandem teller can relate to and loves to tell. She believes the tandem tale will work when each teller has enjoyed planning and preparing for a successful presentation.

Shapiro also relates the importance of timing and pacing when two tellers are planning a tandem tale. She stresses the importance of selecting a story with characters that both tellers can relate to. She laughingly says that she believes that she and her husband, Tom Callinan, have enough real-life experience with conflict to select stories with male/female characters suffering from opposing viewpoints or disputes. They can perform these tales together and enjoy the satisfying endings that result in most tales.

Several questions that arise when selecting the story narration include the following:

- Will one or more of the characters narrate?
- Will the story be treated like a play, with little or no narration?

These are questions worth considering, and Ann's experience is worth sharing (Shapiro, 2008).

Each set of tandem tellers will devise their own techniques for the performance. They will choose a tale, split the parts, plan the timing and pace, and determine any extra setting or lighting elements needed for their performance. It takes more time to plan a tandem tale performance, and each tandem member should allow extra time for practicing.

In a technique for tandem telling, one of the tellers begins part of the tale and ends that section by "freezing" (stopping his or her movements) while the other teller provides background material or fills in or expands the information for a part of the tale. This part could be offered conspiratorially or simply as additional material.

It can be difficult to find a good tale for tandem telling and it is helpful to ask among other tellers.

A Christmas tale that works well in a tandem arrangement is "The Christmas Webs." It is available in books as well as on World

Wide Web sites. Unfortunately, these tales often use various names to distinguish their story.

Books and World Wide Web sites of this story, and other Christmas Spider tales, include the following:

- *Christmas Spider (Legend of):* http://ths.gardenweb.com/forums/load/crafts/msg071219304573.html.
- Christmas Spider: Webs http://powersmuseum.com/exhibits/pastexhibits/spiderweb.html.
- Climo, Shirley and Jane Manning. 2001. *Cobweb Christmas: The Tradition of Tinsel.* New York: Harper Collins.
- Holiday Traditions—Christmas Around the World—Ukraine http://www.msichicago/org/scrapbook/scrapbook_exhibits/catw2004/traditions/countries/ukraine.html.
- Holz, Loretta. 1980. *The Christmas Spider: A Puppet Play from Poland, & Other Traditional Games, Crafts and Activities.* New York: Philomel Books.

Following is my tandem version of the tale, and tellers can choose to split the lines as seems appropriate.

Exhibit 12-1. On a Personal Note: "The Christmas Spider Webs" as a Tandem Tale

My daughter and I had fun planning a tandem tale when she was five years old. We performed a folktale for our Christmas pageant at the Hartford Friends Quaker Meetinghouse in West Hartford, Connecticut, for several years. I had told her tales since she was born, and she had been telling stories herself from the age of three for my husband's and my enjoyment.

We chose a Polish folktale, "The Christmas Spider," for our Christmas tandem tale. There are several versions of this story, and we selected one by Loretta Holz (1980). *The Christmas Spider: A Puppet Play from Poland* is a short book outlining the history of Polish Christmas traditions; explaining craft activities for Christmas ornaments; giving directions for making a *szopka*, or portable puppet theatre; and outlining paper-cutting techniques to use to make stick puppets for the "Christmas Spider" puppet play. The "Christmas Spider" story appears in the book, and we based our tandem performance on that version. I chose to split the tale into two parts based on sections I felt my daughter could remember and ones that flowed well from one person telling to another.

The Christmas Spider Webs

NARRATOR—Welcome to the tale of the Christmas Spider Webs. In the living room of a house on Christmas Eve Day, the spiders are watching the Christmas Eve cleanup.

YOUNG SPIDER—"Mama! I'm scared! They are cleaning and sweeping everything away with brooms! They are cleaning the floors, the walls, and the ceiling! Everything! Where can we go?!?!"

MAMA SPIDER—"Calm down, little one. We will hide in the attic and it will be all right. Let's go now."

NARRATOR—Up in the attic, the spiders watch the cleaning through the cracks.

MAMA SPIDER—"I see they are almost finished and we can go back down."

NARRATOR—Back in the living room.

MAMA SPIDER—"It is SO CLEAN, we can't weave any webs. But, look at the tree in the middle of the room. Imagine a tree indoors! They can't blame us if we spin webs on the tree."

NARRATOR—So, the spiders climbed up the tree, spinning webs as they went and covered the tree with their wonderful webs. Santa came down the chimney and looked at the tree covered with webs.

YOUNG SPIDER—"Santa sees the clean room and he is going to clear the tree of all our webs."

MAMA SPIDER—"No, he knows the webs are our home, and I am sure he'll find another answer."

NARRATOR—Santa raised his hands and turned the spider webs into a shiny, glittering decoration. And, since then, many people decorate their tree with tinsel, in honor of the Christmas Spider Webs.

Source: Adapted by Emily Chasse, who retains the copyright to this version of "The Christmas Spider Webs."

Tandem Tales in the Classroom

Performances of tandem tales by tellers in the classroom can provide much enjoyable entertainment. Tandem tales told in the classroom can also be expanded to cover a number of language arts activities for young people, which are discussed in the following sections.

Listening Skills

Listening is a basic communication skill that takes practice. It involves hearing another person, understanding what they are saying, and deciding what to do with this information. Performing a tandem tale requires both tellers to listen carefully so they recognize the time to begin their part.

Exercise: Children could respond to the multipart story by explaining the different voices:

- Was one voice louder, higher, stronger, etc.?
- Did they have different roles? Explain.
- Did the children have any other comments on the voices?

Writing Skills

It takes a lot of focused time and practice to learn the basic writing skills that include spelling, grammar, punctuation, and writing style.

Exercise: If there was conflict in the story, write it from one person's perspective. Examples include the following:

- If the story was "Little Red Riding Hood," explain why the wolf felt he had a right to eat Little Red Riding Hood.
- Pretend you are one of the pigs in "The Three Little Pigs," and explain why you don't want to move out of your mother's house.
- In the story "The Black Geese of Baba Yaga," explain why Baba Yaga was so angry when Elena took her little brother away from Baba Yaga's hut.

Speaking Skills

Speaking skills can involve speaking one on one to a small group or to a large one. Speaking skills are important when informing, persuading, or teaching someone, as well as to solve problems. The focus can be on basic competencies used every day when asking for information, giving directions, or seeking help in an emergency situation.

Exercise: A student could interview one of the tandem tellers about a character in the tandem tale and ask questions about the story. Remember, interview questions need to encourage answers that are longer than a few words. Examples of questions to Elena might be: "Why did you leave your brother all alone?" and "What was your plan, and did it work?"

Media Versions

Tapes, videos, and DVDs of tandem tales are available from bookstores, storytelling groups, individuals, Web sites, etc. They are not easy to locate, and they may contain many stories, only one or a few of which are being told in tandem. Information regarding several can be found in the "Suggested Resources" at the end of this chapter.

Plays and Puppetry

This section looks at plays and puppetry but will focus specifically on plays and puppetry of folk and fairy tales. There is a tremendous difference between telling tales and presenting tales through drama, theatre, or performance through plays.

Drama and plays can be a wonderful addition to a classroom or other forum with young people as the audience. Drama activities can feel very different from activities that are part of the traditional curriculum, and it may be one of the reasons children are attracted by it and want to participate. Drama experiences range from informal classroom drama to more formal productions.

Children's theatre involves formal productions with scripts, costumes, scenery, makeup, and so forth. It is important for children in many ways, including the following:

- Children can experience the thrill of watching a story come alive.
- They are provided with an opportunity for a strong vicarious experience as they identify with characters.
- They can learn to appreciate the art of theatre (McCaslin, 1987: 7).

Informal Plays, Classroom Drama, and Spontaneous Drama

Often teachers who have tried using drama and acting in their classrooms find them such positive experiences they want to continue to expand these opportunities for their students. It can be intimidating for teachers to try drama and acting if they have never tried them before, but, fortunately there are many resources to help teachers with their first attempts in the classroom. Some of these are included in the "Suggested Resources" section at the end of this chapter.

Drama Techniques

Jo Anne Kraus (2006) uses a technique whereby she shares folk and fairy tales with young people and lets them engage in a storytelling performance of the tale. She uses simple, entertaining tales, including "The Gunniwulf," "The Three Little Pigs," "Little Red Riding Hood," and "Hansel and Gretel." The children enjoyed the stories and gained a feeling of competence as they "played the play."

Another folktale drama technique for the classroom could involve a teller relating a folktale to the group; the teller would then begin to retell it, with the idea that the teller would stop partway through the story and let one or more of the children finish a section of the tale or the complete story by acting it out.

Classroom drama can involve a folk or fairy tale performance. John Stewig (1983: 6) describes four basic components of classroom drama:

- The material or the idea used to motivate the drama. [Note: For the purposes of this guidebook, the material would involve a folk or fairy tale.]
- Spontaneous discussions during and after the presentation.
- Playing of an idea with pantomime, rhythmic movement exercises, verbal fluency exercises, or the complete acting out of an entire play.
- Children considering what was done and discussing their satisfaction with the production.

Simple drama activities can be designed in which children can perform without special costumes, scenery, or makeup. Scripts based on traditional folk and fairy tales can be written with easily remembered lines. Children could volunteer to act as certain characters, remembering a few simple lines. Practice could take place in the classroom, and, if students and teachers feel it is fun and want to share it with a neighboring classroom, they might volunteer to perform the tale for them the next day.

Activity

A classroom could listen to "The Three Little Pigs" and plan a short, amateur play with four characters as follows:

Characters
    Oldest pig
    Middle pig
    Youngest pig
    Mother pig
    Wolf
Props
    Pile of straw
    Pile of sticks
    Pile of bricks
Story: "The Three Little Pigs"

The Three Little Pigs

Mother pig tells her three children that they are getting old enough to build and live in their own houses. She tells them "good-bye" and lets them out the door with their bags of clothing, a blanket, and pillows.

The first little pig sees a man selling straw, and he thinks how easy it would be to pile up straw to make a house. He asks the man for some straw, and he gives the first pig a pile of straw. The first pig arranges the pile into rooms to make a house. When he finishes his house, he looks at it and smiles. This will do fine, he thinks.

The second little pig sees his brother, the first pig, and his straw house. He decides he wants a better house and sees a man selling sticks. He asks the man for a truckload of sticks, and the second pig builds a house from the sticks. When it is finished he enters his new house and smiles. It feels very comfortable.

The third little pig sees the two houses his brothers have built, but wants an even better house. He sees a man selling bricks and buys enough to build a fine brick house. When it is finished, he looks at it and smiles. It feels very warm and secure.

The Big, Bad Wolf has been watching all three pigs and licking his lips. How he would love to eat any or all of them. He walks to the house of the first little pig.

"Little Pig, Little Pig, let me come in."

"Not by the hair on my chinny, chin, chin."

"Then I'll huff and I'll puff and I'll blow your house in!!!"

He looked at that straw and he took a deep breath "Wh-wh-wh-oof" and then he BLEW, "pooooof, ooooof, oooooof." And the straw scattered all around the first pig.

The first little pig ran to the house of his brother, the second little pig and asked if he could come in. "Of course," said his brother.

Then the wolf came and called out,
"Little Pig, Little Pig, let me come in."
"Not by the hair on my chinny, chin, chin."
"Then I'll huff and I'll puff and I'll blow your house in!!!"
He looked at those sticks and he took a deep breath "Wh-wh-wh-oof" and then he BLEW, "pooooof, ooooof, oooooof." Those sticks blew right down. And the first and second little pigs ran to see their brother, the third little pig and his house made of bricks. "Can we come in?" "Of, course!" And the two little pigs joined the third little pig.

The wolf came to the house of the third little pig, made of bricks, and said, "Little Pig, Little Pig, let me come in."
"Not by the hair on my chinny, chin, chin."
"Then I'll huff and I'll puff and I'll blow your house in!!!"
He looked at those bricks and he took a deep breath "Wh-wh-wh-oof" and then he BLEW, "pooooof, ooooof, oooooof." But nothing happened.

Then, the wolf saw a chimney on the roof and climbed up on top the roof. He decided to go down the chimney and eat all three pigs. But the three little pigs heard him climbing up on the roof and they made a quick fire in the fireplace. The wolf threw himself down the chimney and landed in the red, hot fire. "Ow, Ow, Ow . . . that's HOT," and he took off running out of the house of bricks belonging to the third little pig as fast as he could go with his shorts still burning. And the three little pigs laughed at the wolf and knew they would never see him again.

Puppetry

Puppetry originates from ancient cultures and has varied widely in countries and cultures around the globe. There are several types, each of which has its own distinct elements.

Types of Puppets

Marionettes or String Puppets

Operating a stringed marionette is a highly skilled operation. "A simple marionette may have nine strings—one to each leg, one to each hand, one to each shoulder, one to each ear (for head movements), and one to the base of the spine (for bowing); but special effects will require special strings that may double or treble this number" (Britannica Online, 2009). The manipulator plucks the individual strings when a decided movement is required.

The Sicilian culture used puppets of this type, and many were in the form of complete bodies operated by a single puppeteer. The operators of marionettes or oversized marionettes often imitated live theatre in eighteenth-century Europe.

Hand or Glove Puppets

England was known for its hand puppets (e.g., Punch and Judy). These puppets are usually simple in their construction, with the head made of carved wood or papier-mache. The facial features are often exaggerated so their expressions can be seen from a distance. The body is made from a tube of cloth or cardboard so the operator's arm is hidden. Usually only the puppet's upper body is visible, although the puppet may have legs that the puppeteer can use to kick, when needed, or stretch out, if the puppeteer wants the puppet to appear to be sitting. Operators of puppets control the puppet's head and hands with their fingers.

Hand-and-Rod Puppets

Hand-and-rod puppets need to be operated by two or three puppeteers. The rod is attached to the body of the puppet and operated by one puppeteer, while the other operators can move the head, limbs, and/or tail (of an animal) of these three-dimensional puppets.

Japanese hand-and-rod puppets were called *bunraku* and stood three to five feet high and resembled human figures. They were considered serious entertainment for adults, not children.

Shadow Puppets

Shadow puppets are similar to rod puppets except that shadow puppets are two-dimensional. They are jointed puppet characters operated by rods held behind a cloth with a bright light projected behind the puppet. The puppet character appears as a silhouette.

Audiences

In the past, puppetry was adult oriented in many countries. Now, it is used in classrooms, therapy settings, and libraries for educational, therapeutic, and communication formats, with the focus being on children.

Tellers using puppets to tell folktales and fairy tales need to focus on developing their puppetry technique and finding a way to use the puppet to improve the way they tell their tale. Storytellers should minimize the time they spend on constructing their puppet so they can spend time developing their technique. They should learn how to use the puppet effectively to improve the way they tell a story.

Puppets can be used to teach a variety of concepts, but the main purpose of storytelling is not to teach but to entertain. Using puppets to tell stories can be a wonderful option, and storytellers can decide the best way for them to present a tale. Tellers should keep in mind that the important part of the presentation is the story. The puppets can add to a story, but they should not be the primary focus.

The puppet adds visualization, and this can be fun, especially for children who like to *see* characters. A teller knows the importance of children "seeing" the characters in their own minds. The following are ways a puppet can make a story come to life (Champlin, 1998: 5):

- The puppet can add an element of surprise through its voice or its facial expressions.
- The puppet can exaggerate movement by jumping higher or bowing more deeply.

- The puppet serves as a shield for the adult and allows the child to believe the puppet is speaking directly to him or her.
- The puppet show serves as a multimedia experience for children, because the children can use their tactile, visual, and auditory senses.
- The puppet can allow direct interaction between the storyteller and the child. The child can give the puppet a hug or a kiss or can "pin the tail" on a puppet donkey.
- The puppet can teach a variety of concepts, such as speech sounds, numbers, etc.

A teller can decide when it is appropriate to use a puppet to tell a story. Factors might include the following (Champlin, 1998):

- The tale should have a strong action line.
- Cumulative stories often work best.
- Stories with strong lead characters usually make the best tales for puppet presentations.
- A teller doesn't need to include all the characters. Some lines can simply be said without the character present.
- Teller should plan the most appropriate type of puppet.

Once a teller has decided to use a puppet to tell a tale, he or she needs to spend time planning the story performance. Preparation of the puppets should be kept to a minimum. An example of a simple puppet activity could involve the story "The Gunniwulf." This tale is widely available in books and on the World Wide Web, but it is an old tale that comes from many groups, including Native Americans, Germans, Indians, and Africans.

Jan VanSchuyver offers a program for children performing "The Gunniwulf" with stick puppets and simple scenery. She gives directions to make the puppets from popsicle sticks, glue, scissors, and white construction paper. She feels the children (ages 6–8) can learn the story and practice telling it. Each child should be given a chance to perform it to another child in the class (VanSchuyver, 1993: 115).

The Gunniwulf

Once upon a time a long, long time ago in a land far, far away there was a little girl and she lived next to the forest with her mother. Each day, the little girl's mother would say, "You may go out to play but don't go into the woods because there is a GUNNIWULF that lives there and, if he sees you, he may eat you up!"

And every day, that little girl promised she would never go into the woods.

One day the little girl's mother was in town running errands, and the little girl was out playing. The little girl saw some beautiful flowers just a couple of feet into the woods. They had small white blossoms and the little girl wanted some of them, so she tiptoed into the woods a couple of feet and picked a few beautiful white flowers. As she picked the flowers she sang her own little tune, "Kum see, kum saw, kum see, kum saw."

But just then she saw some beautiful red flowers a few more feet into the woods.

She went a few more feet in and picked a few beautiful red flowers. As she picked the flowers, she sang her own little tune, "Kum see, kum saw, kum see, kum saw."

But just then she saw some beautiful pink flowers just a couple more feet into the woods.

She went a few more feet in and picked the beautiful pink flowers. As she picked the flowers, she sang her own little tune, "Kum see, kum saw, kum see, kum saw."

But just then she saw some beautiful blue flowers just a few more feet into the woods.

She went in a few more feet and picked the beautiful blue flowers. As she picked the flowers, she sang her own little tune, "Kum see, kum saw, kum see, kum saw."

But just then, in front of her, she saw, the Gunniwulf! She jumped.

"Little girl! Why you move?"

"I no move!"

"Then sing that good 'n' sweet song again!"

So the little girl sang: "Kum see, kum saw, kum see, kum saw."

And the Gunniwulf fell asleep!

And the little girl ran away, tip, tap, tip, tap.

And, the Gunniwulf woke up and started to chase her!!

Hunka—cha!

Hunka—cha!

Hunka—cha!

"Little girl! Why you move?"

"I no move!"

"Then sing that good 'n' sweet song again!"

So the little girl sang: "Kum see, kum saw, kum see, kum saw."

And the Gunniwulf fell fast asleep!

And the little girl ran away, tip, tap, tip, tap.

And, the Gunniwulf woke up and started to chase her!!

Hunka—cha!

Hunka—cha!

Hunka—cha!

"Little girl! Why you move?"

"I no move!"

"Then sing that good 'n' sweet song again!"

So the little girl sang: "Kum see, kum saw, kum see, kum saw."

And the Gunniwulf fell fast, fast asleep!

And the little girl ran away, tip, tap, tip, tap. And this time she didn't stop and the Gunniwulf didn't wake up and she ran all the way home.

And to this day, that little girl has never gone back into those woods.

And that is that!

Source: Adapted by Emily Chasse from the following sources: Livo (1986), Harper (1967), and Teachers.net (http://teachers.net/lessonplans/posts/123.html).

Summary

Special storytelling techniques and formats offer tellers ways to expand their repertoire and methods. Performances of folktales and fairy tales in tandem or through plays and puppetry can be entertaining and rewarding to tellers and their audiences.

Tandem tales are offered by skilled tellers trained in this technique. Advice to tellers wishing to add this skill involves choosing the right tales, finding a compatible storytelling partner, developing special skills, and much practice.

Plays and puppet shows of folk and fairy tales are wonderful additions to use when performing with young people as well as with adults. Plays and drama can range from informal classroom activities to more formal productions. Various types of puppetry techniques and puppets are available from countries and cultures around the world, and tellers can choose the appropriate type for their performances. Puppets make a story come alive. They add visualization and allow the audience to "see" the characters and are thus very useful when telling to young people.

Chapter 13 discusses a number of issues that are important to storytellers, including copyright, planning events, booktalks, storytelling as a profession, marketing, and a brief history of storytelling.

Suggested Resources

Barchers, Suzanne. 2000. *Multicultural Folktales: Readers Theatre for Elementary Students.* Englewood, CO: Teacher Ideas Press. ISBNs: 156308760X; 978156308760

This series of books for children and young adults provides scripts to help young people learn to "interpret a literary work in such a way that the audience imaginatively senses characterization, settings, and action" (p. xvii). It contains reader's theatre scripts of folktales, fairy tales, and tall tales.

Criscoe, Betty L. and Philip J. Lanasa, III. 1995. *Fairy Tales for Two Readers.* Englewood, CO: Teacher Ideas Press. ISBNs: 1563082934; 9781563082931

This book was prepared to assist children in need of practice with oral reading. The scripts are based on 15 fairy tales adapted for the script in dialogue format for two readers. This fits perfectly since folk and fairy tales are best told orally.

Exner, Carol R. 2005. *Practical Puppetry A–Z: A Guide for Librarians and Teachers.* Jefferson, NC: McFarland & Co. ISBNs: 0786415169 (softcover); 9780786415168 (softcover)

Although Exner mentions nursery rhymes and fairy tales, this is primarily an encyclopedia of information about puppets, puppeteers, building puppets, and working with puppets. Clearly, Exner sees puppets as a way to tell a story, and this is an invaluable reference source for tellers who want to use puppets in their story presentations.

Faurot, Kimberly K. 2003. *Books in Bloom: Creative Patterns and Props That Bring Stories to Life.* Chicago: American Library Association. ISBNs: 0838908527; 9780838908525

This book covers much more than simply plays or puppetry. Faurot explains her belief that tellers should add visual components to a story as a way to enhance the storytelling experience for children. She outlines presentation formats and presents ideas for selecting the type of medium to use. She discusses props, flannel boards, and puppet presentations as ways to dramatize stories and engage audiences. She gives an example of a story or poem that works well with that format. She includes a pattern and instructions for creating it as well as a script for using a flannel or prop story with a group.

Kraus, Jo Anne. 2006. "Playing the Play: What Children Want." *Language Arts* 83, no. 5 (May): 413–421.

Director of "Only Connect" at the Concourse House in the Bronx, New York, Kraus describes her innovative program combining stories and drama in a literary experience for children. She explains a technique of sharing a folktale, fairy tale, or other story with young people in a homeless shelter and letting them decide if they would like to engage in a storytelling performance of the tale. She uses simple, entertaining tales, including "The Gunniwulf," "The Three Little Pigs," "Little Red Riding Hood," "Hansel and Gretel," as well as some books such as Lynn Ward's book *The Biggest Bear* (Houghton Mifflin 1952).

Latrobe, Kathy Howard. 1991. *Social Studies Readers Theatre for Young Adults: Scripts and Script Development.* Englewood, CO: Teacher Ideas Press. ISBNs: 0872878643; 9780872878648

A reader's theatre resource focusing on script development in social studies material and its adaptation into the classroom.

McCaslin, Nellie. 1987. *Creative Drama in the Primary Grades: A Handbook for Teachers.* White Plains, NY: Longman. ISBNs: 0582285992; 9780582285996

McCaslin covers dramatic activities in the classroom and considers them an essential part of school curriculums. Teachers will appreciate her suggestions for creative drama activities, pantomime ideas, choral speaking, puppets, masks, and more. She includes many folktale plays in her activities.

Plays Magazine: The Drama Magazine for Children. Monthly, October through May, beginning with vol. I, September 1941.
This magazine includes plays for young people that are often based on folk and fairy tales.

Polsky, Milton E. and others. 1995. *Drama Activities for K–6 Students: Creating Classroom Spirit.* Lanham, MD: Rowman & Littlefield Education. ISBNs: 1578864445 (hardcover); 9781578864447 (hardcover); 1578864453 (softcover); 9781578864454 (softcover)
Polsky outlines ways to promote dramatic activities with stories and other language arts pieces. These activities, presented within a pleasant, positive, and cooperative atmosphere, can result in children having a deeper understanding of themselves and others. Many of his drama activities involve folktales. This work also suggests warm-up ideas, gives guidance on the development of the story, and provides ways to enrich the tale with other classroom activities.

Saldana, Johnny. 1995. *Drama of Color: Improvisation with Multiethnic Folklore.* Portsmouth, NH: Heinemann. ISBNs: 0435086677; 9780435086671
Saldana uses drama with elementary-aged children as a way to enhance their knowledge of different ethnic groups through folklore, and he summarizes and outlines many activities for using multiethnic folklore with young people. Teachers and children will enjoy following Saldana's plans for dramatizations, activities, and follow-up ideas for grades K–4 and 5–8.

Sloyer, Shirlee. 2003. *From the Page to the Stage: The Educator's Complete Guide to Readers Theatre.* Westport, CT: Teacher Ideas Press/Libraries Unlimited. ISBNs: 1563088975; 9781563088971
Reader's-Theatre Coach Shirlee Sloyer provides teachers and librarians with directions and guidelines for using reader's theatre material in the classroom and library.

Stewig, John W. 1983. *Informal Drama in the Elementary Language Arts Program.* New York: Teachers College Press, Columbia University. ISBNs: 0807726478; 9780807726471
Stewig discusses classroom drama and focuses on many different areas of spontaneous and creative drama.

Storycrafters. 1996. *Apples, Corn & Pumpkin Seeds.* South Norwalk, CT: Galler West Productions. DVD.
Storycrafters have recorded numerous CDs and a DVD, displaying their storytelling skills.

———. **1996.** *Ladder to the Moon.* South Norwalk, CT: Gallery West Productions. Compact Disc.

Storytelling for all ages, including the tales "Sambalele"(Brazilian), "Sea Girl"(Chinese), and "Polar Bear & Hunting Dog"(Inuit).

———. **1997.** *Straw into Gold.* South Norwalk, CT: Gallery West Productions. Compact Disc.

A collection of international tales, chock-full of laughter, music, and thought-provoking themes. Included are "Rumpelstiltskin Rap," "A Gourd of Palm Wine"(Africa), "A Bundle of Sticks," and others.

———. **1998.** *Gather Round the Fire.* South Norwalk, CT: Gallery West Productions. Compact Disc.

This collection of world folktales begs for participation, including "The Naga" (Burma), "Tipingee" (Haiti), and others.

———. **2001.** *Classics with a Twist.* South Norwalk, CT: Gallery West Productions. Compact Disc.

Winner of the Parents Choice Silver Honor, the Storycrafters provide a collection of special stories, including new versions of "The Gingerbread Man," "Three Pigs Trap," and other favorite stories with a new twist.

———. **2004.** *The View from Here: New York State Stories.* South Norwalk, CT: Gallery West Productions. Compact Disc.

The Storycrafters tell some of their favorite tales from the Hudson Valley in New York State, including "Milk Bottles," "Zack the Dog," and "The Princess and the Pea Rap."

VanSchuyver, Jan M. 1993. *Storytelling Made Easy with Puppets.* Phoenix, AZ: Oryx Press. ISBNs: 0897747321; 9780897747325

VanSchuyver provides a basic introduction to puppets and gives instructions to use when children are telling stories with puppets. She offers group activities for helping children make and use puppets and gives ideas of possible problems and solutions for those beginning to use puppets. She also lists helpful puppet resources for teachers. This book is full of valuable information for tellers who want to expand their repertoire of story presentations with puppets.

Zipes, Jack. 2004. *Speaking Out: Storytelling and Creative Drama for Children.* New York: Routledge. ISBNs: 0415966604 (hardcover); 9780415966603 (hardcover); 0415966612 (softcover); 9780415966610 (softcover)

A master storyteller, Zipes speaks about the positive place of storytelling and creative drama for children ages 5–12.

Bibliography

Barchers, Suzanne I. 2000. *Multicultural Folktales: Readers Theatre for Elementary Students.* Englewood, CO: Teacher Ideas Press.

Baylor, Byrd. 1976. *And It Is Still That Way. Legends.* New York: Scribner.

Britannica Online. Available: www.britannica.com (accessed May 3, 2009).

Brown, Fred. 1992. "Seniors: Telling Tales to Life's Upperclassmen." *Storytelling Magazine* (Fall): 18–20.

Champlin, Connie. 1998. *Storytelling with Puppets.* Chicago: American Library Association.

Chasse, Emily. 1991. "Sharing Folktales with Seniors." 15.30 *Activities, Adaptation & Aging,* v. 13, no. 3: 109–113.

Cinderella. 1959. Burbank, CA: Walt Disney Home Video. Video recording 76 min. VHS.

Cinderella. 1987. Faerie Tale Theatre. Livonia, MI: Playhouse Video. Videorecording 53 min. VHS.

Criscoe, Betty L. and Philip J. Lanasa, III. 1995. *Fairy Tales for Two Readers.* Englewood Cliffs, CO: Teacher Ideas Press.

Exner, Carol R. 2005. *Practical Puppetry A–Z: A Guide for Librarians and Teachers.* Jefferson, NC: McFarland & Co.

Faurot, Kimberly K. 2003. *Books in Bloom.* Chicago: American Library Association.

Harper, Wilhelmina. 1967. *The Gunniwolf.* New York: Dutton.

Holz, Loretta. 1980. *The Christmas Spider: A Puppet Play from Poland & Other Traditional Games, Crafts and Activities.* New York: Philomel Books.

Johnson, Malcolm. "Fairy Tale as Film." *Hartford Courant,* December 29, 2000.

Johnson, Pam and Flora Joy. 1993. *The Water Troll: Story and Lesson,* Classroom Corner. *Storytelling World* 2, no. 1 (Winter/Spring): 27–29.

Kraus, Jo Anne. 2006. "Playing the Play: What the Children Want." *Language Arts* 83, no. 5 (May): 413–421.

Latrobe, Kathy Howard. 1991. *Social Studies Readers Theatre for Young Adults: Scripts and Script Development.* Englewood, CO: Teacher Ideas Press.

Livo, Norma. 1986. *Storytelling: Process and Practice.* Littleton, CO: Libraries Unlimited.

McCaslin, Nellie. 1987. *Creative Drama in the Primary Grades: A Handbook for Teachers.* White Plains, NY: Longman.

McCullough, L.E. 1998. *Plays from Mythology: Grades 4–6.* Lyme, NH: Smith & Kraus.

Plays Magazine: The Drama Magazine for Children. Monthly, October through May, beginning with vol. 1, September 1941.

Polsky, Milton, Dorothy Napp Shindel, and Carmine Tabone. 2006. *Drama Activities for K–6 Students: Creating Classroom Spirit.* Lanham, MD: Rowman & Littlefield Education.
The Princess and the Pea. 1987. Faerie Tale Theatre. Livonia, MI: Playhouse Video. Videorecording. 50 min. VHS.
Puss in Boots. 1985. Faerie Tale Theatre. Farmington Hills, MI: CBS/FOX Video. Videorecording. 51 min. VHS.
Rumpelstiltskin. 1987. Livonia, MI: Playhouse Video. Videorecording. 48 min. VHS.
Saldaña, Johnny. 1995. *Drama of Color: Improvisation with Multiethnic Folklore.* Portsmouth, NH: Heinemann.
Shapiro, Ann. Personal interview, April 2008.
Sloyer, Shirlee. 2003. *From the Page to the Stage: The Educator's Complete Guide to Readers Theatre.* Westport, CT: Teacher Ideas Press/ Libraries Unlimited.
The Snow Queen. 1986. Faerie Tale Theatre. Farmington Hills, MI: CBS/FOX Video. Videorecording. 48 min. VHS.
Stewig, John. 1983. *Informal Drama in the Elementary Language Arts Program.* New York: Teachers College Press, Columbia University.
Storycrafters. 1996. *Apples, Corn & Pumpkin Seeds.* South Norwalk, CT: Gallery West Productions. DVD.
———. 1996. *Ladder to the Moon.* South Norwalk, CT: Gallery West Productions. Compact Disc.
———. 1997. *Straw into Gold.* South Norwalk, CT: Gallery West Productions. Compact Disc.
———. 1998. *Gather Round the Fire.* South Norwalk, CT: Gallery West Productions Compact Disc.
———. 2001. *Classics with a Twist.* South Norwalk, CT: Gallery West Productions. Compact Disc.
———. 2004. *The View from Here: New York State Stories.* South Norwalk, CT: Gallery West Productions Compact Disc.
Teachers.net. "Lesson Plans." Available: http://teachers.net/ lessonplans/posts/123.html (accessed May 3, 2009).
Toy, Ellie. Personal interview, May 2008.
VanSchuyver, Jan M. 1993. *Storytelling Made Easy with Puppets.* Phoenix, AZ: Oryx Press.
Ward, Lynn. 1952. *The Biggest Bear.* Boston: Houghton Mifflin.
Zipes, Jack. 2004. *Speaking Out: Storytelling and Creative Drama for Children.* New York: Routledge.

Chapter 13

❊ Final Considerations: Storytelling Course, Copyright, Planning Tale Events, Storytelling as a Profession, and a Brief History of Storytelling ❊

This chapter will cover a number of items of interest to storytellers that haven't been covered fully in this book so far. These include a storytelling course; copyright information that storytellers need to know; planning storytelling events; professional storytelling and fees; and the history of storytelling.

A Storytelling Course

The benefits of storytelling to children, young adults, and adults that were covered in Chapter 1 are considerable and offer many positive results. Learning to tell is a wonderful skill, and storytelling courses are valuable to children, adolescents, and adults, especially adults in the fields of teaching, social work, psychology, and anyone in the helping professions. Storytelling is an invaluable art that offers a multitude of benefits in the areas of entertainment, passing on cultural ideas, as well as education, in terms of reading, language arts, the humanities, the social sciences, and other curriculum topics.

It is most advantageous for the storytelling instructor to be an accomplished storyteller, but an instructor could be an amateur teller learning to expand his or her storytelling skills. Storytellers from other disciplines on campus or local, national, or internationally known storytellers could also be invited to present tales to the storytelling class or provide demonstrations of storytelling techniques.

The course described in this section follows a sixteen-week semester schedule in higher education for Teacher Education, Reading & Language Arts, English, or other departments. This section includes samples of a course description, goals and objectives, syllabus, course requirements, and additional class material. These samples could be revised to meet the needs of students in primary or secondary education as well.

Sample Course Description, Goals, and Objectives

Catalog description:

> Study of the history, art, and technique of storytelling. The skills involved in mastering the art of storytelling are discussed in an effort to develop the student's competency in this oral tradition. This course is designed to enable the student to build a personal repertoire of stories for performance.

Course objectives:

1. Student will learn to understand and appreciate the value and tradition of storytelling.
2. Students will recognize the fundamental elements of tales.
3. Students will learn to distinguish among the characteristics and purposes of different types of stories for children, young adults, and adults.
4. Students will learn how to locate, access, and evaluate stories for their own use and performance.
5. Students will build a collection of story cards reflecting their selection of stories for performance.
6. Students will deliver tales confidently and successfully.
7. Students will develop an understanding of storytelling styles and techniques for presentation to groups of different sizes, ages, and purposes.
8. Students will learn about the history of storytelling, including classical myths, legends, family tales, ballads, folk and fairy tales.
9. Students will plan units on topics using tales as an integral part of that presentation.

Sample Syllabus

Course: Folktelling Art & Technique, Reading 569
Instructor: Emily S. Chasse
Location: 2nd floor, Spec. Collections, Burritt Library
E-mail: chasse@ccsu.edu
Phone: 860/832-2063
Office hours: M–W, F—8–3:30
            Thursday 12–8:00

Required textbooks:
Chasse, Emily. 2009. *Telling Tales: A Guidebook & DVD.* New York:
  Neal-Schuman.

On reserve:
Livo, Norma J., and Rietz, Sandra. *Storytelling Activities.*
Livo, Norma J., and Rietz, Sandra. *Storytelling: Process & Practice.*

Other reserve readings are available in the reserve collection.

Week 1   General introductions, purposes & values of telling
        tales, selecting tales, and storytelling questionnaires.
        Syllabus, objectives, and requirements.
        Assignment: *Telling Tales,* ch. 1, "Background and Ba-
        sics."

Week 2   Library/Curriculum Lab tour, locating tales, developing
        story memory, story structure, participatory storytell-
        ing, ages, and classification.
        Students sign up for one or two stories, and Special Proj-
        ect.
        Assignment: *Telling Tales,* ch. 2, "Locating and Select-
        ing Tales."
        Santino, Betsy H., 1991. "Improving Multicultural Aware-
        ness and Story Comprehension with Folktales," *Read-
        ing Teacher,* 45 (September): 77–79.

Week 3   Designing stories, story mapping, types of tales, editing,
        rewriting, life experience stories, family tales, oral his-
        tory, recording interviews.
        Life experience stories; family tales; oral history.

Assignment: *Telling Tales,* ch. 5, "Family Tales, Life Experience Tales, Reminiscences, and Oral History."

Week 4   Preparing and delivering stories; evaluating tales and storyteller.

Developing characters, point-of-view, dialect, voice.

Play *Telling Tales* DVD story "The Storm," by Eshu Bumpus.

Assignment: *Telling Tales*, ch. 3, "Preparing and Performing Tales"; ch. 11, "Telling Tales with Young People in the Community and Classroom."

Week 5   Presentation of practice tales.

Planning units on countries.

Play *Telling Tales* DVD, Chinese folktales: "Why the Sea Is Salty," "The White-Hair Waterfall," and "The Golden Sheng."

Assignment: *Telling Tales,* ch. 8, "Folktale Country Studies"; Chasse, Emily. 1992. "Chinese Folktales: A Librarian's Contribution to the Elder Hostel." *Activities, Adaptation & Aging,* 16(4).

Week 6   Stories from news sources, historical and art museums, and other institutions.

Assignment: *Telling Tales*, ch. 10, "Other Resources for Locating Tales."

Begin Folktale and Special Project Presentations.

Week 7   Student presentations of activities from *Creative Storytelling* or another source.

History of storytelling.

Props, plays, and puppetry.

Student volunteers perform an impromptu play of "The Three Billy Goats Gruff."

Assignment: *Telling Tales*, ch. 12, "More Fun! Tandem Telling, Folktale Plays, and Puppetry."

Week 8   Homer (*Iliad, Odyssey*), Chaucer, *Beowulf.*

Assignment: *Telling Tales*, ch. 4, "Storytelling with Classical Mythology"; Reserve: *The Adventures of Wishbone: Be a Wolf* by Brad Strickland.

Students will plan the "Trojan Horse" performance for April 8—background, props, name tags, etc.

Week 9 SPRING BREAK!!!

Week 10 Classical mythology.

Assignment: Cronin, Jim. 1996. "Teaching Astronomy with Multicultural Mythology." *Science Scope*, 20(3): 15–17. (RESERVE)

Week 11 Play performance—THE TROJAN HORSE

Assignment: Choose a Greek god or goddess to present to class on April 11 (2–3 mins.). Include name, brief history, short story. Use one of the following:

Grimal, Pierre. 1989. *Larousse World Mythology*. New York: Gallery Books.

Hansen, William F. 2004. *Handbook of Classical Mythology*. Santa Barbara, CA: ABC-CLIO.

Leach, Marjorie. 1992. *Guide to the Gods*. Santa Barbara, CA: ABC-CLIO.

Mercatante, Anthony S. 2009. *The Facts on File Encyclopedia of World Mythology and Legend*. New York: Facts On File.

Week 12 Gods and goddesses presentations; legends.

Assignment: Telling Tales, ch. 6, "Storytelling with Legends and Epics": Read one legend each from Part I, Part II, Part III, and Part IV of Legendary Connecticut by David Philips (RESERVE) or an appropriate state book of legends.

Week 13 Epic stories; new stories; stories with music; ballads.

Assignment: *Telling Tales*, ch. 7, "Ballads."

Week 14 Helping children with stories; planning folktelling events.

Children telling stories (guest); tandem storytelling (guest teller).

Assignment: *Telling Tales*, ch. 12, "More Fun! Tandem Telling, Folktale Plays, and Puppetry," and ch. 13, "Final Considerations."

Week 15 Professional storyteller—guest.

Copyright; fables; fees—The FABLES CONTEST!!!
Catch-up; review for final.
Assignment: *Telling Tales*, ch. 9, "Digital Storytelling"

Week 16   FINAL.

Sample Graduate Course Requirements

1. Tale Card Collection (10 story card sets)
2. Practice Storytelling Performance (3–5 mins.)
3. Storytelling Performance (5–10 mins.): 15%
4. Special Project Presentation (20–30 mins.): 30%
   This can be on any topic of your choosing. It should include 3 relevant tale card sets (at least 2 of which should be included in your presentation), related storytelling classroom activities, 5 typed pages, including bibliography of sources.
5. One of the following: 15%
   a. Special Project (no presentation): This should include 3 relevant folktale card sets, 2–3 typed pages, related storytelling classroom activities, and a bibliography of sources. OR
   b. Extra Story Performance (10 mins.)

Ideas for special project topics, and type of information to be included:

   a. Country or state (Greece, Canada, Connecticut, etc.) Short history, overview of their folktales, ideas of folktelling activities that could be used in a presentation on the country or state, bibliography of sources in your research. OR
   b. Subject (elderly, non-sexist folktales, oral history, event in history, holiday, curriculum unit, etc.)—overview of the subject, folktales relevant to the subject, ideas of folktelling activities that could be used in a presentation of your subject, bibliography of sources used in your research.

6. Attendance at a Public Storytelling Performance AND Written Summary, Evaluation, and Criticism of performance: 10%
7. Final: 15%
8. Class Participation: 15%

Sample Undergraduate Course Requirements

1. Folktale Card Collection (5 story card sets)
2. Practice Folktale Performance (2–3 mins.)
3. Folktale Performance (5–10 mins.): 15%
4. Special Project Presentation (15–20 mins.): 35%

   This can be on any topic of your choosing. It should include 3 relevant folktale card sets (at least 1 of which should be included in your presentation), 2–3 typed pages, including bibliography of sources.

   Ideas for special project topics, and type of information to be included:

   a. Country or state (Greece, Canada, Connecticut, etc.). Short history, overview of their folktales, ideas of folktelling activities that could be used in a presentation on the country or state, bibliography of sources in your research.

   OR

   b. Subject (elderly, non-sexist folktales, oral history, event in history, holiday, etc.)—overview of the subject, folktales relevant to the subject, ideas of folktelling activities that could be used in a presentation of your subject, bibliography of sources used in your research.
5. Attendance at a Public Folktelling Performance AND Written Summary, Evaluation, and Criticism of Performance: 10%
6. Midterm: 10%
7. Final: 15%
8. Class participation: 15%
9. Class Attendance Is Required. Grade will be lowered 1 point for each 3 class sessions missed.

Extra Class Ideas

Week 1 The goals in the early storytelling class meetings are as follows:
- Help students feel relaxed with the instructor and other students.
- Make certain the students understand the course goals and objectives as well as the course syllabus.
- Immerse the students in stories and assist students as they immerse themselves in stories on their own by exposing them to as many tales as possible. Include folktales, fairy tales, legends, family tales, classical myths, etc. Preferably, the instructor should perform many stories throughout the class and show videos and DVDs of storytelling performances. Play *Telling Tales* DVD tales— "Jack and the Northwest Wind," "The Smell of Food and the Jingle of Coins," and "Mollie Whuppie"— during the first three class meetings.

Week 2
- Explore campus library facilities for folktales and fairy tales with the students. Focus on the 292 and 398.2 sections in the Dewey Decimal collection and the GR sections in the Library of Congress. Encourage the students to investigate those collections in their public libraries.

Week 3
- Conduct a sample oral history interview with students.
- Help students map the tale "The Three Little Pigs."

Week 4
- Class discussion focuses on storytelling and storyteller evaluation. Students will understand the important elements of storytelling and storyteller evaluation.

Week 5
- As students begin to perform tales, most will be understandably nervous, but allowing students to present tales will increase their self-confidence. Once students have performed stories before their fellow students, they will want to continue to improve their performances. Students involved in the teaching pro-

fession may want to perform and practice tales with other classrooms in their school building. This will continue to increase their self-confidence.

Weeks 6–7 • Tell or read "Anne Ryland's Guadanucci Violin" story from *Telling Tales*, ch. 10.

• Student volunteers perform an impromptu play of "The Three Billy Goats Gruff."

• As students present their country study or subject study, they generally become more actively involved with class participation and input on other students' performances. The instructor should ask students to limit their evaluative points to positive criticism. The instructor can provide constructive criticism and evaluation as needed.

• The presentation of storytelling activities during week 7 is especially helpful to teachers, as they recognize the benefits of entertaining storytelling games and exercises for their classrooms.

Weeks 8–12 • These units can be exciting and fun for the students. Instructors should be aware that this course is not expected to provide an in-depth coverage of classical mythology but will be limited to the use of Greek and Roman myths in storytelling. Because of these tales' importance to the field of storytelling, the instructor should also provide basic information on the history of classical mythology. Students will have had varied experiences with classical mythology and the topic makes a good discussion.

• Instructor can perform or read the Greek story of creation.

• Students will enjoy planning for the *Trojan Horse* play or other similar performance that will involve designing backgrounds on poster board or panels, props, name tags, or set design, as needed. Chapter 12 on plays in *Telling Tales* points out the importance of keeping the preparation of this type of additional material to a minimum. The story is the most important part and extras are fun but don't need to be elaborate.

Class discussion should examine use of this play in the classroom.

- A discussion of Greek gods and goddesses can follow the play, and students will present their favorite god or goddess, including information and a story about them.

Week 13 • This week will cover additional aspects of storytelling. A student might want to focus his or her special project on ballads and perform several for the class. The instructor should locate new stories, epics, and ballads and perform them as appropriate. Play Tom Callinan's ballad on the *Telling Tales* DVD.

Week 14 • This lecture should include a tandem story performed by the instructor or another teller, or the instructor can play Ellie Toy and Sharon Lynch's tandem tale on the *Telling Tales* DVD.

Week 15 • A guest teller should be invited for week 15 and asked to comment on copyright and fees. The instructor's lecture can cover those topics as well as fables. A class activity for fables is included in Exhibit 13-1.

Exhibit 13-1. Fables Activity

As stated in Chapter 10, "Other Resources for Locating Tales," fables may best be used with older elementary-aged children or adolescents. The moral development of younger children hasn't matured sufficiently to understand or appreciate the finer points of fables, but older children, adolescents, and adults can enjoy activities with fables. Students could read from a selection of fables:

Aesop's Fables. 1981. New York: Viking.
LaFontaine, Jean de. 2007. *Fables: The Complete Fables of Jean de la Fontaine.* Urbana, IL: University of Illinois Press.

Either by organizing teams or allowing individuals to answer, students could offer morals for the fables. The game could be played simply for fun or scores could be kept.

Some fable selections have been designed for or written for children. These can be read, discussed, or just enjoyed by younger audiences:

Lobel, Arnold. 1980. *Fables.* New York: Harper & Row.
Paxton, Tom. 1988. *Aesop's Fables.* New York: Morrow Junior Books.

Copyright Information for Storytellers

Copyright is an especially important concern for tellers. Copyright is a lengthy and complicated area of law. Most important for storytellers are the sections dealing with the exclusive rights of the copyright holder. Important points that storytellers need to remember concerning copyright include the following:

- The copyright holder has control over the public performance of his or her copyrighted material.
- The copyright holder has the exclusive right to perform his or her copyrighted version of the story, and he or she also has the right to record that performance.
- The copyright holder can create new, derivative works of his or her copyrighted version of a story.
- The copyright holder of a story can make copies of his or her story to distribute and sell.
- If a storyteller is benefiting financially from using another's copyrighted work, the storyteller must obtain a signed permission form from the copyright holder or the copyright holder's agent.
- A librarian, teacher, or teller must ask the copyright holder for permission to produce a DVD, videotape, audiotape, or any other electronic form of the copyright holder's version of the story for distribution, including broadcast or posting on a Web site.

Kendall Haven explains how to determine if a story is copyrighted, and, if it is already copyrighted, how to obtain permission from the author to tell that tale.

He notes, "If you can find three different versions of the same story, even though they are each individually copyrighted, you are free to tell the story without permission" (Haven, 2000: 67). Betty Lehrmann, from The National Storytelling Association, states a similar opinion: "It is difficult to know whether or not a folktale is protected by copyright, but . . . if there are three or more published versions of the tale, it is probably in the public domain" (Lehrmann, 2005: 38).

Generally, librarians and teachers don't need to worry about copyright when they share tales as part of their professional position. For example, children's librarians can tell stories to young people in the schools or during club or community activities, because they are offering this service as part of their regular job description.

This would also be true for teachers when, as part of their professional duties, they tell stories to students within the school system. Teachers tell many tales of various types (e.g., folktales, fairy tales, life experience stories) both as part of the curriculum and for the students' entertainment. In such cases, librarians and teachers are well within the copyright law and should feel free to carry out storytelling activities whenever they seem appropriate.

As a matter of courtesy and to provide information for their students, the librarian or teacher should provide the source of the story (i.e., tell the title and author of the book the story came from). They should also show a copy of the book, when possible, to their audience.

If a librarian or teacher is paid to tell tales for a special program outside their normal professional work activities, however, there are legal issues involved. If a storyteller is benefiting financially from another storyteller's copyrighted work, he or she must have a *signed permission form* from the copyright holder or the copyright holder's agent. This may involve paying the author a fee for the right to tell his or her version of the tale.

A librarian, teacher, or teller needs to ask the copyright holder for additional permission to produce a DVD, videotape, audiotape, or any other electronic form of the copyright holder's version of the story for distribution, including broadcast or posting on a Web site. Even if the teller has received permission to tell the story, producing an electronic version of the tale takes it to a different level and requires further permission. Fair use guidelines are worth consulting, but a teller cannot be assured of his or her right to make an electronic copy for broadcast under fair use.

Nancy Schimmel discusses some other important points of copyright law. She states, "Folktale plots cannot be copyrighted, but the particular words used to convey the plots can be copyrighted, and are the property of the copyright holder" (Schimmel, 1992: 12).

Exhibit 13-2. Storytelling Permission Form

Permission to Retell a Story

I hereby grant permission to _____ (storyteller's name) to tell the following story:

_____

_____

I am authorized to grant this permission.

Permission granted by:

_____ (Signature)

_____ (Print name)

_____ (Title)

_____ (Date)

For example, there are numerous folktales, fairy tales, and life experience stories about Baba Yaga, a witch in some Russian tales. The story of "The Black Geese of Baba Yaga" is included in several books by Allison Lurie. She has an exclusive copyright to her exact version of the story, and another teller cannot perform her version without written permission from her.

The form in Exhibit 13-2 can be used to obtain permission to tell a story. Tellers should make copies of the form and use it to seek permission when they are performing a copyrighted version of a tale in a commercial program where they will be paid a fee for telling it. This permission must be obtained before the storytelling performance. Tellers should send two copies of the form to the copyright holder and ask the copyright holder to sign both forms and return one to them and keep the other.

Planning Storytelling Events

Planning storytelling events is a topic worthy of an entire book in itself and is beyond the scope of this guidebook. There are books and

Web sites that describe the steps involved when planning special story presentations. Caroline Feller Bauer (1993) has published a wealth of information about storytelling performances of all types. She skillfully inserts stories she has used successfully in programs and exhibits her knowledge of tales as she points out information useful in preparing events. It is interesting to hear about her experiences in an incredible range of situations. Things do not go perfectly every time, but you will laugh as you see her deftly making the best of the situation, and you will, hopefully, gain from her wisdom.

R. Craig Roney (2000), a storyteller and teacher of storytelling classes at the university level, provides wonderful information for storytellers, including illuminating the value of storytelling and explaining the preparation, selection, practice, and delivery needed to successfully present tales. He guides tellers in planning story performances while focusing on the setting, location, audience, and other relevant variables. Librarians, teachers, or individual tellers can use this information to plan storytelling programs for children, young adults, adults, and special groups.

As mentioned, each teller will develop his or her own style. Tellers will choose appropriate tales for specific occasions, and they will arrange different formats and structures of their storytelling programs. Tellers should select story programs in a manner similar to the way they choose their favorite stories. They should be certain it is an area they *love* to share with others and will contain the best stories for the program.

Librarians generally have an audience always ready for stories. Children's librarians can be assured there are preschool, elementary-aged, middle or high school–aged young people who enjoy story programs. People who use the library generally enjoy all types of literature, and a program involving oral literature would be welcomed. Librarians will be aware of topics of interest to their users.

There are some important points to keep in mind when planning programs. The following areas should be considered and organized to suit the intended purpose.

Locations

The library would most likely be the most appropriate setting for a storyhour, because the books, craft materials, videos or DVD, equipment, and other necessary items are located there. The space could be quiet for picture book readings but also spacious enough for movement, craft, and singing activities during other parts of the story program. Storytelling space needs can vary by group or type of event.

Many other programs involving stories can be held within the library. Martha Seif Simpson and Lucretia Duwel (2007) offer helpful ideas and guidance for bringing elementary grade groups to the library. They provide suggestions for working out scheduling with the schools cooperatively and cover budgeting, staffing, and other needs for the visits.

When a librarian wants to explore stories with new groups or large groups, it might be more appropriate to choose a location convenient for that group. Events for teenagers or adults could also be held in the library, unless the program is expected to draw an unusually large crowd. In that case, librarians could plan programs at local schools or community centers.

Ages and Scheduling

Young peoples' attendance may be restricted to certain times of the day. Morning is a good time to offer preschool storyhours, with parents present or nearby. In the morning, children are usually awake and active. Their older siblings may be in school, and one of the parents might appreciate time for the child to play with other children.

Afternoon programs on school days can attract preschoolers, elementary school–aged children, or junior or senior high students. Early evening could be reserved for older elementary, junior, and senior high school–aged young people and adults. Later evening might be a time for programs attracting senior high school students or adults. Events may be single or a series of events lasting in length from one to two hours and possibly continuing for a number of weeks or months, but with a scheduled end date.

Groups

A community will be home to many individual groups and town groups from schools and clubs. Also consider subgroups of national associations, such as Girl Scouts, Boy Scouts, professional associations, young men's or women's associations, boys and girls clubs, and so forth.

Occasions

Usually, there is no need for a special occasion to add stories to an already scheduled program or meeting. A librarian, teacher, or teller could offer to tell a story at any program. Regularly scheduled clubs or group meetings can often use a story at the opening or as part of the meeting. The librarians, teachers, or tellers who are part of the group can volunteer to provide a tale as they see an opportunity.

But, tellers who want to see storytelling added regularly to a program or meeting would need to find a way to convince the group of its benefits. The tellers might need to offer stories without charge in the beginning and hope their services are seen in such a positive light that the group will hire them for a future performance.

As noted in Chapter 10, tellers need to be careful that the storytelling doesn't lose its value, or the tellers may lose the admiration and respect of the group because the tales are offered free of charge. It can be difficult to find a balance between offering free tales, because tellers like to share their expertise, and saving tellers' self-respect because they should be paid when they tell stories.

Booktalks

Booktalking and storytelling work well together and could be considered when working with school classes. Booktalks can be enlightening to children and teachers, promoting further reading by the young people or their teachers. There are numerous books available on designing and planning booktalks.

Joni Bodart Richards (2002) has found that adolescents are attracted to books that deal with the excitable and touchy themes of teenage pregnancy, substance abuse, sexual and physical abuse, gangs, and suicide. She encourages teachers and librarians to find relevant books to explore with adolescents. She discusses some of these books, giving ideas for booktalks and book reports and other ideas for working with this age group.

Storytelling as a Profession

Tellers of tales love storytelling, but making it a fulltime profession isn't always an easy task. The tellers highlighted here chose different paths in their professions, and this flexibility may be necessary. Catherine Conant (www.4astoryteller.com), a Connecticut storyteller, described different types of storytelling performers:

- Platform tellers perform in front of large audiences and often spend a lot of time on the road. Examples of platform tellers include Jay O'Callahan, a long-standing teller with broad appeal from New England. Bill Harley, another platform teller, is a singer of ballads telling wonderful stories. Harley's recorded CDs and DVDs have received many positive reviews in the literature and on the World Wide Web. He is also the winner of several Grammy Awards.
- There are tellers who specialize in storytelling to pre-primary and elementary school–aged groups. These tellers need to register with state agencies that provide funding for storytellers in the schools and other institutions.
- Some tellers focus on performing for children and young adults through the schools. Often these tellers need to rely on the school systems to obtain grants to cover the costs of the storytellers' classroom or school visits.
- Librarians and teachers who perform tales to preschool and elementary school–aged children can usually be counted on to cover storytelling to middle school and high school groups as well.
- Social workers, ministers, psychologists, psychiatrists, and others in the helping professions may incorporate storytelling into their work.

Marketing Performances

A storyteller can offer to tell stories to groups of varied sizes and organization. In the past, tellers would send brochures out to schools and groups describing the types of programs they offered in terms of stories and activities. Tellers report that most schools and groups now use the World Wide Web to locate storytelling performers. Therefore, all tellers should have a presence on the Web, preferably a distinct and attractive site.

As noted above, it might be tempting to offer your storytelling skills for free, but it can unfortunately cause the craft to be under-valued. Most tellers list their fees as negotiable, but those who offer price ranges can charge from $200 to $1,000 or more, depending on the presentation and the size or type of the group. It is a topic for consultation with other local tellers.

Professional Storytellers

The following are tellers from New England I have been fortunate to have had the chance to experience and enjoy. They have taught me much about life, people, and our storytelling journeys.

Eshu Bumpus

⊙ Eshu generously allowed me to include his story "The Storm" on the accompanying DVD.

Eshu grew up in Boston and Connecticut and developed a love of stories and work-ing with children. Early in his work with young people, he discovered that he en-joyed combining stories with acting and drama. An accomplished storyteller, Eshu has performed at the National Festival in 1998, in 36 sold-out shows in 13 days at the Smithsonian in 1997, and in storytelling venues in 18 different states across America.

Now, located in western Massachusetts, Eshu continues to spend time with children and young adults, focusing on drama and the arts in the schools and within the many workshops he offers in Massachusetts. On his Web site (http://eshu.folktales.net), Eshu says, "My hope with this is to encourage literacy, communication, and forge a strong sense of community with what I see as our most human of activities, storytelling." He does all of that and more wher-ever and whenever he performs. Children love his stories, and the young people and adults appreciate his humor and warmth as he delivers tales from Africa, African-American stories, and world folktales with style, grace, and charm.

Catherine Conant

Catherine Conant grew up in a large Italian family. Family members shared much food and conversation, including many, many stories from Catherine's mother and seven aunts and uncles.

Catherine believes that storytelling is a powerful communication tool and that it shouldn't be limited to those of us lucky enough to have grown up in a family of tellers or who have learned to be practiced storytellers. She encourages everyone to tell their stories and believes that those tales should be valued.

She shares her stories with audiences of all ages, specializing in work with older adults, intergenerational groups, and others who work in nonprofit agencies. She also teaches storytelling at the Greater Hartford Academy of the Arts, in Hartford, Connecticut.

Catherine feels that the most powerful stories are often those told by individuals who may consider their lives to be "ordinary." She believes those stories reflect universal human experiences that we all share and that they convey values and principles that are essential for all individuals. Most important, she believes that children need to hear stories or else they will risk growing up feeling rootless and unguided.

Catherine completed a project with fifth graders that she considers her most successful. The children interviewed World War II veterans and wrote stories of their military experiences. She feels that through the act of sharing stories the children and elders grew to have a greater understanding of each other and discovered how humor, integrity, honesty and patience are essential parts of life. Visit her Web site at www.4astoryteller.com.

Ann Shapiro and Tom Callinan

Ann Shapiro is director of the Connecticut Storytelling Center in New London, Connecticut, and she spoke with me about her decision to work with Barbara Reid, at the Connecticut Storytelling Center (CSC), and, later, to become the Director. Ann was active with the CSC from the first Storytelling Festival in 1981 and, after five years, was asked to serve on the Board of Advisors. Ann helped coordinate school visits in New London and nearby Middletown, and the Center continues to work with schools in Connecticut and sends storytellers to perform at those schools.

Ann and her husband, Tom Callinan, work with stories, folk music, and ballads at the Connecticut Storytelling Center. Tom was designated as Connecticut's first "Official State Troubadour" in 1991. Barbara Reid recognized the power of story coming through their ballads, and both Ann and Tom continue to provide programs for children through CSC.

Ellie Toy

Ellie grew up in New Jersey, but her family often visited her grandfather in Virginia, a colorful man who told stories and played folk-type games with his grandchildren on the porch. Ellie says she has great memories but does not remember any particular stories.

Her sister said Ellie was always a storyteller. Actually, Ellie says she just used to describe movies to her sister. In 1982, Ellie started a storytelling group, and Sharon Lynch quickly joined. Both Ellie and Sharon told tales, and at one point they decided to tell a tandem tale.

In school settings, Ellie often offers older historical tales. After the telling, she asks students, "What did he look like?" or "What do you think that would that have felt like?" and other questions that make the children think about different parts of the story and the feelings and emotions surrounding it.

Ellie noted that, often, historical centers, such as Connecticut Historical Society, offer legendary tales performed as tandem tales. She feels they tend to be "performance pieces" more than actual storytelling between teller and audience. Performance pieces are more often memorized.

For younger children, of preschool age, she recommends telling a strong story, followed by a short and fun story-related activity. She suggests sharing another story and letting the students know you want them to notice descriptive words you are going to use in the story. After you are finished with the tale, ask "What words did I use when I told that story?" List the words and then use them to make a poem. Ellie also often combines storytelling with puppets.

Ellie feels that a professional teller needs to appear on several lists of storytellers. For instance, the Connecticut Commission on

Culture & Tourism (CCCT) provides a list of storytellers in Connecticut. They have a Web page that describes the agency, news and events, programs and services, funding opportunities, resources, and how to contact the agency. The Arts division of the CCCT promotes Connecticut's cultural and tourism programs and activities throughout the state. They include a list of storytellers and, through its grant programs, promote tellers and other artists for appearances in schools, for organizations, and for individuals. Their Historic Preservation and Museum Division offers some storytelling programs as well.

A Brief History of Storytelling

It might appear out of place to offer information on the history of storytelling at the end of this book. But in fact, students and others learning about telling tales can appreciate its history better *after* gaining some understanding of the development of storytelling over time.

Once a teller hears about the hundreds of different versions of "Cinderella" and other tales, it makes sense that stories develop from universal emotions that are common to all people. People can understand the need to tell tales that explain strange phenomena of nature, or stories about people whom others quickly recognize as someone they know who behaves in a similar manner, and tales told the world over that display similar themes. Folktales, or tales of the common folk, reflect ordinary behavior and happenings, where people recognize the fact that the tales reflect a wide range of cultures.

Anyone can watch a young person today, making up stories that reflect what they are doing, how they feel about it, possibly showing their fears and their pride. Children's stories are usually incredible, imaginative, and somewhat boastful. It makes sense that the earliest stories show the same type of design.

An Expanded Timeline of Storytelling History

Many early stories were told over and over because the people did not have the means to write them down. For example, *The Iliad* and *The Odyssey* were told for hundreds of years before they were transcribed.

Storytelling is older than history, but this chapter will outline basic events in the history of storytelling from the ancient story discovered and written on papyrus called "The Tale of Two Brothers" (discussed in Chapter 1), through Greek mythology, the birth of Christ (one of the most prolific storytellers!), Roman mythology, Norse tales, European myths, the arrival of the printing press and its effects on stories, stories traveling to the New World in the 1400s, and the results on storytelling with the advent of the Internet and the World Wide Web. Clearly these events are only a small part of the history, but they comprise some of the most important episodes in the overall growth of storytelling.

Greek and Roman mythologies revealed fantastic tales of gods and goddesses, fabulous beasts, and stories about why things and people are the way they are. After the fall of the Roman Empire, stories were spread across Europe by traveling nomads and gypsies. Tales traveled through many countries, including Afghanistan, Britain, Finland, North Africa, and Asia. More stories were told as the various Christian Crusades made their way around Europe from 1095 to 1291.

Over the years, countries have responded to storytellers in different ways. Some treated them with respect and offered them special tribute, depending on the quality of their tales. Others considered tellers less worthy of admiration and undeserving of their regard.

As the field of storytelling in the British Isles grew, the communities recognized the value of their art. Beginning in the thirteenth century, tellers from Wales and Ireland offered numerous tales and training for tellers. Novice tellers were told many stories and were taught techniques of telling and ways to create their own tales. The Cymric School of Bards in Wales and the Gaelic school Ollamhs were divided into categories or ranks, and, based on the tellers' skills, they were given special privileges involving land ownership, the right to wear special clothing and colors, and other favors. Storytelling students were taught to gather the stories they had been told, remember them, and create new stories; as a result, the "Celtic tradition has provided the world with a larger and more ancient body of folktales than any other single source" (Maguire, 1992: 34).

By the Middle Ages (500–1500 AD), it was apparent that stories would continue to be told, and they were carried throughout Europe and Russia. In the fifteenth century, the advent of a moveable type printing press changed the world of storytelling. Tales were written to be read, even before the majority of the people were literate. But that changed very quickly, and many tales were passed around in print rather than by word of mouth. At one point, the printed story was given more prestige than one told orally. Some thought the printed tale was "better" than the oral version.

At the same time, there were events that resulted from the printing press that benefitted stories. Collections were published from the Grimm Brothers in Germany, from Spenser in England, Perrault in France, and others that allowed these tales to be read and told from the printed page.

With the discovery of America in 1492, tales came to the New World from all over. There were Native American tales here originally, and stories were added from England, Europe, Africa, and other countries. May Hill Arbuthnot and Zena Sutherland (1972: 82) point out in *Children and Books* that "Grandmothers have always been the custodians of traditional tales, both of families and of the larger tribe or village."

Summary

The entire profession surrounding storytelling involves offering tales to individuals or groups. As tellers perfect their skills and offer storytelling to young people and adults, they will need to be aware of the importance of preparation, selection, practice, and delivery. They need to consider the logistics of the location and how the overall age of the audience members affects scheduling. And they must learn marketing skills and how to negotiate fees.

Tellers need to be aware of the significance of copyright laws and be as informed as possible about this area. Original stories are protected by copyright, and tellers must request permission to use those stories as needed.

Storytelling as a profession can be both rewarding and challenging. Making it as a fulltime teller isn't always an easy endeavor.

Many incorporate storytelling into their primary professions. For example, besides librarians and teachers, social workers, ministers, psychologists, psychiatrists, and even business people tell stories.

The history of storytelling, which has been referred to in several chapters of this book, has always had an effect on the stories being created and told. Knowing of that history across time allows tellers to appreciate all that storytelling has offered and will continue to offer communities throughout the world.

Suggested Resources

Birch, Carol. 2007. "A Storyteller's Lament: A Librarian Looks at the Rights and Wrongs of Sharing Literature Orally." *School Library Journal* (August): 26–27.
Birch discusses the responsibilities of storytellers when using stories composed by other people.

Classical Myth: The Ancient Sources. http://web.uvic.ca/grs/department_files/classical_myth/index.html (accessed May 3, 2009).
This Web site is intended for students from University of Victoria, British Columbia, but is accessible to all. It draws together the ancient texts and images available on the Web concerning major figures of Greek and Roman mythology.

Connecticut Storytelling Center. www.connstorycenter.org (accessed May 3, 2009).
The Connecticut Storytelling Center was founded in 1984 and is based at Connecticut College in New London. Its mission is to promote the art of storytelling in all its forms and to serve storytellers and story listeners throughout the state.

Freeman, Barbara and Connie Regan-Blake. 2007. *Storytelling Tales for Children & Techniques for Teachers.* [United States]: Folktellers. Videorecording: DVD video, 1 videodisc (90 min).
Dynamic storytelling performance for K–5 students and an entertaining in-service workshop for teachers, parents, and librarians; previously recorded live for PBS Studios, now released in DVD format. Freeman and Regan-Blake are two former children's librarians who chose to leave that field to become fulltime storytellers. They have produced a DVD of a workshop that covers storytelling techniques for teachers. They echo the advice given earlier to locate tales you really love when selecting stories to tell others. They suggest some memory techniques for new tellers and offer all types of tales, including perform-

ing tandem tales, and they describe their entry into the practice of tandem telling.

International Storytelling Center. www.storytellingcenter.org (accessed May 3, 2009).
The International Storytelling Center's goal is to infuse storytelling into the mainstream of our society and to promote the power of storytelling and its creative applications to build a better world.

Langemack, Chapple. 2003. *The Booktalker's Bible: How to Talk about the Books You Love to Any Audience.* Westport, CT: Libraries Unlimited. ISBNs: 1563089440; 9781563089442
This is a sensitive book to help a person working with teens through books.

National Storytelling Network. www.storynet.org (accessed May 3, 2009).
The National Storytelling Network works to bring together individuals and organizations that use and promote the power of storytelling. It offers information on the art of storytelling, opportunities for training and networking, a calendar of events, and a directory of tellers, and it publishes *Storytelling* magazine.

Richards, Joni Bodart. 2002. *Radical Reads: 101 YA Novels on the Edge* Lanham, MD: Scarecrow Press. ISBNs: 0810842874; 9780810842878
Richards speaks about ways to convince young adults to read and enjoy literature. She is known for highlighting new, edgy, and controversial fiction for teens.

Seif Simpson, Martha and Lucretia Duwel. 2007. *Bringing Classes to the Public Library: A Handbook for Librarians.* Jefferson, NC: McFarland. ISBNs: 0786428066; 9780786428069
The authors cover books for grades K–8 and present about 350 nonfiction books organized in seven chapters by themes such as "Biggest, Fastest, Weirdest, Grossest: Quirky Books Kids Love." This is definitely a place to find books that appeal to teenagers.

Storyfest Journeys. www.storyfest.com (accessed May 3, 2009).
Storyfest offers travel adventures into legendary places through stories, drama, art, and more, with a personal guide and mentor.

Bibliography

Arbuthnot, May Hill and Zena Sutherland. 1972. *Children and Books,* 4th ed. Glenview, IL: Scott Foresman.

Bauer, Caroline Feller. 1993. *New Handbook for Storytellers: With Stories, Poems, Magic, and More.* Chicago: American Library Association.

Baxter, Kathleen A. and Marcia Agness Kochel. 2002. *Gotcha Again! More Nonfiction Booktalks to Get Kids Excited about Reading.* Greenwood Village, CO: Libraries Unlimited/Teacher Ideas Press.

Birch, Carol. 2007. "A Storyteller's Lament: A Librarian Looks at the Rights and Wrongs of Sharing Literature Orally." *School Library Journal* (August): 26–27.

Haven, Kendall. 2000. *Super Simple Storytelling: A Can-Do Guide for Every Classroom, Every Day.* Englewood, CO: Teacher Ideas Press.

Lehrmann, Betty. 2005. *Telling Stories to Children: A National Storytelling Guide.* Jonesborough, TN: National Storytelling Press.

Maguire, Jack. 1992. *Creative Storytelling: Choosing, Inventing, and Sharing Tales for Children.* Cambridge, MA: Yellow Moon Press.

Richards, Joni Bodart. 2002. *Radical Reads: 101 YA Novels on the Edge.* Lanham, MD: Scarecrow Press.

Roney, R. Craig. 2000. *The Story Performance Handbook.* Mahwah, NJ: Lawrence Erlbaum Associates.

Schimmel, Nancy. 1992. *Just Enough to Make a Story: A Sourcebook for Storytelling.* Berkeley, CA: Sister's Choice Press.

Seif Simpson, Martha, and Lucretia Duwel. 2007. *Bringing Classes to the Public Library: A Handbook for Librarians.* Jefferson, NC: McFarland.

❋ Story Index ❋

✳ Subject Index ✳

Page numbers followed by the letter "e" indicate exhibits.

A

Accents, language, 52–53
Activist ballads, 121–122, 131
Adults, story selection for, 40
Age
  scheduling performances, 243
  story selection and, 36, 38–40
Allen, Katherine, 85–86
American Folklife Center, 91
Appearance, storyteller, 49
Arbuthnot, May Hill, 251
Art museums, 174, 175
Art studies stories, 141, 191
Arthurian legends, 97
Asbjørnsen, Peter Christen, 30–31
Astronomy studies stories, 192
Audiences
  participation by, 7, 54–55, 56e
  and story selection, 36–40
  types of, 243–244

B

Baker, Augusta, 30, 39, 194
Balladeers, 112
Ballads. *See also* Ballads, types of
  composers, 130–131
  definition, 2e, 111, 131
  format, 113–116, 131
  meter, 114, 131
  musical accompaniment, 113
  performance and performers,
    112, 130–131
  purpose, 113
  refrain in, 115–116, 131

  repetition in, 115, 131
  research, 113
  resources, 132–134
  rhyme, 114, 131
Ballads, types of
  activist, 113, 121–122
  broadsides, 112
  cowboy, 116–118
  folk, 112, 113
  geographic, 129–130
  historical, 118–119
  labor, 128
  literary tales, 112
  maritime, 119–121
  oral tradition, 112
  patriotic, 121
  religious, 122–125
  sea shanties, 119–121
  sea songs, 119–121
  tragedy, 125–127
  work, 128
Bauer, Caroline Feller, 242
BBC, digital storytelling and, 162
Beasley, Augie, 89–90
Beekman, Jeannine Pasini, 8
Benefits
  children, 10–11, 31, 187–188,
    195–196
  entertainment, 6–7
  psychological, 10–11
  sense-making, 7
  teaching, 8–9, 196
  teens, 187–188
  therapeutic, 10–11
  at worship services, 15

✳ About the Author ✳

Emily S. Chasse is a librarian, teacher, and storyteller from West Hartford, Connecticut. Married, with one daughter, she works as a librarian and teacher at Central Connecticut State University. She has taught storytelling courses in the English and Reading Departments at Central Connecticut State University for the past 20 years and tells stories to young people and adults in the schools and within her community. Emily hopes that this book will encourage others to try telling stories and to enjoy sharing tales with others of all ages.